Southern Africa Since 1800

NE WEEK LOAN

Southern Africa Since 1800

New edition

Donald Denoon and Balam Nyeko

Pearson Education Limited
Edinburgh Gate, Harlow,
Essex CM20 2JE, England
and Associated Companies throughout the world.

First edition published 1972
This edition first published 1984
Tenth impression 2000

British Library Cataloguing in Publication Data

Denoon, Donald
    Southern Africa since 1800-2nd ed
    1. Africa, Southern-Social conditions
    2. Africa, Southern-History
    I. Title   II. Nyeko, Balam

ISBN 0-582-72707-3

Library of Congress Cataloging in Publication Data

Denoon, Donald.
    Southern Africa since 1800.

    Bibliography: p.
    Includes index.
    1. Africa, Southern—History. 2. Africa, Southern—
Politics and government. 3. Africa, Southern—Economic
conditions. I. Nyeko, Balam. II. Title.
DT740.D46 1984   968   83-14907

ISBN 0-582 72707-3 (pbk.)

Printed in China
GCC/10

Contents

List of maps

Acknowledgements

The publishers are grateful to the following for permission to reproduce photographs in the text:

BBC Hulton Picture Library for pages 16, 80, 86, 98, 102 and 121; Camera Press Limited for pages 38, 173, 193, 203, 213 top, 213 bottom, 228 and 231; John Hillelson Agency for page 194; Illustrated London News Picture Library for page 166; Mansell Collection for pages 77, 88 and 134; Popperfoto for pages 50, 113, 154 and 218; Thomson Newspapers for page 216; Brian Willan/The Wykeham Studios Limited for page 188.

The publishers regret that they are unable to trace the copyright holder of the photo on page 212, and apologise for any infringement of copyright caused.

Preface

Southern Africa has been in one crisis or another for the last hundred years. Conflicts between states and societies were often bloody and violent. These conflicts have been succeeded by struggles between races and between social classes within a single economic and social system. Recent attempts by the South African government to partition the country politically, according to race and language, have not changed the pattern of persistent conflict within a single, complex framework. As these tensions have developed, they have attracted an ever-wider audience. Southern African crisis used to involve only the people living in the region itself, and a few imperial officials. For the past half century however, these affairs have affected the whole of Africa, and attracted the attention of governments and people throughout the world. People who believe that human beings should be able to live together humanely – and governments which claim humane values – are necessarily involved in struggles for equality and for tolerable living conditions in southern Africa.

Because of this concern and attention, the authors of this book have taught courses in southern African history in several parts of Africa, in North America, Australia and the Pacific. The book is part of our attempt to make southern African affairs familiar to students, who are always puzzled by the survival into modern times of a government committed to racial separation in political and social life but to an integrated economic system for the whole region. As far as possible, we have compared southern African conditions and events with those of the rest of Africa, but we also acknowledge the unique conditions and actors in southern African history. Our aim is to introduce the subject, to make a clear first statement which can be modified as students read more widely. We do not attempt to have 'the last word' on the many arguments which rage among scholars, observers, and participants in the struggles.

As more people have taken an interest in southern Africa, so the quality of the books on the subject has improved and become very diverse. That process had begun when we wrote the first edition in 1972, but it has now developed much further. One important result is the revival of a point of view which considers the struggle between social classes to be the driving force in events.

Other scholars have been obliged to do more research and better analysis in defence of their belief that it is conflict between races which mainly inspires events. Both the 'revisionist' and the 'liberal' scholars in these debates have taken much more interest in ordinary people than they used to – black as well as white, poor as well as rich, women as well as men. We have tried to incorporate this impressive new research within the framework of the second edition. But perhaps the most awesome change in the subject during the past dozen years has been the achievement of independence, after a very long and bitter struggle, by the people of Mozambique, Zimbabwe and Angola. They have transformed inter-state relations throughout the region, and have forced us to look more carefully at the structures of repression which they have overthrown. By changing present reality, they throw a quite new light on the realities of the past.

These are very great changes in the quality and in the quantity of information available. In order to accommodate the new evidence, and the new ideas which have been circulated, we could not simply make the small changes which are often introduced into the second edition of a book. Instead, we found we had to re-write the book, developing a new framework for this evidence and for these ideas. Only one aspect of the book is absolutely unchanged. It is our belief that the living conditions of the majority of the people must be transformed as soon as humanly possible; and that a reasonable understanding is the necessary first step towards achieving that change.

Chapter 1

The environment and the strategies of pre-capitalist production

Every human being, throughout human history, has been anxious to have a little bit more to eat, to enjoy rather more leisure time, to live in more comfort than he or she is used to. Small changes are constantly being made, to see whether more can be produced – or less labour and time spent on production. Not all experiments are successful: sometimes the material circumstances simply do not permit improvements in production, and sometimes the experiments make life worse than it was. Nowadays, these changes usually involve the use of large sums of capital (for machinery), and they are usually controlled by the State, which employs experts to conduct the experiments and to manage the new production system. When a lot of capital, political power, and expertise are used in these innovations, economic change is likely to be very swift and the results dramatic – for better or worse.

When we look at changes in production before capital became available, we find that change was rather different. For one thing, almost everybody lived on the land, and most changes had to do with different uses of the land. For another, there was no capital for the invention and mass production of ingenious tools: rural production was carried out by people using very simple tools combined with a great deal of intelligence (whereas agricultural development now is conducted by unskilled people using very sophisticated implements). Third, if a mistake was made, it was not possible to import bulk food from some other country; so people were rather cautious about innovation, just in case they destroyed their food supplies entirely.

In general, then, social and economic changes were made, but the changes were usually smaller, and always slower, than we would expect today. Increasingly, human beings have been able to change the landscape – bringing water to dry areas by irrigation, draining water out of swamps, introducing new crops and trees and

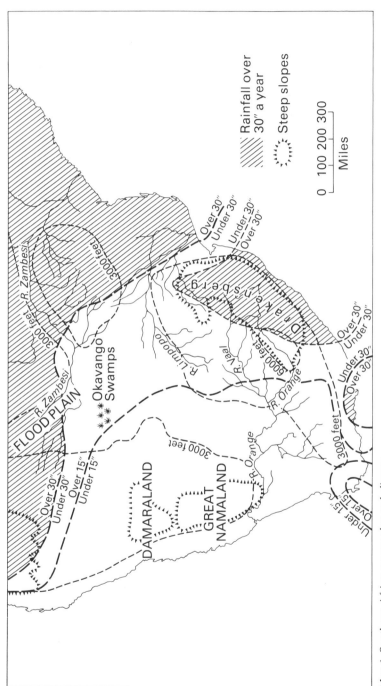

Map 1 Southern Africa: geography and climate

animals from the other end of the world – but before the development of capitalism these dramatic changes were simply not possible on a large scale. People were more closely linked to their environment than they are now. In order to understand how people in southern Africa made a living before capitalist production was introduced, we must therefore pay some attention to the environment in which they lived, and from which they must extract regular supplies of food, clothing and shelter.

The most crucial feature of the southern African environment was the distribution of rainfall. There have been changes in the amount of rainfall over the whole region, but always the eastern coastal belt (east of the Drakensberg mountains) has enjoyed more rain, and more regular rain, than the rest of the country. Roughly speaking, the amount and the reliability of rainfall declines from the east (which usually has had plentiful rain) to the west (much of which is desert or semi-desert). There is also more rain in the north than in the south. The reliability of rain is just as important as the quality. It is no use having good crops for nine years out of ten if everyone starves to death in the tenth year when drought occurs.

Another dimension of the rainfall question is the quality of the soil. Parts of the western half of southern Africa (notably northern Namibia) usually receive sufficient rain for crop production – but the water evaporates so quickly, and runs away through the earth, that it has been impossible to use it for cultivation in large areas.

In other words, without large irrigation and water conservation projects, southern Africa is rather drier than the rainfall statistics would make us expect; and a lot of the rainfall is too unreliable for pre-capitalist crop production (see map 1).

Although much of the eastern coastal belt has had a natural cover of forest, and there have been patches of forest even to the west of the Drakensberg range, in fact for several centuries these forests have been shrinking, being replaced by grassland. There are several reasons for this, including the fact that people have usually grown cereal crops (sorghum, then maize) rather than root crops (like yam), and cereal cultivation makes it more difficult for forest to recover after a period of farming. In any case, most of the land surface has been transformed to grassland, so it is important to establish the nature and the uses of different kinds of grasses. Once again, the eastern coastal belt contains more useful qualities than the rest of the country: a lot of the pastures in the east are described by herdsmen as 'sweet', while to the west more of the pastures are described as 'sour'. Herded animals living on sour grass need feed supplements or (before that was available) some period each year eating the sweet grasses, which seem to have better nutritional qualities. Once again the advantage lay with people living along the eastern coastal belt, where it is not necessary to travel such a great distance as in the west, to find winter pastures (see map 2).

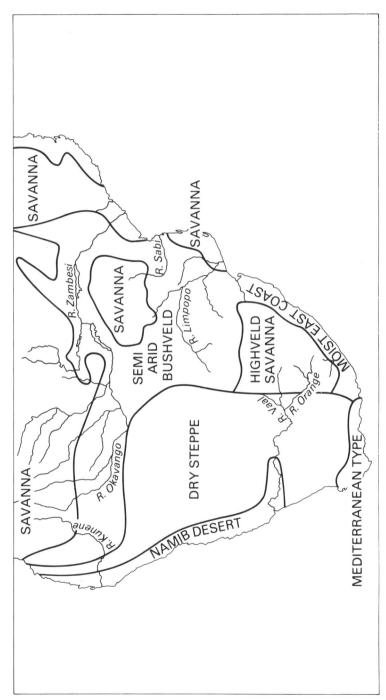

Map 2 Southern Africa: natural vegetation and major rivers

Most of the interior of southern Africa is high tableland, sloping down from the Drakensberg dividing range towards the west coast. During winter nights on this tableland frost is a normal occurrence, and in the mountain ranges snow is not uncommon. Most of the crops which have been developed throughout Africa are adapted to tropical conditions: so at the southern extremity of the continent there are extensive areas which simply will not support the crops which were most readily available. In some of the colder parts of this region, it is also necessary to protect animals from the cold night air, enclosing them within a structure which will keep out the wind. On the other hand the prevalence of frost also kills off a number of plant and animal diseases which endanger crops and herds in the hot and humid eastern coastal belt. Tsetse fly was perhaps the most dangerous of the disease vectors of the humid regions, where it flourished in bush conditions; and the movements of wild animals throughout southern Africa have complicated the task of isolating diseased animals from healthy herds. In general then, southern Africa contains a range of rather different environments, each with distinct dangers and opportunities, and each requiring its inhabitants to build up a very large body of knowledge and skill in order to survive and to accumulate a surplus.

Of course the environment is not passive and unchanging, but rather a series of conditions which plants and animals and humans can modify in various ways. The absence of root crops for example, and the common reliance of most agricultural communities upon grain crops, means that the bush-fallow system of crop production (common throughout the West African forest belt) has not occurred. The grain crops make it more difficult for the forest to re-colonise a patch of land after cultivation. Sorghum seems to have been the most widely used crop until it was supplanted by maize which probably entered the region through the Zambesi valley – though sorghum is more resistant to cold, so it can still be found in the cooler regions of the interior plateau.

Equally important is the fact that cattle and sheep have been available for several centuries. The organisation of ordinary life around cattle and sheep herds, finding pastures for them and fending off predators, is one of the most decisive conditions which made African life so different in quality from that of the Pacific, or the Americas. And in turn the presence of herds of domestic animals, and the cultivation of particular crops, have transformed the social landscape.

We may also note in passing that there was sufficient iron ore for the manufacturing of iron tools (for agriculture and cooking and defence), so that the inhabitants of the region could move quite easily from early iron age (when iron tools are rare) to late iron age (when they are common) without any technical bottleneck. Iron implements seem not to have been useful in hunting and gathering;

but for every other purpose iron ore and iron processing was quite widely distributed, and does not seem to have been difficult to obtain.

Strategies

As we shall see later in this chapter, it was most unusual for one strategy for survival to be practised in isolation from all others. For the sake of convenience though, we may describe these strategies separately, before looking at the interactions between them. The mode of production which is most difficult for most modern people to understand is nomadic hunting and gathering, relying upon the capture of wild animals and the collecting of wild foodstuffs. (In coastal areas, the collection of shellfish, or the catching of fish, also involves the taking of food directly from nature, without any intervening process of cultivation or herding.) Hunters and gatherers in southern African history have been expelled from most of the land, and it is tempting to think of San hunters as 'primitive'. Very short in stature, they looked quite different from most other Africans, and their nomadic style of life exaggerated the differences. Certainly they accumulated very few material possessions, since a nomadic lifestyle made people think twice before carrying goods around with them. On the other hand it seems that skilled hunters and gatherers, who had been brought up to understand the habits of animals and the rhythms of plant life, could count on a reliable and quite good standard of nutrition. In areas which were impossible for agriculture or for pastoralism, hunters and gatherers could live reasonably well. The acquisition of skill, however, was a long and serious business, involving not merely locating and harvesting food, but also some measure of management of resources. It is likely, for example, that San required more skill to live by the hunt than farmers did to grow one or two crops.

There were, however, two extreme disadvantages in the San mode of living. One was that population had to be very severely controlled, because over-population would destroy the natural resources which everyone relied upon. The other was that a thin population of San would find it impossible to prevent the occupation of their lands by other communities, putting the land to new uses. San communities almost certainly occupied most of the southern African region, before the intervention of agricultural and pastoral specialists; and gradually they were forced to concentrate mainly (though never exclusively) on environments which made agriculture and pastoralism impossible.

In recent times, almost all speakers of Bantu languages have been associated with the use of iron and with agriculture; and this seems to have been true for many centuries. Archaeologists are constantly analysing fresh evidence for the early use of iron and agriculture, and it seems likely that the people who left traces of iron-working and cultivation spoke Bantu languages of some kind. It is beyond the scope of this book to consider the evidence for the settlement of agricultural people in southern Africa; but it is evident that some communities have been present for well over a thousand years, and that there were quite dense settlements parallel to the eastern coast by the sixteenth century at the latest. By that time the speakers of the 'Nguni' branch of the Bantu language family were securely established. European sailors who were shipwrecked on that coast sometimes chose to settle there, in peaceful and well-organised societies. Nguni communities cultivated grain crops and kept herds of cattle, both of which were favoured by the good rainfall and warm, moist climate, though it was unwise to rely on either one of these for the staple diet: milk production fell off in the winter, and plant and animal diseases had to be reckoned with. A community which required a spread of different environments for winter and summer pastures, and for cultivation, did not need to secure a very large area of land.

In the absence of severe population pressure, it was not necessary to tolerate dictatorial leadership and control. Most of the Nguni societies appear to have consisted of a few thousand people at most, and they exercised a wide latitude in local self-government in ordinary times. The trade in ivory from elephant tusks, which was linked in eastern Africa to the emergence of powerful chieftaincies, did not produce the same effect in southern Africa, perhaps because the trade through Delagoa Bay was too small and too erratic to sustain merchant princes. During the late eighteenth century the quality of political life became more vigorous among the northern Nguni, and in the long run (see Chapter three) there emerged centralised, expansionist and militaristic kingdoms in that region. Until the eighteenth century, however, there were evidently no great crises in the environment or the economy to provoke a more intense system of politics.

Until the crisis of the late eighteenth century, then, speakers of Nguni languages could live quite comfortably by cultivation and herding, with a family household as the most important production team. The clans consisting of related families were often grouped together under the authority of the patriarch of a senior clan, to whom tribute was paid. However, a patriarch who attempted to extract more tribute than people thought reasonable had to run the risk of whole clans simply transferring their allegiance to a more generous leader. Leadership therefore required close attention to the wishes of the heads of households, and especially to the heads of clans.

West of the Drakensberg dividing range, where rainfall declines sharply and is less dependable, people placed greater emphasis upon their herds and less upon cultivation, although the

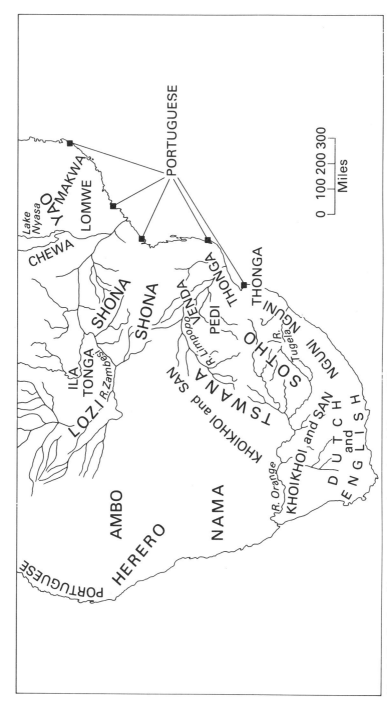

Map 3 Distribution of language groups in southern Africa, c. 1800

rivers which flow into the Orange River and the Vaal enclosed some areas where agriculture was particularly productive. Pastoralism was specially attractive in this region, since tsetse fly and other animal pests were rare. Some measure of political authority was useful, if only to reduce or control the raiding of cattle herds by young men eager to establish themselves as independent heads of households; but the Sotho-speaking people who lived here did not form anything like the large and centralised communities of their northern relatives, the Shona.

Further west, however, along the eastern fringe of the Kalahari desert which marks the limit of agricultural production, Tswana-speaking people tended to converge into large settlements sometimes exceeding 10 000 inhabitants, deserving the description of towns. Urbanisation may have been encouraged by the fact that water was available only in riverine regions where natural springs reached the surface. In these urban settlements – as in similar population concentrations throughout Africa – it was much easier for a chief to exercise authority, especially in the allocation of pastures and the remote cattle posts where herds converged for drinking water. Such concentration also permitted a greater degree of economic specialisation than further east. Craftsmen skilled in iron-work and stone construction found regular clients. Considerable trade was conducted north to Zimbabwe and eventually to the east coast; and that also encouraged a measure of specialisation in production.

Even further west, in what is now central Namibia, there were other speakers of Bantu languages separated from the Tswana by the Kalahari desert. On the central plateau of Namibia, bounded by the Kalahari desert on one side and the Namib coastal desert on the other, Herero communities specialised almost exclusively in cattle and sheep. Since the Herero language is very closely related to Ovambo, and Ovambo speakers were cultivators of the soil in the well-watered Kunene River valley, it seems likely that the Herero had taken to pastoralism only in order to cope with the very arid conditions in which they found themselves.

To over-simplify matters, it may be useful to conceive of Bantu speakers settling southern Africa in three distinct environments, each requiring a rather different adaptation: the Nguni along the eastern coastal belt combining agriculture and pastoralism on a small scale; Sotho and Tswana in the interior plateau laying greater emphasis upon pastoralism than cultivation; Herero in the far west relying almost exclusively upon their herds. In each case, however, hunting provided an additional source of food (and of trade goods such as ivory): where human settlement was particularly dense, or where herds of cattle and sheep needed extensive pasture, the supply of wild animals naturally declined. Nevertheless hunting was always important, especially where it permitted the establishment of trading links to the north (in Zimbabwe) and towards the east coast. Venda communities for example, lived in an area which permitted good hunting, and that in turn enabled them to keep in contact with the affluent Shona communities of Zimbabwe.

There was little encouragement for these communities to expand further south, since (for example) the quality of pastures declines steadily to the south along the eastern coastal belt, and anyone moving south would be entering marginal agricultural conditions. South of the Sotho and the Herero lay almost desert conditions. Nevertheless some pastoralism was possible even in those conditions, and for several centuries (perhaps since about 1400 AD) a form of nomadic pastoralism had been practised in the southern half of the interior plateau. The Khoi people who developed this specialisation possessed most of the hunting and gathering skills of the San, and they certainly needed these skills in order to be sure of finding pastures each season, and water supplies in an emergency, and wild animals to hunt to supplement their diet. As nomadic people, they accumulated few possessions apart from their herds of cattle and sheep; and the size of each nomadic band was limited by the difficulty of finding water and pasture for large herds in a small area.

Interactions

When Europeans began to visit the Cape peninsula regularly, it was the Khoi communities which they first encountered. Later they came across Bantu mixed farmers, and San hunters. Their immediate response to these different strategies was to see them as distinct *stages* in human evolution, and to assume that human communities all began as hunter-gatherers, then evolved into nomadic pastoralists, and later into agriculturalists. Once this idea had been accepted, then obviously the San (Bushmen as they were called) must be the most primitive; Khoi (Hottentots) must be the next stage; mixed farmers (Kaffirs) must be an evolved form of the others. This very simple and convenient theory of human history is still very popular; but it does not help us to understand the dynamics of southern African history.

If we begin with the San, we may see the range of activities which were available to them. Some of course lived their whole lives in independent hunting-gathering bands. Others attached themselves as semi-permanent clients to Herero or Tswana or Sotho or Nguni patrons, exchanging the products of hunting, for regular supplies of grain or milk. Others again lived in the hills, raiding not only wild animals but also the herds of pastoralists, and relying on their well-developed skills of tracking and camouflaging themselves to remain free. They had every opportunity to see how pastoralism and agriculture were practised, but they did not 'evolve' away from hunting even after several centuries of interaction. We must assume that they lived well enough from hunting and gathering not to need to change their mode of living.

Khoi were also involved in a wide range of activities at different times. A band of Khoi might lose their herds entirely – through disease or through raiding – and in that crisis some would 'become' San hunters (since they were familiar with the necessary skills), others survived by fishing and collecting shellfish (the Strandlopers, or beachcombers as they were termed by Europeans). Others again could become the clients of Bantu patrons, receiving land or small herds in exchange for tribute. In one case, Robert Ross considers that a whole community of Khoi became a Nguni 'tribe' – the Gqunuqwebe. A certain amount of trade was also conducted through the Khoi communities, particularly in dagga (marijuana) and in cattle and sheep and metal; so they were easily able to keep in touch with events over a large region. Once again we should notice that most Khoi remained nomadic pastoralists for most of the time, with periods of hunting or fishing or cultivation when they had lost the herds on which they relied. In spite of all opportunities, they did not usually think it was worthwhile to abandon their mode of livelihood.

The mixed farmers along the eastern coastal belt were rather more stable in their production systems, but the societies were not entirely static. The most southerly of the Nguni languages (Xhosa) includes four of the clicks which are so characteristic of Khoi and San languages; and that implies a long period of very close contact, including some measures of inter-marriage. If Khoi could be absorbed as mixed farmers, it was also possible for adventurous (or unpopular) Nguni to abandon mixed farming and make some kind of living as marauders with the San, or as nomadic pastoralists with the Khoi. Hunting expeditions took them out of the well-settled valleys in search of elephant especially, and that was another way in which contact with San could be maintained. The Xhosa (and Sotho, and Tswana and Herero) patrons who enjoyed the services of San clients, often liked to think of themselves as the owners of their servants; but the reality was quite different. In broken country, San were formidable guerrillas; and in all cases the San preserved their ability to live independently of their patrons. San were often thought to possess powerful magic and familiarity with medicinal (or poisonous) plants; and that too made it necessary to take them seriously. In other words, the idea that San and Khoi were in some way innately inferior to mixed farmers, is a recent idea which does not explain real, historical relationships.

These interactions linked many of the farming and pastoralist communities to the south-west: equally important were the trading links which ran to the north-east, to Zimbabwe and to Mozambique.

The Shona seem usually to have been much more prosperous than their southern neighbours, having a wide range of crops, good pasture, and small quantities of alluvial gold for external trade. The Shona supported an elaborate (and presumably expensive) state structure; and when the Mwene Mutapa confederacy collapsed, it was soon replaced by the Changamire dynasty of rulers. Here was a reliable market for ivory from the south, and for copper as well. Stone buildings, craftsmen working metals, and the management of alluvial gold working all imply that the Shona formed the focus of the regional economy. Some ivory was certainly traded out to the southern coast of Mozambique without the knowledge of the Changamire, through the Thonga communities which had direct access to occasional European traders; but much more of the trade from the southern African interior passed through the Zimbabwe region. The two leading examples of early state formation in the region – among the Shona and among the Lozi – both occurred where two distinct specialised production systems were linked together. Extensive pastoralism and intensive agriculture became inter-dependent activities in Zimbabwe; the Zambesi flood-plain required seasonal specialisation. Elsewhere in the region, relations between specialists were much more casual.

Interaction among the peoples of southern Africa was promoted by the fact that all the communities were mobile, both seasonally (to take advantage of pasture variations) and for the purpose of hunting and trading. The Bantu languages of southern Africa are, for example, very closely related to each other, by comparison with linguistic diversity elsewhere in the continent; and that would suggest that contacts between them were quite common throughout the centuries of their settlement. The Drakensberg mountains certainly limited human and animal movement, but did not prevent it. More serious barriers were the Kalahari desert and the Zambesi flood plain inhabited by the Lozi. Khoi and San languages – which are very difficult for outsiders to learn – suggest a long period of separate existence from the Bantu language-speakers; but again it is clear that language barriers did not prevent a great deal of sustained interaction over a long period.

In general, then, the wide range of environmental circums-tances which prevail in southern Africa certainly encouraged people to specialise in quite different ways; but it also permitted sustained cooperation even between people whose languages and ways of life were very different from each other. Hostility, and even warfare certainly occurred; but there was nothing in the environment to make that hostility an essential part of day-to-day living. Rather the environment permitted a great range of specialisations to develop, and encouraged a range of relationships between the specialists, such that each of them could live slightly better in harmony with each other than in isolation.

Chapter 2

International contacts to 1800

Like most of Africa – and most of the non-European world – southern Africa came to be dominated by European powers. In southern Africa, however, European domination has been more intense and complex than in most other parts of the world, and the differences are obviously important in any account of the region's history. This chapter considers two questions which are more closely related than they seem: why was European influence so late; and why was it so massive when it did begin? To explain the intensity of post–1800 influence, we need to consider briefly events before 1800.

By the year 1500, different Europeans had found their way across the Atlantic to the Americas, and around the Cape of Storms (later re-named the Cape of Good Hope) to India. During the following half-century the Spaniards conquered the whole of central America and launched expeditions across the Pacific Ocean, seizing the Philippines as an off-shore island for trade with China: the Portuguese established a series of small settlements along the coast of West Africa, and began to chase Arab merchants out of the Indian Ocean, while they themselves established trading stations in India and began the penetration of Japan. For more than a generation these two European powers led the way in the conquest and conversion of vast areas of the world. Portuguese vessels all rounded the Cape on their way to the East, and it was not long before Dutch and English and French trading expeditions followed them, to destroy their brief monopoly of the trade of the Indies. What is surely remarkable is the fact that 150 years passed before any attempt was made by Europeans to establish a permanent settlement on the southern African coast.

This strange avoidance begins to make sense when we look for a pattern in Portuguese navigation and settlement. Like other European powers of the same period, they sought densely populated regions, where the people were already under the control of a centralised state system, and which would yield commodities of high value and little weight and volume. The ideal trading commodities were precious metals and minerals (gold, silver, jewels) or tropical spices, because these commodities could easily be fitted into the small sailing ships of the period, and commanded such high prices in Europe that they would repay the huge transport costs incurred by the slow sailing ships. The Portuguese were powerful at sea, thanks to their sailing skills and their cannon: on land they were far less secure, since their armour and guns would not always compensate for their very small numbers. To make any kind of profit at all, they must rely upon influence over some ruler whose people were already committed to pay tax and tribute, and who could therefore be coerced to grow the spices or hunt the elephants or mine the metals which were in such great demand. In Asia, therefore, they attempted to control trade with Japan (which proved too powerful for them) and with India (where the Mughal empire was a centralised state, but not a very stable one). In Africa, they sought Prester John, a Christian king who would no doubt facilitate international trade for their mutual advantage; and when Prester John proved hard to find, they concentrated on other centralised societies including the kingdom of Kongo on the west coast, Mwene Mutapa behind the east coast, and the long-established Arab trading towns of the Swahili coast. Most of southern Africa, from a Portuguese point of view, was simply a nuisance which lengthened the trading voyage between the Atlantic and the Indian oceans.

From all these points of view, southern Africa has no attraction at all. When ships landed at any point on the Cape peninsula (which offered sheltered anchorages from the powerful winds which are common at that latitude), the crew found only Strandlopers or San or Khoi – and not many of them either. This small population seemed to have no great kings, and nothing very valuable to trade. Once the landing crew had filled its water containers and bartered for a couple of sheep or cattle (or stolen them, if the owners did not want to barter for iron), they had obtained everything which could easily be extracted from the region. Essentially the Cape was nothing more than a hazard to shipping – and a major hazard, which caused many cumbersome Portuguese vessels to founder on unexpected rocks in rough weather. Some would put in for water at Algoa Bay (on the way to Goa), or at Delagoa Bay (on the way back), but they would have been much happier if Africa had come to an end at the Kunene River. Even Delagoa Bay, where ivory could sometimes be acquired, was much less important to the Portuguese than Beira or Quelimane which offered access (albeit difficult and precarious) to the markets of Zimbabwe.

The entry of the Netherlands, France and especially England into the Indian Ocean trade greatly increased the number of ships sailing round the Cape, although it did not lead immediately to any settled relationship with the inhabitants. Whereas the Portuguese merchants operated under the direct control of the Crown, their competitors evolved a rather different manner of organising trade. Within each European country, merchants committed to the Asian trade formed themselves into large joint stock companies, which enabled them to pool their resources and spread the risks, and to consolidate a very tight control over a defined Asian region. Steadily the English squeezed the French and the Dutch and even the Portuguese out of most of India; and the Dutch entrenched their control over the Spice Islands which were the core of the later Dutch East Indies. English trade with India was monopolised by the London-based East India Company; Dutch trade with the Indies by the Amsterdam-based Dutch East India Company. In each case the company was owned and controlled by merchant capitalists in the metropolitan country, and behaved overseas as if it were a sovereign and independent government. The large capital invested in these companies, and the long-term responsibilities they assumed, encouraged them to make greater provision for their trading expeditions than the earlier adventurers. After considerable research and consideration, the Dutch company determined that a supply station at the Cape would add to company profits by providing fresh meat and vegetables, and by caring for sick sailors, both of which would reduce the costs of the journey to and from Batavia. At last, in 1652, that station was established, under the command of a surgeon, Jan van Riebeeck. A permanent European presence had been planted, a century and a half after the site had been put on the map.

The company, unlike most governments, was required to make a profit in every year of its operations, and the governing Heeren XVII were constantly alert to any opportunity for reducing the running costs of their enterprise. The Cape, which was not expected to contribute profits directly, was most carefully scrutinised: the commander's reports were supplemented by reports written by company officials who stopped at Cape Town in mid-passage, and unnecessary expense was quickly pointed out. Only a well-capitalised company could undertake the settlement at all, and even a wealthy company found itself committed to a great deal of annoying expense.

The station was a garrison, which had to build a castle and protect itself against Khoi or against any European power which showed an interest in the station. It was also a food-producing centre, charged with supplying company fleets with fresh meat and vegetables. In addition, it was responsible for providing 'rest and recuperation' for those sailors and passengers who were too ill to continue their journey. Finally, the personnel of the station, many of them non-productive, had to be administered and coerced into

Late-eighteenth century impression of the Cape of Good Hope, 1796, the year after it was seized by Britain

16

fulfilling their allotted functions.

The essential purpose of establishing this little settlement was not to initiate the transformation of southern Africa – that was much too large and too speculative an enterprise for a cost-conscious merchant company – but to service the existing and expanding trade between the Netherlands and the Dutch East Indies. The character of Cape Town throughout the company period reflected that commitment. Elphick and Shell describe it in these terms:

> Cape Town was a seaward-looking community, a caravanserai on the periphery of the global spice trade. European and Asian cultures flourished in the port; so, too, did Christianity and Islam...

Cape Town retained that quality for a century and a half, until the company itself was destroyed during the French revolutionary and Napoleonic wars.

Even then, when Britain seized the Cape (in 1795 and again in 1806) the character of the town was not immediately changed. The Dutch saw the Cape as a half-way house to the East Indies; the British regarded it as a half-way house to India; at first the authority of the Dutch East India Company was replaced by British officials conscious of the English East India Company's monopoly rights. The early commanders of the company garrison indeed thought of insulating the settlement from the rest of the continent, either by a hedge (Van Riebeeck's idea) or by a canal (Van Goens's notion). However, even though the merchants of Amsterdam deplored the expansion of the Cape settlement, it kept on growing, and its impact upon the whole region increased steadily.

We should now consider the immediate impact on the region, of the establishment of an outpost of merchant capitalism at Cape Town.

Kraal and castle

The people most affected by the establishment of the garrison-outpost were Khoi; and during the generation before 1652 they had experienced increasing contacts with the crew of ships putting in to the anchorages. A tradition had already been built up whereby Khoi would exchange some stock for pieces of iron; but there were strict limits to that exchange system, because the Khoi did not need a lot of iron, and they did not have a lot of surplus stock to exchange. Once the settlement began to make regular demands for stock, the limits of voluntary exchange were soon reached. Company officials needed fresh meat on a scale which could not be matched by the exchange system, and inevitably conflict broke out. If cattle would not be offered voluntarily, then they would be seized anyway, leaving the Khoi with the choice of robbing cattle from more remote regions, or else to become San or Strandlopers. The garrison had to grow its own vegetables in any case, and as soon as possible they tried to grow wheat as their own staple diet: that system was quickly expanded to the herding of their own slaughter animals. Even within the peninsula region, with its essentially European Mediterranean climate, quite large areas of land were needed in order to provide the full range of pasture types, and soils and environments to sustain vegetable and wheat production. Inevitably, the effect of more intensive pastoralism and of agricultural production was to drive the Khoi out of the area of company settlement; and the further away they were driven, the more difficult it became to continue the tradition of barter. Very rapidly the Khoi became marginal to the expanding settlement.

Within a century of the founding of Cape Town, the Khoi communities of the western Cape had been displaced. We have seen that the loss of herds had happened to Khoi communities in earlier times, and they had either become San for a period, or attached themselves to Bantu patrons until they could re-establish themselves as nomadic pastoralists. The impact of the Cape Town settlement made such recovery impossible. Whenever Khoi abandoned territory which they had used as pasture, it fell into the hands of the immigrant community and it could not then be recovered, so that the amount of land available to Khoi was constantly diminishing. When they lost their cattle and sheep, they could no longer build up their herds once again, since company officials or unofficial immigrants were constantly on the look out for fresh stock to purchase or to appropriate. Then in 1713 an epidemic of smallpox – to which the Khoi had no immunity – swept away large numbers. The survivors found it difficult to reconstruct their old societies, so some individuals attached themselves to the immigrants as wage labourers or as clients, and many others migrated out of the western Cape altogether, either to the north or to the east where conditions were more settled.

The catastrophe of the Khoi is difficult to measure, but in the course of less than a century they declined from the dominant community of the western Cape to a few survivors who could no longer live as Khoi unless they left the region entirely. The most obvious cause of this decline was smallpox, but that will not serve as an explanation, because the Khoi could presumably have recovered from that disaster if circumstances had favoured them. More important were the immigrants' persistent demands for cattle, and for land, and the removal of any possibility of recovering land and herds once they had been bartered or robbed.

Perhaps the fate of the Khoi can be seen more clearly if we consider what has happened to other nomadic communities when commercial pastoralism has intruded upon their lands. Indians in North America, Indians on the grasslands of Argentina and

Uruguay, Aboriginals in most of Australia, and hunters and gatherers throughout Siberia, have all shared the same fate as the Khoi: commercial pastoralism has made an old and satisfactory way of life impossible, dispersing the nomads either to a few corners of land which the new pastoralists do not need, or distributing them as individual labourers among the new owners of the land.

A settler society

In one important respect the crumbling away of Khoi society and its replacement by an immigrant society involved rather little change. Apart from some strictly limited areas near the peninsula, the land was still impossible for agricultural production with the technology then available: the land continued to be used as pasture – often enough for exactly the same cattle and sheep which the Khoi had hearded, but under new ownership and management. The decisive change was not from pastoralism and nomadism to settled production (a transformation which occurred only very much later) but from subsistence production to market conditions. Commercial pastoralism involved a slightly different relationship between people and animals and land – and a drastically different relationship between people and people. The company and its servants emerged from that part of western Europe which had been most completely transformed by the development of agricultural and merchant capitalism, and inevitably they approached colonial problems in the light of their own experience. (Spain and Portugal, the earliest of European colonial powers, remained much more feudal in their own societies, and imposed something rather like feudalism on their colonies.)

What distinguished European influence upon southern Africa, from almost all other African colonial situations, was the establishment of a quite new society which entirely replaced its Khoi predecessors, and which was committed to capitalist and commercial relationships from the moment it was established. The immigrant community contained within itself only three kinds of people: company officials governing the whole community, then the owners of productive property (land, cattle, sometimes slaves), and finally those who performed labour for the owners of property (either as slaves or as wage labourers). Company officials were often able to become property-owners, either in their spare time (and often illegally), or when they resigned from company service. The essential division within the immigrant society, then, was ownership of productive property.

To understand the unique nature of this form of society, we may briefly consider the kind of society which .the Portuguese attempted to plant in the Zambesi valley of Mozambique. There the land and its inhabitants were parcelled up, and each parcel (or *prazo*) comprised the *prazeiro* who held it for the Crown, and the inhabitants who rendered feudal service to him (or her). The kinds of personal obligations and social ties which formed on a *prazo* were therefore very different from those which formed on a farm in the western Cape, even though the company was always reluctant to provide the land registration facilities, and the rural police, to make commercial pastoralism work smoothly and productively.

If capitalism worked imperfectly at the Cape, nevertheless it worked more effectively there than in other regions of the world where the colonial power introduced European feudal ideas, or where production was complicated by the survival of pre-colonial and pre-capitalist society with its own social traditions.

Paul Baran (in *The Political Economy of Growth*) states the relationship in this way:

> one cannot distinguish sharply enough between the impact of Western Europe's entrance into North America (and we could add the western Cape) on one side, and the 'opening up' by Western Capitalism of Asia, (the rest of) Africa and Eastern Europe. In the former case Western Europeans entered more or less complete societal vacua, and *settled* in those areas . . . From the outset capitalist in its structure, unencumbered by the fetters and barriers of feudalism, that society could single-mindedly devote itself to the development of its productive resources.

Elsewhere there was the problem of re-shaping a feudal society, to suit the needs of capitalist production.

The term capitalism implies the private ownership of means of production, and the employment of labour for wages. How were these innovations established at the Cape? As Khoi society crumbled, so the company acquired all rights to land. However it was impossible for the company itself to conduct agriculture and pastoralism, and within five years of his arrival, Van Riebeeck allocated land to the first freeburghers. The freeburghers were employees of the company who were released from their employment and authorised to own land, and to sell their products to the company (which insisted on a monopoly control over the market). The freeburghers had virtually no capital (otherwise they would not be living at the Cape in the first place), and the most reliable and profitable way of using their land rights was to herd slaughter stock. The freeburghers could not afford to improve their pastures, so their pastoralism exploited extensive areas of land. The hinterland of the peninsula rapidly became (or became again) a region devoted to pastoralism; and the production of sufficient grain, for the settlement itself, evolved only very much more slowly. In practice, the new farmers seldom owned the freehold title to the land they used; but the practice of renting land for a small annual rent gave the farmers quite sufficient control of the land. More important, they were the absolute owners of their stock.

The provision of labour was a much more difficult issue. It was difficult to attract Europeans to the Cape at all, since the economic opportunities in the East Indies were much more attractive; and in practice the company had to rely upon small numbers of Dutch, Belgians, West Germans, and French Protestants, to recruit settlers. These settlers would certainly not stay at the Cape if their prospects were limited to wage labour on the new ranches. A more accessible source of labour was the disintegrating Khoi communities, which did provide individuals, though the employers always feared that Khoi herdsmen might vanish with the herds, and try to regain their independence. A further source of labour was African slaves, mainly from Madagascar, Angola and West Africa; and the Indies themselves provided some slave and some 'free' wage labour for the Cape employers.

From the point of view of employers, there were difficulties in all these sources of labour. Pastoralists could seldom afford to buy slaves, who were much more common in Cape Town itself and in the agricultural areas nearby. Slaves were less likely to run away to the interior than were Khoi – but some did escape, and not all were recaptured. If slaves were driven too hard, they might resort to violence and the destruction of property. Male slaves outnumbered females at all times by a very large margin, so the slave population had constantly to be increased by fresh importations. In any case, since the company maintained a monopoly on sales of meat and grain and vegetables to passing ships, very few of the new farmers could afford either to purchase slaves or to pay regular wages. Even wage labour had to be enforced by threats and punishments to the labourers – which of course made labour even less attractive to anyone who had an alternative. In spite of these difficulties however, the slave population of the Cape throughout the period of company rule, kept pace with the freeburgher population: by 1800 there were more than 20 000 people in each of these conditions. Because of the prevalence of slavery, the legal conditions of free labourers were little better: employers would opt for slaves if the wages or allowances of wage labourers made them less profitable.

In several ways then, the new community centred upon Cape Town differed from any previous African society. Almost all its members were immigrants, either from western Europe or from the Indies or from Madagascar; and even those descendants of indigenous Khoi, had been violently separated from their societies. Cape Town, the focus of the community because it was the central market for all produce and for labour, depended almost entirely upon the Europe–Asia trade, and the company ensured that no money was spent which did not contribute directly to the profits of that trade. Land, cattle and sheep (as well as personal property) were privately owned, and property relationships were governed by legal principles and procedures which had evolved with capitalism in western Europe. Most of the productive labour was performed by slaves – and that was true of the early development of capitalism in North America as well – but some was performed for wages, and in either case the feudal labour relations of Portuguese Africa were not to be found at the Cape. None of these relationships was much influenced by any previous African practices. Instead, the new community was dependent upon a European merchant capitalist company for all its external contacts; and the external contacts were the essential dynamic of the society as a whole.

Expansion

In one further respect the new settlement differed radically from any previous society on the continent, and that was the speed of its expansion. The Nguni and Sotho and Herero colonisation of land for cultivation or for pastures was commonly, as we have seen, a slow business: only during the Mfecane would the pace increase to something like that of the Cape settlement. For the first fifty years, the settlement expanded rather slowly, scarcely beyond the immediate hinterland of the peninsula. Between 1700 and 1780, however, commercial nomadic pastoralism swept through the whole coastal belt of the south, to the Great Fish River, and spread into those areas of the hinterland which enjoyed sufficient rainfall to be worth owning. To some extent the speed of the expansion was illusory: areas of semi-desert were by-passed, and the new pastoralists occupied mainly those areas which could be appropriated from the Khoi. Dry areas, or regions already occupied by agricultural people, posed much more difficult problems for the frontier pastoralists. Even so, the expansion was dramatic, affecting an area perhaps 700 km from west to east, and as much as 200 km from south coast to northern extremities. The dynamic for this expansion was within the pastoral economy.

Once the Cape settlement was widely known, and could produce reliable quantities of meat and vegetables, more and more ships stopped at the Cape for supplies. The production of fresh meat was therefore a dependable source of cash income, even if Cape Town butchers and company officials skimmed off some of the profits which the pastoral farmers might otherwise have enjoyed. Furthermore cattle – unlike vegetables or wheat – could walk to the market. It was quite feasible to breed and raise cattle on the frontier, bring them back to Cape Town, perhaps fatten them in the well-watered areas near Cape Town, and then sell them. The proceeds of these sales would provide clothing, wagons, domestic utensils, and especially firearms and gunpowder to sustain the trekboer for a year or two in the interior. In order to sustain this trade however, the trekboer required great areas of land. Often he needed access to sweet grass as well as sour, and always the unimproved pastures would carry only a very limited number of animals. The company recognised that 6 000 acres was a reasonable size for each property – almost 2 500 ha. There frontiersmen were prolific, and their children could not sub-divide the property and still make a living; so in each generation every son except one must find a new piece of land. Now the Khoi who had previously occupied this region had not been obliged to purchase clothing or firearms or indeed anything else, and they had been able to collect food from the countryside; so the effect of the transition to commercial pastoralism was to *reduce* the population density of the pastoral region. It was the commercial dimension of the pastoral industry which made it so greedy for land, and so restless in its expansion: and it was only when the pastoralists reached the vicinity of the Great Fish River that it was feasible to exploit countryside north of the dividing range. Until that time the sparse pastoral settlement had mainly been a thin ribbon development along the coastal fringe.

The rapid expansion which occurred almost throughout the eighteenth century, came to a halt in the generation before 1800. One very obvious reason for the change in pace was that the trekboers had entered into territory occupied by more densely settled mixed farmers. After a century of easy expansion at the expense of patoralists, the trekboers were ill-equipped to deal with this obstacle, and the old techniques of encroachment worked badly against a population which would not simply melt away. Second, the Khoi who had retreated ever further eastward in the face of settler expansion, were no longer the dispirited and broken communities of a century earlier, but had begun to practise commercial pastoralism on their own account (as we shall see in Chapter 5). Caught between the trekboers from the west and the Xhosa mixed farmers on the east, between the Indian Ocean and the mountain ranges, they put up a strenuous resistance to further encroachment. Third, the company itself was unable to control events beyond the hinterland of Cape Town. A frontier war in 1793 demonstrated that the company was unable and unwilling to support the frontiersmen in an attempt to expel the Xhosa from the contested territory – and that it lacked the power to discipline the frontiersmen themselves. In 1795 a frontier rebellion broke out, which had not been suppressed by the time the British occupied the Cape later that year. Fourth, the more prosperous among the colonists were increasingly frustrated by the continuing control of company officials, and the frontier rebellion of 1795 was part of a series of assertions by groups of colonists, from Cape Town to the frontier, that they ought to play a larger role in the management of the colony. By that time – the 1780s onwards – it becomes impossible to see the new settlement as merely an extension of external

European influence. It had acquired a dynamic of its own, and had begun to interact with a settled, agricultural population.

It should now be clear why the Cape was settled so long after it was first observed: successful occupation required a great deal of capital, manpower and reliable external communication, all of which had to be imported into the region. Only a successful merchant capitalist company could afford the expense involved. Having imported capital and landowners and labourers from outside the region however, and having initiated commercial production for the market, the company had unleashed formidable forces for the transformation of the region as a whole. In both respects the Dutch settlement was quite different from the Portuguese settlements on the eastern coast, which required little capital or manpower, which led a very precarious existence, and which had much less impact on the well-established societies of the interior.

So far, we have emphasised the dynamic and expansive quality of the new settlement. That description now requires modification. The dynamism of the new society was limited by two sets of circumstances, both of which became clear in the last years of the eighteenth century. First, the expansion of the pastoral frontier created some problems of its own: a dispossessed and disaffected Khoi population around the frontier, some struggling to become trekboers and others fighting a guerilla war with San tactics; the formation of quite distinct interest groups within the colonial society itself; and the vulnerability of a sparsely settled pastoral society when it collided with dense populations of mixed farmers. Second, in spite of the rapid growth of the colonist and slave population, the society as a whole was still substantially dependent upon Cape Town and its links with Europe and Asia. Whoever controlled Cape Town controlled the export market for meat, and the import trade in firearms and gunpowder, and could therefore enforce its will upon the hinterland. Thus in 1795 a British expedition occupied the Cape; in 1803 it was returned to the Batavian republic which now ruled the Netherlands; in 1806 it was again occupied by British troops; and in each case the frontiersmen could do little more than grumble, and then adapt themselves to the new authorities. There were occasional, and limited, rebellions among the frontiersmen; but the authority of Cape Town was not seriously threatened by these rebellions. Rather the most serious obstacle to Cape Town's continued authority was a revolutionary uprising of frontier Khoi, in alliance with Xhosa across the colonial frontier, challenging the distribution of landed property throughout the frontier regions. We will consider that event in Chapter 5, once we have seen what was happening beyond the pale of settlement, among the Nguni and Sotho communities.

Chapter 3

The Mfecane and the rise of the Zulu Kingdom

This chapter examines the rise of the Zulu state and its consequences during the first three decades of the nineteenth century. The evolution of the kingdom under Shaka, its founder, till his death in 1828 was accompanied by numerous major changes in society, described by the Zulu as the *Mfecane* ('the crushing') and by the Sotho as the *Difaqane* ('forced migration'). The Zulu kingdom is an example of the social and economic strength that pre-colonial states and peoples often derived from the particular relationship that existed between themselves and their environment. In the case of the Zulu, the ability of the physical environment to support its population was of great importance in shaping the people's way of life: the river system, the vegetation, rainfall and climate were all suited to the life of the farming and cattle-keeping Zulu. As will be shown later, all these factors played a crucial part in determining the nature of the changes that took place in northern Nguni society during the reign of King Shaka (1816–28). Following a summary of the pre-Mfecane situation, we shall describe the changes that resulted from the rise of the Zulu kingdom before attempting an explanation of them and a discussion of some of their consequences for the Zulu people's African neighbours.

African societies in pre-Mfecane Southern Africa

There were certain common characteristics among the southern Bantu, of whom the northern Nguni groups were cattle keepers as well as agriculturalists. The significance of cattle went beyond the mere provision of food; it was also a source of wealth since it was often used as a currency that could fetch many things. As a people practising both pastoralism and agriculture, the southern Bantu had a distinct advantage over their Khoisan counterparts with whom they now came into contact. For the mixed economy gave them the capacity to construct rather more intricate social and political systems than those enjoyed by the Khoi and San peoples, even though (as we saw in the previous two chapters), the Khoi had by

1800 embarked upon commercial pastoralism. It should be remembered that this difference in social and economic organisation did not necessarily imply that the Khoi and San were inferior to the Bantu. (See Chapter 1.)

Information on the exact origins of the Zulu kingdom is scanty and there has been no agreement among historians about it. Numerous accounts of the career of Shaka, its founder, and a clear outline of the main events of the story do exist, however. In the region now known as Natal and Zululand were a northern Nguni group known as the Mthethwa. Dingiswayo assumed the chieftianship of the Mthethwa in about 1795, at a time when two other contemporary northern Nguni leaders (Zwide of the Ndwandwe and Sobhuza of the Ngwane) were experimenting with the idea of amalgamating various small political units into larger entities. Dingiswayo's contribution to socio-economic changes in northern Nguni society was quite substantial. His innovations were not unique; rather, his major achievement was the degree to which he succeeded in carrying them out. Two such major innovations introduced by him were the abolition of circumcision, an old Nguni practice, and the formation of age regiments, embracing all young men in his chiefdom, to supplant the previously existing kinship groups. The new age-grades, comprising initiates who were usually in the same age-brackets, approximated to a standing army, with each regiment being allocated a particular uniform and using shields of a particular colour to identify it. The impact of these changes was to place the Mthethwa immediately at an advantage over the neighbouring African groups. The Methethwa were now able to conquer and absorb the others systematically. However, Dingiswayo's innovations did not go as far as they might have: he usually left the women and children of the conquered groups alone, and took only their men who were then conscripted into the expanding Methethwa army. A major function of the army now was the production of men with a loyalty transcending the kinship allegiance of the past. By the end of his rule in 1818, Dingiswayo had succeeded in transforming the Mthethwa chiefdom into a comparatively large, multi-chiefdom confederacy that extended from the Mfolozi River in the north to the Tukela in the south. But Dingiswayo is remembered as having been of a gentle disposition. It is true that he was an expansionist and that he achieved his aims by forcing others to submit to his rule. However, he is reputed to have used force sparingly and was known for his generosity towards subjugated peoples.

Before Dingiswayo's death, a young recruit called Shaka had joined the Methethwa army in about 1809. Shaka was born in about 1787, the illegitimate son of Senzagakhona, the ruler of the small Zulu clan which was tributary to the Mthethwa confederacy. His early life was somewhat unhappy and insecure because of the

circumstances of his birth. From the time he joine
army to serve his apprenticeship, however, Shaka
himself as an efficient and able soldier and tactician. He
that army till the death of Senzagakhona in 1816. A co.
Dingiswayo's court led to the elimination of Sigujana, th
heir to the Zulu chieftianship, and the imposition of Shak.
new chief of the Zulu clan. Having achieved political power, .ka
began his own military and political reorganisation of the Zulu
chiefdom. The soldiers discarded the long throwing spears, and
relied upon the short stabbling spear, which was already common
throughout the Nguni societies, but nowhere used so effectively.
Shaka intensified military training, abandoned sandals and made
his men go barefoot for greater mobility, forbade men to marry till
the age of 40, perfected the enveloping method of attack, and
employed surprise tactics using spies and smoke signals. These
methods were not new, but the discipline and the scale of the armies
were unprecedented. He dispensed with limited warfare and
replaced it with total warfare, involving everyone in either
combatant or supporting roles and aiming to eliminate completely
the enemy's ability to resist. A major result of the military
reorganisation undertaken by Shaka was the emergence of strong
military regiments which also became the units of social life. Men
lived in the regimented headquarters until such time as Shaka
permitted them to marry and retire from active service, when they
were obliged to marry women from the equivalent female regiment.
However, as Jeff Guy points out, it is incorrect to suggest that the
restriction on marriage that Shaka imposed on his soldiers 'led to an
accumulation of sexual energy' which was then translated into
military strength. Since military service was drawn out for many
years and men retired only in their forties, the regiments were a
focus of social and political life in the way the old lineage-groups
had been before the military revolution.

It is doubtful whether Shaka could have remained a
subordinate of Dingiswayo for very long, since his personal
ambition was so great and Dingiswayo so close a neighbour. It has
been suggested that Shaka conspired to betray Dingiswayo to his
enemy Zwide. At any rate in 1818 Zwide did capture and execute
Dingiswayo, thereby leaving Shaka as the strongest military leader
in the old Mthethwa confederacy. Just as Dingiswayo had imposed
Shaka on the Zulu, so Shaka now imposed one of his followers on
the Mthethwa, and consolidated his authority throughout
Dingiswayo's sphere of influence. The following year he led
Dingiswayo's old armies in a successful and devastating war against
Zwide, and so extended his power over all the Nguni in what is now
Zululand, and his influence over a vast area from Swaziland in the
north to the Transkei in the south, and from the Drakensberg
mountains to the sea. Military control had been established, and the

27

, cleared for the political revolution which was about to begin. What distinguishes Shaka from Zwide and Dingiswayo is not so much his military power (though his was certainly greater than theirs) as the use which he made of that power to bring about political change.

Many of these changes had already been attempted on a small scale in the pure Zulu community. Even then they had a different effect when applied on the larger scale of the whole Zulu state. The regiments, for example, had been organised before: but now they served a nation-building purpose as well as a military one. Recruits from all over the new state were mixed up together in each regiment, where they built up a loyalty to the regiment and to Shaka as king, and tended to forget their separate individual origins. By living and fighting together, they grew to understand and to trust each other. In addition, promotion could only be achieved through the military organisation, so that ambitious young men devoted their efforts to zealous service under Shaka as commander-in-chief. Moreover, since most of the able-bodied men at any given time were to be found in these regiments, local chiefs were unable to build up any dangerous organisation against the state itself. Since the regiments were so often successful in the following years, the members steadily developed a pride in the regiment and in the state which it served, to the exclusion of prior political identity: Methethwa and Ndwandwe young men could take common pride in belonging to the most powerful state any of them had ever encountered. Very quickly therefore a degree of political and social unity was achieved which replaced the political fragments of the earlier era. The Zulu dialect of Nguni became standard throughout the country; the traditions of the Zulu dynasty became the traditions of all the citizens; people thought of themselves as Ama-Zulu instead of the remnants of the earlier political units.

At the same time, military and social unity were accompanied by a centralisation of the economy. Each barracks of a regiment was also the location of one of the royal herds. Cattle and captives from the raids were distributed by the king himself. External trade was strictly controlled by him. The problem of feeding so large a standing army required state control over food production. Though each soldier had a home to go to on retirement, he spent most of his active life entirely dependent economically upon the ability of the state to organise food supplies, and the homesteads were no longer the focus of economic activity and interest.

Not only the economy, but also religious beliefs were transformed into instruments of nation-building. Shaka, making himself ritual as well as political and military head of the system, devoted his attention to rooting out sectional religious beliefs and exterminating sectional religious officials. The famous 'smelling-out' of witches exercise emphasised the fact that the king was supreme even over the religious institutions. That supremacy was symbolised when the annual first-fruits ceremony became a national event; an event which also symbolised the new economic centralisation. Naturally, Shaka also took care that his local chiefs (some of whom had ruled before the conquest) remained absolutely loyal, by bringing them frequently to his own court, and by dismissing or executing potential and real enemies of the new state system. Loyal subjects could win prestige and wealth through service to the king: those suspected of disloyalty ran the risk of swift execution. Chiefs were further controlled by the fact of having to spend much of their time at the royal court and in any case Shaka's female relatives were often posted to provincial centres.

The most striking attribute of Shaka was the thoroughness which marked all his most characteristic decisions. Having decided upon his ends, he was unswerving in pursuit of them. He was fearful of fathering sons, since these might eventually turn against him and succeed him: but unlike any other ruler of his day, he made sure that he had no children. His mother, who had quarrelled with his father, occupied a massive place in Shaka's consciousness. When she died, he found it difficult to express his grief adequately. That in itself is not unusual; but what is most unusual is Shaka's determination to make everyone else mourn, and his willingness to sacrifice other lives to make sure that mourning should be complete. It was sensible to insist that the men in the regiments did not marry, but remarkable that Shaka was prepared to over-rule human nature in his soldiers (and in himself) in order to create an effective military machine. Finally, he set no apparent limit upon his ambitions for his new Zulu nation: there were no neighbouring communities which could be left to themselves. No doubt it was sensible to keep the regiments fully occupied, lest they turn their attention to internal politics, but it is nevertheless striking that the Zulu state had no external allies whatsoever. Neighbours of the Zulu state could be enemies or they could be vassals, but no friendly equality was permissible.

Ultimately the Zulu paid a great price for Shaka's policy, since none of their neighbours were prepared to assist them, and some were prepared to join the incoming colonists in alliance against them. Such singleness of purpose is probably necessary in the creation of a new and unprecedented political system. However, it is difficult to see what Shaka would have done had he not been assassinated. His neighbours were beginning to learn Shaka's own military tactics and to use them against his regiments; and the regiments themselves were growing discontented with their lives. It may well be the case that his death spared Shaka the necessity of re-considering his attitudes – just as it spared him the knowledge that his army in the Gaza empire had failed in its mission. It is doubtful whether any community can indefinitely accept such thoroughness, even in the course of revolution and external conquest.

Explaining the emergence of the Zulu Kingdom

One of the earliest popular explanations offered by the local Zulu people for the emergence of the Zulu state stresses the personal qualities and contributions of individuals such as Dingiswayo and Shaka. The charismatic and heroic personalities and qualities of these men, according to these Nguni traditions, enabled them to introduce the changes they made in their societies. But these heroic traditions are an inadequate explanation of the whole spectrum of changes in northern Nguni society at this particular moment in time. It is clear that no single person acts in a vacuum; yet the theory of heroic achievement is completely silent on the circumstances leading to the emergence of particular individuals. Any historical explanation that eulogises individuals quite out of proportion to the times in which they lived will therefore not do. The Nguni people were also, apparently, in a mood to tolerate this immense change in their manner of life. Had their mood been different, Dingiswayo and Shaka would have worked in vain, since soldiers can be trained but cannot be made to fight with enthusiasm, and people can be ruled but cannot be forced to welcome or love their rulers. In a poorer agricultural country, there would have been neither the food nor the man-power required to operate such a system.

The theory that Dingiswayo of the Mthethwa was influenced by what he saw in the white settler society of the Cape can be equally quickly dismissed. The earliest propagators of the theory were Henry Francis Fynn, Theophilus Shepstone and the Reverend A. T. Bryant. The explanation suggests that Dingiswayo met a certain Dr Cowan in the Cape, that Dingiswayo received the gun and horse from the doctor, and that the two men's conversation about the white regimental system prompted Dingiswayo to copy it. But Fynn, the original author of this idea, mixes up his dates, making it highly improbable that his evidence about the alleged meeting between Dingiswayo and Cowan can be trusted. The 'white inspiration' theory (as Leonard Thompson refers to this idea) is the kind of racist whiteman's view of Africa which saw nothing good ever coming out of the continent – a view which has now long been discredited by historians and other scholars. Not only is there no evidence whatever to support the 'white inspiration' theory, Dingiswayo's state and Shaka's bear hardly any resemblance to the white communities that were then being established at the Cape.

A third hypothesis is related to the desire for the control of trade, which the social anthropologist Monica Wilson was the first to suggest as a possible explanation for the emergence of the Zulu and other northern Nguni kingdoms. According to this theory,

Dingiswayo's and Shaka's desire to control the trade of the African chiefdoms with the Portuguese in the late eighteenth century might have dictated to the two leaders the need to establish their political jurisdiction over larger areas. It was in response to this need that they would have launched the process of amalgamation and their expansionist programmes of the late eighteenth and early nineteenth centuries. But this explanation is based more upon conjecture than on any firm evidence. A further objection to this kind of hypothesis is that in this period the Portuguese presence in the region of south-eastern Africa was very limited; their power here was declining rather than growing. Equally limited also was the trade that was going on through Lourenço Marques, suggesting that trade was not a very important factor. Moreover, the trade that existed was mainly in slaves, and we know that the Nguni did not participate in the export of slaves.

The fourth type of explanation is that there was population pressure at the time, and that it was necessary to reorganise the economic structure in order for everyone to make a living. Though not explaining all, this theory has attracted increasing attention from historians since it can be linked with the whole issue of the importance of the relationship between the northern Nguni and their environment as a factor in the emergence of the Zulu state. But we must begin by stating the theory as it was originally presented by Gluckman. He suggested that there was evidence in the Zulu traditions as well as data left by shipwrecked European travellers that the northern Nguni population had multiplied to the extent that by the end of the eighteenth century matters had reached crisis proportions. The existing land could no longer support the population. The rapid growth of the Nguni population was attributed to the eminent suitability of the south-eastern coastal strip of the land for human settlement: it had reliable rainfall, good grazing, good soil, and good yields of food such as maize and millet. All this led to rapid population growth and overcrowding. Hence, so the theory concludes, both Dingiswayo and Shaka were responding to these circumstances and through there amalgamation of chiefdoms into larger political units, they were seeking a solution to the problem confronting them.

It has already been suggested that though there is probably some truth in this kind of explanation, by itself, however, it is not convincing. It rests on rather flimsy evidence as the demographic figures for the region in this period are rather shaky and unreliable. Nevertheless, recent research by Jeff Guy into Zulu history suggests that by the end of the eighteenth century there was an ecological imbalance between the population density of the northern Nguni and the environment. An analysis of the environmental factors (especially with regard to the grazing capacity of the vegetation of Zululand) indicates that in this period there was a serious

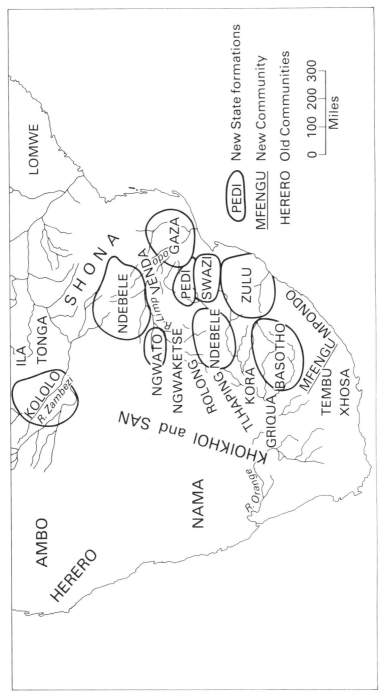

Map 4 African states and communities during and after the Mfecane

competition for diminishing resources. Though not going as far as arguing that 'the environmental crisis of the late eighteenth century led to the creation of the nineteenth-century kingdom which solved this problem', Guy's work nevertheless shows that the Zulu techniques of production, the environment, and population pressure were all inter-related factors in the rise of the Zulu kingdom under Shaka.

It is not enough, however, to enumerate the factors which may have assisted Shaka in the construction of the Zulu kingdom: his understanding of the situation and his ability to turn factors to his advantage are equally important. We might perhaps suggest that the crucial factor explaining the success of Shaka in Zululand was the fact that the political and social traditions of the northern Nguni were crumbling at the relevant time and that people were therefore unusually willing to accept charismatic leadership and the construction of a very different political regime. Why the people were so willing, however, is a question beyond our power to answer.

The effects of the creation of the Zulu state

In the immediate neighbourhood of the Zulu themselves, other communities could feel secure only if they had a safe place of refuge. To the south, the white traders at Port Natal stayed close to the shore, hoping to find refuge in ships if a Zulu *impi* (regiment) approached. The African communities in the open country inland from the Port were either absorbed into the new nation, or retreated into the foothills of the Drakensberg mountains, or fled south into the territory of southern Nguni peoples. To the south of the Tukela River, therefore, there stretched a belt of country which was almost depopulated. The Hlubi, for example, had retired further into the hills; the Bhaca had crossed the Mzimkhulu River to establish themselves near the Mpondo. To the north-east, the Thonga were very vulnerable to Zulu raiding parties, and were in fact raided, but since they possessed very few cattle and presented no interesting military challenge, they were less harried than they might have been. To the north, beyond the Pongola River and partially sheltered by the Lebombo mountains, refugees were able to establish themselves over and among Ngwane people, where they built up the Swazi nation which will be considered in the next chapter. To the north-west, the open pasture country of the interior tableland offered an attractive raiding ground, whose Sotho inhabitants were obliged to move away from their grazing lands and seek refuge in the mountains or further away to the north. To the west, the Drakensberg offered a refuge in which the Sotho could and did find security and established one of the most interesting and successful political systems of the nineteenth century, under

Moshoeshoe who will be considered in the next chapter.

The area affected was very much larger than the area directly raided by any of Shaka's raiding parties. Refugees from his rule fled the country, taking their immediate followers with them, often travelling immense distances, and almost always adopting the military system which had originally driven them away. In about 1823, for example, one of Shaka's generals, Mzilikazi, having failed in an expedition, thought it best to flee from the wrath to come. He was unusual in being also the chief of one of the pre-Zulu communities and therefore enjoyed a personal following. He and his followers, who were very familiar with Zulu military and political methods, fled onto the interior plateau, and eventually settled beyond the Limpopo River in what is now Zimbabwe. They were described by the Sotho name for all Nguni speakers, Ndebele. Their numbers were expanded by conquest and absorption of the conquered people into the Ndebele community.

Similarly Soshangane, a Ndwandwe refugee, in about 1820 fled northwards with a few dozen followers, and established himself as ruler of the Gaza kingdom, over conquered Thonga and Shona peoples in the hinterland of Lourenço Marques. Two similar groups of Nguni, one led by Zwangendaba and the other by Nqaba, both describing themselves as Ngoni, fled northwards, crossed the Zambesi, and eventually settled around Lake Malawi.

Secondary movements of people can also be traced, though less clearly than the primary movements already mentioned. Large numbers of refugees flowed into the Transkei area; and although many were absorbed into the existing communities, most seem to have established a separate identity for themselves as Mfengu (or, as the colonists called them, Fingo). Finding life difficult in the already densely populated areas near the white frontier, some groups crossed into the colony themselves, helping the white settlers to assert themselves against the southern Nguni. Another group, the Ngwane under Matiwane, preserved their old identity despite a very eventful career; around 1818 they retreated in the face of Zwide and Dingiswayo, and dislodged some of the Hlubi who then crossed the Drakensberg onto the interior plateau. In 1822 another raid – this time by Shaka's armies – sent the Ngwane themselves over the mountains onto the plateau. Once on the plateau, these two refugee communities in turn displaced indigenous communities, until it became very difficult to grasp precisely who everyone was, where they had originally come from, how they had travelled and where they were going. Best known of the displaced peoples is a Sotho-speaking community known as the Tlokwa, and ruled at that time by MaNthatisi, widow of the previous chief and mother of the later chief Sekonyela. Three major streams of refugees – led by MaNthatisi, Matiwane and Mpangazita (chief of the Hlubi) – proceeded to pillage the southern interior plateau, between the Vaal and Orange rivers, for two years or more. Eventually in about the middle of the 1820s, all three communities established themselves in strong defensive positions along the Caledon River, one of the tributaries of the Orange River, flowing from the Drakensberg mountains south-westwards. This settlement and the relative security it offered tended to reduce the severity and frequency of raiding activities. Nevertheless the *Mantatees* has become an English expression to describe any desperate and ruthless roving band.

The Sotho communities had been disastrously affected by these movements, and many of these little communities, in turn, fled to the west or the north, spreading the dislocation even further. Only in the area which is now the northern Transvaal were the Pedi and the Venda able to defend themselves successfully and consistently, making use of the mountainous country in which they lived. In the whole country between the Limpopo and the Orange rivers, between the Kalahari desert and the Indian Ocean, only communities blessed with natural defensive positions were able to withstand the flood of raiding and flight. Moreover, the refugees were often obliged to adopt Shakan tactics in order to survive. In this way, people who might never have heard of Shaka nor of the Nguni peoples, found themselves profoundly affected all the same.

While all these movements were taking place, the original agent of the changes was assassinated. Shaka had taken care that no son should be able to challenge his position, but had neglected to take sufficient precautions against his father's other sons. In 1828, during one of Shaka's campaigns to the north – this time against Soshangane in Gaza – two of his half-brothers absented themselves from the army, returned to the capital and assassinated Shaka at his own home. These two brothers – Dingane and Mhlangana – then turned against each other, and Dingane organised Mhlangana's assassination as well.

Having already killed another brother, Ngwadi (a maternal brother of Shaka), Dingane was reasonably secure in possesssion of the kingdom by the time the army returned from the Gaza campaign. That was the crucial moment of the coup, since the army might well have avenged Shaka's death. However, finding the coup accomplished and Shaka dead, and being already discouraged by the failure of the military campaign, the army was in no mood to attempt a counter-coup. Shaka's campaigns had imposed a great strain on them, and since Dingane promised some relaxation of the campaigns and a reign of peace, the regiments were prepared to accept the new state of affairs.

However, it soon transpired that Shaka's revolution was incomplete. Perhaps even Shaka himself could not have completed it, but the un-warlike Dingane certainly could not. The military campaigns which he did conduct were often unsuccessful, and the army grew demoralised. It was dangerous to leave the army idle; on the other hand many of the neighbouring communities had adopted Shakan tactics and were difficult to defeat. Internally, one of the component groups of the Zulu nation – the Qwabe – rebelled and escaped to the south, while Dingane's regiments were powerless to prevent them. Dingane decided that the solution to these problems lay in acquiring firearms from the traders at Port Natal. It is doubtful whether that course of action did represent a solution to the internal political problem, but in any case Dingane's relations with the white traders at the port were not very happy. Increasing numbers of refugees from Dingane's rule sought refuge around the white community: this encouraged Dingane to regard the traders as a possible focus of discontent, and naturally the refugees painted a very unflattering picture of conditions within the kingdom.

Despite Dingane's resolution to govern peacefully, he found himself ruling with greater reliance upon fear than Shaka had required. Many political organisations have survived an incompetent monarch, and perhaps the Zulu might also have preserved Shaka's achievements despite Dingane's reign.

Unfortunately the Zulu state was about to encounter its most serious challenge so far, in the form of white settlers migrating from the Cape into what later became Natal. In 1837, when they arrived and sent a deputation to meet Dingane, the Zulu state was in sad disarray. Power was centralised in the hands of a monarch whose political control was both arbitrary and unsure, and whose military limitations were such that he could devise no sensible plan to deal with the trekkers. Where Shaka might possibly have devised successful tactics and would probably have kept the community more united, Dingane failed on both counts. He had, in addition, alienated the sympathy of the white traders at the port, whose support would have been very useful. As it was, neither missionaries nor traders saw any reason for trying to avert the destruction of the kingdom.

But far the greatest weakness of the Zulu state on the eve of the great crisis of 1837 was its failure to form any friendly alliance with neighbouring communities. Neither Swazi nor Ndebele, Sotho nor Mfengu, were prepared to mourn the misfortunes of the Zulu, much less to assist them in their time of trouble. The Zulu state was the only one in the sub-continent which could have led a confederacy of African communities. Because of the manner of its creation, such an alliance was unthinkable, and neither the Zulu nor their neighbours thought of it.

Chapter 4

African reactions to the Mfecane: the Basotho, Swazi, Ndebele, Gaza and Kololo

The emergence of the Zulu state created immense problems for their African neighbours and the reactions of these groups varied. In this chapter we examine first the 'survival tactics' adopted by two such societies: the Sotho under their king Moshoeshoe, and the Swazi under the leadership of Sobhuza I and then Mswati. Secondly, we discuss the experiences of the Ndebele, Gaza and Kololo, all of whom reacted by moving away and becoming themselves invaders and attempting to establish states away from their original homes. The first kind of reaction, which may be described as defensive nation-building, ensured a high degree of social cohesion and loyalty among the followers of the respective leaders during the period of the *Mfecane* crisis, which in turn helped the societies to survive. Although it is self-evident that no individual person's actions are independent of the society in which he lives, it seems reasonable to suggest, nevertheless, that the story of the Sotho and Swazi reactions to the Mfecane (*Difaqane* in the Sotho language) was very much the story of the personal careers of the leaders of the period.

This seems particularly true of the Basotho, whose efforts to grapple with the crisis and whose general foreign policy in this period appear to have been dominated by Moshoeshoe as a person to a remarkable degree. However, as we turn to examine the career of this Sotho leader, it will be useful to remember (as Peter Sanders points out) that to explain the fortunes of the Basotho during the Difaqane purely in terms of the character of Moshoeshoe as the 'good chief' (as opposed to Sekonyela of the Tlokwa as the 'bad chief') without reference to the circumstances surrounding his career would be unsatisfactory and misleading.

Statue of King Moshoeshoe I, founder of the Basuto nation, unveiled during Lesotho independence celebrations

Moshoeshoe and the Sotho nation

Born about 1786, Moshoeshoe had a humble origin, his father being a mere village headman of the Mokotedi, an insignificant Sotho chiefdom. Following Sotho tradition, Moshoeshoe was circumcised before he began to engage in cattle raids like many other Sotho youth. A famous Sotho chief named Mohlomi is said to have dreamt that Moshoeshoe would one day become a great chief. He is further reported to have exhorted Moshoeshoe to be a kind and reasonable ruler who should discourage witchcraft. Although this wise man had recognised Moshoeshoe's potential at an early age, it was in fact the Difaqane that provided him with the opportunity to show his talents to a wider public. When the southern Sotho chiefdoms began to collapse as a result of the Shakan disturbances, Moshoeshoe distinguished himself as a man of great ability in the realm of both military and political organisation. Around 1820, he moved from his father's original home to Butha–Buthe mountain in northern Lesotho, from where he defended his followers from the first attacks upon them by the Hlubi, Ngwane and Tlokwa refugee hordes. However, in doing so – and in founding the Sotho nation in the process – Moshoeshoe always remained strongly attached to the values and institutions of the society in which he had been born. He is often remembered as the chief who used Sotho traditional ideas to help him found the Sotho nation in the face of very serious threats from his African neighbours as well as his European contemporaries. A biography of him published in the 1970s is entitled *Survival in Two Worlds*. How did he ensure the continued existence of the Sotho nation?

Following the invasion of the Sotho by the various refugee groups, Moshoeshoe had done exactly what many of his contemporaries were doing: he took his followers up on top of one of the flat-topped mountains that are common in Lesotho. When the Tlokwa attacked his new headquarters at Butha-Buthe in 1824, destroying all his crops, Moshoeshoe decided to move to Thaba Bosiu, an inconspicuous but particularly strategic mountain, 50 miles south-west of Butha–Buthe. Thaba Bosiu had a sizable flat top too, and was well-provided with water for humans as well as good pasture for cattle. Here Moshoeshoe and his father established their new headquarters, with the rest of their followers living at the bottom and running up to the top in times of emergency.

From this position Moshoeshoe was now exceptionally well-placed to exploit the *mafisa* system of the Sotho, the custom of cattle ownership and use, as a means of boosting his following. By this custom, all cattle were owned by the chief, who merely loaned them to his followers for their use. Hence the more cattle a leader possessed, the greater his following was likely to be as he had a greater capacity to provide both food and cattle to the needy. (This also explains the importance of cattle raids as a source of political power and influence in mid-nineteenth-century Sotho society.) In the wake of the series of raids by Hlubi, Ngwane and Tlokwa hordes during the first two decades of the century, Moshoeshoe was able to provide for the large number of refugees that poured into his stronghold. All such refugees were obliged to pay allegiance to him in gratitude. Moshoeshoe's early career thus demonstrates the way in which wealth could be used to build up a political following. He could provide not only food for the hungry, but also security and hope for the destitute.

Another traditional method of building a state among the Sotho was through polygamy, whereby alliances could be cemented with numerous powerful communities and factions. Polygamy was an accepted form of political action, but it is doubtful whether any previous ruler had been quite as polygamous as Moshoeshoe eventually became, having probably more than 100 wives. Inevitably a large number of sons were born to him, all of whom had to have some administrative post in the system, and in course of time that proved a severe strain upon the system itself. That was in the future, however, and in the short run polygamy was a successful technique for consolidating political power.

The maintenance of the old Sotho political culture was also seen in the way in which Moshoeshoe strove to avoid building a community in which political power was concentrated in the person of the monarch. This was in sharp contrast to the situation of Shaka and his successor Dingane among the Zulu. When whole communities arrived to seek refuge from Moshoeshoe, he permitted them to settle in their existing organisation, retaining their existing chiefs and methods of government. Moshoeshoe became the head of a confederation, not the monarch of a united state: some groups near the headquarters were directly ruled by the central government; other groups further away conducted their own internal administration; and some groups on the periphery were independent in all but name (and sometimes independent in name as well, when it suited them to be so). Political and economic allegiance were, in an important way, voluntary. If sections of the new community chose to go away, there was nothing to prevent them from doing so. Moshoeshoe had no standing army worth mentioning, and the defence of the community depended upon the ability of the people to defend positions rather than destroy enemies. The Basotho therefore never achieved (nor did they attempt to achieve) anything like the unity and uniformity of the Zulu. Dialects continued unstandardised, customs remained peculiar to the particular community within the state; and the identification of the people as Basotho was a very slow process indeed.

All these characteristics of Moshoeshoe marked him out as a

bearer of the old standards; not only a refuge in the political storm, but also an outpost of traditional chiefly generosity and hospitality and traditional good sense. Even though the state system was a patchwork of variable and voluntary relationships, Moshoeshoe was an attractive focus of the dispossessed Sotho peoples.

Moshoeshoe's relations with other African peoples

The great success of Moshoeshoe's survival tactic can best be illustrated by the manner in which he conducted his relations with the various African groups that were constantly fighting for supremacy in the region. That success becomes more striking when it is remembered that Moshoeshoe's following in 1833 was estimated at only 25 000, and in 1848 at 80 000 only. It must be remembered, too, that like Moshoeshoe and his followers, the Tlokwa under MaNthatisi and the Ngwane people of Matiwane as well as the Hlubi followers of Matiwane had also occupied hilltops in the region. The threat to Moshoeshoe's survival came not only from these rival groups but also from much bigger powers such as the Zulu and the Ndebele. Such a situation naturally called for astute political calculation on the part of Moshoeshoe.

Ultimately, his policy of sending tribute to potential enemies paid handsome dividends: when in 1825 Matiwane's Ngwane defeated Mpangazita's Hlubi and appeared to be planning to attack Moshoeshoe next, Moshoeshoe responded by despatching presents to Shaka. This diverted Shaka's attention to other enemies, while the two rivals (Matiwane and Mpangazita) forgot that they faced common danger from both the Zulu and the Ndebele. The two groups soon went to battle with each other, each side incurring severe losses, and in due course Mpangazita was killed and his followers were dispersed. The Hlubi too lost their coherence and identity, becoming either refugees in other communities or allowing themselves to be subjected to the victorious Ngwane.

Though Matiwane had apparently won the battle, he had seriously weakened his power of resistance and continued to over-estimate his military strength. Meanwhile, Moshoeshoe continued sending tribute to Shaka and others.

In 1827, however, Matiwane was attacked in quick succession first by the Zulu and then by the Ndebele. These attacks dislodged him from his mountain refuge, and he was obliged to retreat from the area altogether. The only remaining direction for him and his followers was south, and they duly moved into the territory of the southern Nguni, creating so much havoc that the forces of the Cape Colony were despatched against them. In 1828 the colonial forces defeated and dispersed his army: Matiwane himself was obliged to return to Zululand where Dingane had no hesitation in putting him to death; his followers found what refuge they could by breaking up and throwing themselves on the mercy of Xhosa and Thembu who had recently been victims of their raiding.

Moshoeshoe, who had played no part in these affairs, was immensely strengthened by the removal of these uncomfortable neighbours, and by the addition of many of their people to his expanding community. All that had been necessary was to avoid giving offence to stronger groups, and to repel a feeble attack by Matiwane between the Ndebele campaign and his flight into the border lands of the Cape Colony.

The Tlokwa, however, represented a much more serious problem. Though they were one of the most powerful chiefdoms on the high veld at the beginning of the nineteenth century, they (like the Mokotedi) were merely one chiefdom among more than twenty or so Sotho-speaking chiefdoms in the region. Before the 1820s, while Sekonyela (born in 1804) was still in his teens, his mother MaNthatisi acted as regent of the Tlokwa. She was at least as astute as Moshoeshoe himself, and she enabled the Tlokwa to survive the Difaqane by developing a most effective method of defence: like Moshoeshoe, she established herself on top of a hill and defended it by rolling stones down upon her attackers. She also attracted new followers from the remnants of the scattering and scattered Nguni and Sotho. As long as MaNthatisi remained in control, therefore, the Tlokwa continued to pose a serious threat to the followers of Moshoeshoe and the other Sotho-speaking peoples. But she was only a regent, who had to step down once Sekonyela had achieved his majority in the late 1820s.

Though Sekonyela attempted to continue his mother's policy of extending control over various groups, he was far less successful. In fact, during Sekonyela's rule the leadership of the southern Sotho, which had been in Tlokwa hands, passed to Moshoeshoe. Some white witnesses reported that Sekonyela made an unfavourable impression, alienating his own followers not only by his cruelty but also by his constant interest in warfare. He was therefore seen by contemporary observers as a warmonger, for whom his own followers had more fear than love. Being envious of the upstart Moshoeshoe, Sekonyela decided to storm Thaba Bosiu in 1829 while Moshoeshoe and many of his followers were away on a cattle raid to the east. Though he failed to capture the station, Sekonyela succeeded in taking some of Moshoeshoe's wives and cattle. However, he was forced to surrender the cattle by some of Moshoeshoe's men who had remained behind.

Sporadic warfare between the two communities continued for the next twenty years. The dispute was further complicated by the arrival of the missionaries and of white governments in the vicinity, and it was not until 1853 that Moshoeshoe found the opportunity to destroy the power of the Tlokwa, most of whom now joined the Basotho.

Moshoeshoe's relations with whites

From 1830 onwards, Moshoeshoe faced additional problems: his followers began to be harried by coloured parties from the Cape Colony, attempting to establish themselves in what had been Sotho territory. These groups were equipped with firearms, horses and often with missionaries as well, and they brought a wider experience of warfare and modern military techniques than the Sotho possessed. On the other hand, Moshoeshoe was quick to perceive the advantages which these groups enjoyed, and adopted a policy of acquiring riding horses, firearms and even missionaries. Although he was unable entirely to dislodge these immigrants from the Caledon valley, and although he failed to assert his political supremacy over them, he was at least able to contain them and prevent them from expanding into the heartland of the new Basotho community.

In his policy towards the white communities, however, Moshoeshoe was far less successful. His great new state had been built mainly by means of traditional policies. These methods of state-building were quite inadequate to deal with the situation created by the whites. At this time there were two types of whites that Moshoeshoe encountered: the missionaries and the settlers.

The earliest missionaries arrived at Thaba Bosiu in the early 1830s, at about the same time that the Griqua threat to the Basotho was subsiding. The Sotho king was prompted to investigate these whites. Learning of their presence among certain Griqua groups, Moshoeshoe decided to invite them to his land too, despatching presents of cattle with the invitation. So it was that French Protestant missionaries, led by Casalis of the Paris Evangelical Missionary Society, came to Moshoeshoe's country. Other missionaries followed, notably the Wesleyan Missionary Society. In the long run their presence was to prove of immense advantage to the Sotho leader in his defence scheme. He positioned the missionaries, for example, on the outskirts of the Sotho community, where their presence might discourage attacks by his enemies. Moreover, though he took great interest in the missionaries' religious beliefs, and encouraged his sons to receive instruction, he ensured that he himself was not converted, lest this should risk outlawing polygamy as a means for building the nation. By the 1850s, Moshoeshoe was probably better informed about the ways of the white groups than any contemporary African ruler, even though in the long run that knowledge was of little value.

The second, and much more dangerous, group of whites were the settlers. From about 1810 onwards, white farmers had begun to cross the Orange River into the interior to graze their cattle. Initially, the white farmers had come in small groups and were therefore not a threat to the Basotho. However, once they began to move in greater numbers and to settle more permanently in Transorangia, they proved a menace. For one thing, they were unwilling to be assimilated into Sotho traditional society. Secondly, they were reluctant to stick to specific areas of open country, preferring instead to wander all over the place. This situation was compounded by the differences between Bosotho and European concepts of land tenure, particularly during the days of the Great Trek in the 1830s. Moshoeshoe's idea was to grant the white farmers permission to graze their herds on the land until they could move again. This was done, in Moshoeshoe's own scheme of things, on a purely temporary basis and he believed he had granted the white farmers mere usufructs, and not permanent occupancy. Many of the white farmers did not heed this, and hence the misunderstanding between them and the Basotho. Among the latter there was no such practice as the individual ownership of land, since land was seen as belonging to the entire community, controlled and administered on its behalf by the chief.

Moshoeshoe's relations with whites were further complicated by the difference in the two sides' interpretation of the ownership of property, such as cattle for example. As we have seen, the Basotho operated the *mafisa* system, by which Moshoeshoe loaned cattle to his followers, who would use them but not own them. The centrality of cattle and cattle raiding in Sotho political life is obvious. Moreover, cattle raiding was an accepted practice and a chief could not punish his subordinates for engaging in it. This made for immense difficulties for Moshoeshoe in his relationships with the white farmers, who could not tolerate the numerous cattle raids upon them by the followers of the Sotho leader.

The loose political structure created by Moshoeshoe, with no clearly demarcated boundaries, permitted the recurrence of such troubles, despite his determination to forge friendly relations with the whites and to avoid hostilities. Unlike the Zulu, his people were not a united community, nor was the political system centralised. It depended upon a network of differing obligations between Moshoeshoe and a multitude of local chiefs. The *pitso*, or national assembly, was a crucial decision-making body throughout Moshoeshoe's reign. The network of alliances was a personal creation, depending to a great extent upon the personality of the paramount chief: the term king does not apply to Moshoeshoe in the way that it applied to some of his contemporaries. As Moshoeshoe advanced in age, so the system became harder to operate.

Further, a consequence of polygamy was a multitude of sons, all of whom felt entitled to chiefly position and prestige. In pre-colonial times, many of these sons would have broken away and formed independent chiefdoms: but in the 1850s there was nowhere for them to go. Nor was there any way – in Sotho tradition – of ensuring that succession passed to one son. As the years passed, more and more of Moshoeshoe's sons clamoured for some of their father's power. Some could be appointed over people who accepted Moshoeshoe's authority completely: but very often such a group of people resented the imposition of an 'alien' chief in place of a kinsman. Inevitably also, following Sotho tradition, these sons were anxious to acquire fame for their courage and raiding ability. Whatever policy Moshoeshoe might adopt towards his neighbours, there was little chance of his sons behaving in a peaceful manner. The high spirits of these sons immensely complicated the task of conducting foreign relations.

By the 1840s, Moshoeshoe had achieved a traditional Sotho ambition through the application of traditional Sotho wisdom, in a situation of unprecedented difficulty. It was very much a personal achievement and, in the event of his death, it might have fragmented like other charismatic states. The durability of his creation was largely a consequence of events in the last twenty years of his life. If he had died in the 1840s at the end of a sufficiently remarkable career, it would not be necessary to say any more about him. However, he lived on into the 1860s, through an even more difficult period for his people, and with increasing domestic problems to contend with. We have noted briefly the increasing white threat to his creation; how he dealt with this particular problem will be discussed in subsequent sections

The Swazi and the Mfecane

In what became the Swazi nation, the core comprised the ruling Dlamini clan and some ten other subordinate clans. This small community lived north-eastward of present Swaziland, until a conflict with the Ndwandwe – another Nguni-speaking group – obliged them to move southward to their present location towards the close of the eighteenth century. Under Ndungunya (1780–1815) the community closely resembled its neighbours both in size and in the nature of political authority. Decision-making was shared between the ruler, a council of chiefs (*liqoqo*) and a national council (*libandla*) and the ruler never became an autocrat in the manner of the Zulu kings. The balance of power between these bodies changed over time, but essentially the Swazi people survived the Mfecane by means of altering, rather than overthrowing, their pre-existing political system.

Sobhuza I, who became king in 1815, steered the community through a series of crises until his death in 1836. During the Mfecane it was clearly necessary to provide for the stream of refugees from broken communities, and if possible to build up the size of one's following. During Sobhuza's reign a further eight clans accepted the authority of the Dlamini. However, these were Sotho-speaking, with rather different political and social traditions. Sobhuza's followers therefore classified themselves into three groups: the 'true Swazi', those 'found ahead' in Swaziland by the Dlamini, and those who were absorbed later on, as a result of conquest or seeking refuge. Such a division was obviously dangerous. Unlike Shaka, but in the Dlamini tradition, Sobhuza permitted the newcomers to retain any chiefs they possessed, and to retain a distinct culture if they so wished. Political authority, in other words, was very loose. So long as the Zulu continued to menace the area, the clans were happy to remain part of the Dlamini following.

Sobhuza I appreciated that his following was not strong enough to challenge the military power of the Zulu, nor of the Ndebele, and therefore that the Swazi must retain friendly relations with their neighbours as far as possible. Partly, that object could be achieved by living in mountainous and broken country, presenting difficulties for invading armies.

Sobhuza also applied the traditional remedy of marriage-relations. After the clashes with the Ndwandwe, for example, he married the daughter of Zwide, their ruler. He also sent a number of Swazi girls to Shaka, including princesses of the Dlamini clan. Even when Shaka ordered the killing of some of these once they had become pregnant, Sobhuza refused to be provoked into warfare. With a measure of peace abroad, the internal process of national integration could continue.

His successor, Mswati, enjoys a more aggressive reputation among the Swazi, who have taken his name as their own. Unlike his father, Mswati had matured during the revolutionary years of the Mfecane and was less interested in tradition and more interested in military organisation, than any of his predecessors. His succession to the throne in 1840 was preceded by two successive Zulu attacks – in 1836 and 1837 – which underlined the importance of creating a reliable military machine. Military power still depended upon the clan leaders and chiefs who would mobilise their immediate followers. The system was cumbersome and unreliable, since it depended upon decisions by a series of military authorities without centralised command. Mswati set about adapting the Zulu military organisation to his people. Age-set regiments were introduced, and quartered in barracks throughout the country. Officers became directly responsible to central command. District authorities were now more closely controlled in the exercise of administration. Female relatives of the king could be used as informers in the provinces, reporting on any potentially subversive activity – in much the same way as Shaka's female relatives served him.

The new regiments needed practice, since the encounters with the Zulu had normally involved retiring into the mountain caves, rather than venturing upon open battles which would almost certainly be lost. Concentrating on weaker communities, the Swazi regiments began to raid throughout a large area to the north. The Sotho, to the north-west, were raided and robbed of their fine herds of cattle. An ambitious attack was also launched against the Pedi further north, but the Pedi in their hill defences were able to repel the invaders. An attack was also sent against the Shangane kingdom in southern Mozambique, but also unsuccessfully. Only when the founder of the kingdom – Soshangane – died in 1859, were the Swazi able to intervene safely in that direction. Even then the Swazi were less than effective, and despite their support Mawewe lost the succession war against his brother Mzila. Nevertheless the training was useful, and if the Swazi were not entirely successful, they did at least keep warfare at a safe distance from their own border. More important, as in Zululand, national service proved a powerful instrument of nation-building, and it is no accident that the Swazi accepted Mswati's name as their new national identity.

Mswati was, in fact, much more successful internally than in his foreign military adventures. A polygamist himself, he encouraged polygamy among his followers as well: partly to provide homes for female captives, but partly also for a subtler purpose. Mswati's wives were drawn from a wide range of society; and his female relatives were similarly distributed as wives throughout the clans and lineages of the community. When his followers accepted and imitated this practice, a great change was initiated: inter-marriage had the effect of blurring the old divisions between the clans of the nation, and the effect was felt very swiftly. Though the Swazi continued to suffer occasional raids from Zulu regiments (especially in the 1840s and 1850s) and although these attacks could not be defeated militarily, the Swazi nation nevertheless preserved its unity. Again, the regiments may not have been impressive in warfare, but they served an economic purpose as well.

They performed construction work, and each military camp was economically self-sufficient. In this way the soldiers were prevented from becoming a superior, powerful but unpopular caste in the society. Altogether, a collection of friendly clans was transformed during Sobhuza's and Mswati's reigns into a coherent and centralised kingdom, able to survive even so close to the centre of Zulu military power. That ability, in turn, resulted much more from internal unity than from the indifferent success of the Swazi regiments.

Though the development of the Sotho and Swazi nations followed very different procedures, they do show that an intelligent adaptation of traditional political attitudes and practices could assist particular communities to survive the crisis. It is also clear that the rulers found it necessary to expand the scale of their ruler, beyond any previous size; and they were assisted in this development by the existence of large numbers of refugees seeking some powerful patron. The expansion of the political system naturally imposed some strain, and it became necessary at least to modify the old political structure.

Having a standing army also involved some changes in the balance of power within the community. The king, as commander-in-chief, was inevitably more powerful than his predecessors. The authority of Mswati was that of a monarch advised by national councils: Ndungunya's authority had rested very largely upon the consent of clans which preserved a sense of separateness. In Lesotho, Moshoeshoe's authority resembled that of a chairman at a meeting of chiefs; but even so, his power was greater than that of any Sotho leader before him, and he can fairly be described as the first Sotho paramount chief.

These changes did not only influence the chiefs: ordinary people were also profoundly affected. In varying degrees throughout the new communities, the politics and economics of kinship were supplemented (and sometimes replaced) by the politics and economics of nation-states. There was a difference in kind between being a subject of Ndungunya and being a subject of Mswati, since many decisions previously made by a family or by a group of kinsmen were now influenced by policy and power emanating from a central government. It is possible in the mid-nineteenth century to speak of Zulu, Swazi and Sotho states, and perhaps nations, in a manner which was impossible half a century earlier.

The emergence of the Ndebele state

The remaining three Mfecane states to be considered in this chapter – the Ndebele, Gaza and Kololo – all established empires away from the focus of trouble. They became 'imperialist refugees' whose activities contributed to the creation of new political system where they settled. However, it is possible to exaggerate the power of these immigrant communities over the pre-existing groups they encountered: historians have recently come to see the Ndebele-Shona relations, for example, in a different light, noting that Ndebele raids on the Shona were not as devastating as had been thought earlier.

The Ndebele were led by Mzilikazi, the son of a young pre-Mfecane chief. He entered military and administrative service under Shaka, becoming one of his generals, but eventually fled from Zululand in 1823 at the head of two or three hundred soldiers and their dependents, refusing to hand over to Shaka the loot he had captured from the Sotho. Other refugees joined Mzilikazi and his followers, and Sotho groups, whom they had conquered, were absorbed. First these refugees settled near where Pretoria now stands, and the indigenous Sotho people described them as Ndebele – the Sotho name for the Nguni – a title which was accepted. Mzilikazi's followers were defeated by white emigrants from the Cape, and in 1838 moved northwards into what is now western Zimbabwe. There Mzilikazi built up the new Ndebele nation until his death in 1868, when he was succeeded by his son Lobengula. Decades earlier, other Nguni groups had migrated inland and been described as Ndebele; but Mzilikazi's Ndebele differed from the earlier groups in almost every important respect. This was a new creation, and it is worth asking how it was created.

Mzilikazi had increased his following by conquering and absorbing people as he proceeded. Because he was familiar with Zulu military techniques, he was able to ward off his Zulu pursuers, and in addition to employ their very methods to build up a new state on the Shakan model. Chiefs were responsible to the monarch, who could and did dismiss them. The new society was geared to war, and the basis of political power was the regimental system (although recent research work suggests that the military aspects of the Ndebele state have sometimes been exaggerated). The *amabutho* (regiments of young men assembled together into separate groups) were, in fact, more production units than full-time professional soldiers: they played an important role in the state economy by herding the nation's cattle, for example.

As in Zululand, the economy was as centralised as the polity. Mzilikazi controlled not only the herds of his followers, but also a number of captured girls, who were (in one sense) an important form of wealth. Royal cattle could be used to reward loyal servants and soldiers, or to underpin the political loyalty of whole communities. The girls could be given as brides, and Mzilikazi himself sometimes provided the bride-price if the bridegroom were too poor to do so. Also following Nguni tradition, the female relatives of the monarch performed a useful role in supervising the administration of other chiefs in areas far removed from the king's court.

However, it was not simply Nguni tradition, but more precisely Zulu tradition, on which the new state tended to draw for experience. At first the state was more like an army of occupation than a civil organisation. When civil administration became necessary, it was the regimental system which provided it. However, the essential problem facing the Ndebele was more complex than that facing the Zulu. Unlike the Zulu, Mzilikazi's subjects were not homogenous in origin. Nguni, Sotho, Rozwi and Tswana, all comprised his following. The regimental system was not, by itself, sufficient to create a new and durable nation.

To the problem of assuring the loyalty of distinct groups of subjects was added the problem that the Ndebele quickly developed into a caste society. The original Nguni members regarded themselves as the proper ruling caste – the Zansi – with monopoly rights over responsible positions. The Sotho who had been

Lobengula succeeded his father Mzilikazi as leader of the Ndebele. Photographed here are members of his bodyguard

absorbed in the 1820s and 1830s – the Enhla caste – were steadily working towards their own acceptance into the aristocracy. Those conquered from the Shona states – the Rozwi or Holi caste – were very recent additions and had no status within the community. What made that problem particularly dangerous was that most of the original Shona communities of the Rozwi confederacy, and even the Rozwi Mambo himself, remained unconquered and hostile to the intruding Ndebele. Any alliance between the independent external Shona and the internal Holi caste would threaten the survival of the Ndebele state. Though many Shona communities agreed to pay regular tribute to the Ndebele, these theoretically subordinate communities were more likely to be hostile than friendly towards the interlopers. Finally, the risk of attacks from the south was never far from Mzilikazi's mind; and to resist these, it was obviously sensible to bring about as great a degree of unity within the state as humanly possible.

Zulu experience offered a partial remedy, in the form of the age-regiments. Promising young men from the lower castes and volunteers from neighbouring communities were enlisted into these organisations, which served to assimilate all the servicemen into Ndebele customs, the Sindebele language and loyalty to the regime of Mzilikazi. Promotion and honour within the army were available to any serviceman of whatever ethnic origin; and so the regiments provided a nation-building, as well as a nation-protecting, function. Since civil administration was normally conducted by ex-soldiers, success in the army opened out even greater prospects after a man's retirement, if he proved competent first as a soldier and then as an administrator. The great test of the assimilation policy came in 1868, when Mzilikazi died and Lobengula succeeded him after a disputed succession and a civil war. At this point, the lower castes could have rebelled against Ndebele authority altogether, and perhaps have overthrown the state. They did not; and the state and the society survived intact. By that time the Ndebele were a nation-state rather than an empire, and the army could concentrate on external affairs rather than internal order.

External dangers were always a lively possibility. Attack from the Zulu quarter was an obvious risk; but so, too, was attack from the south. Mixed communities of Griqua and Kora, as we have seen, settled quite peacefully along the Orange River banks; but the pastoral frontier also attracted energetic and violent men. In 1829, for example, an alliance was formed specifically to attack the Ndebele. In the alliance were Jan Bloem – a half-caste outlaw – several Kora and Griqua individuals bored by agriculture, and several groups of Tswana. Armed with muskets, and taking the Ndebele by surprise, the allies had an easy victory, but were then pursued and ambushed by Ndebele regiments which had been absent during the initial attack. In this case, only the over-confidence of the allies and their failure to post sentries saved the Ndebele from great loss.

Shortly afterwards a similar alliance was formed by Barend-Barends, another half-caste, who achieved exactly the same temporary success, and met exactly the same fate. The Ndebele position was clearly perilous, and even before the fatal encounter with the white trekkers in the 1830s, Mzilikazi was thinking of a further retreat beyond the range of the armed and mounted coloured communities.

Soshangane and the Gaza empire

The Gaza state north-east of the Swazi differed from the Ndebele state in many respects: the quality of leadership available to them was less impressive; the extent of the area over which they exacted tribute was wider than that of the Ndebele; and ultimately the relationship that the Gaza established with the people they conquered was less smooth than the Ndebele's relations with those they absorbed. The fate of the Gaza empire is therefore an illustration of the perils of empire-building when the leadership of the empire was less sensible and thoughtful than Mzilikazi and Lobengula.

Soshangane, the head of the Gaza clan of the Ndwandwe, fled before Shaka's attack in 1821. Like Mzilikazi, his followers numbered only a hundred or so soldiers and their dependents. These people became known as the Shangane, derived from the name of their leader. At first they raided throughout the Thonga country, and into the easternmost chieftaincies of the Shona, but then settled down to dominate the Thonga on a more systematic basis. Unfortunately, the territory they chose was extremely unhealthy, and the new rulers had no resistance to the diseases which were endemic. While they could consistently control the disunited Thonga they had no defence against malaria or cattle diseases. Furthermore, they gained few followers from Zululand, and were destined to remain a very small minority within their sphere of power. Nor was it possible to absorb the Thonga piecemeal, by making some of them honorary Nguni. Their sense of insecurity may perhaps explain why they felt it necessary to demonstrate their power so frequently. Other Nguni refugees were driven off; the Portuguese settlements on the coast were destroyed; and there was little respite for the Thonga during Soshangane's reign. As a consequence, the Shangane people made unnecessary enemies for themselves.

The empire at its height was a very considerable power. In 1828 they defeated a Zulu army shortly before the assassination of Shaka, when it was still extremely difficult to resist Zulu military power. The decline and collapse of the Gaza empire cannot be explained in terms of military incompetence. On the contrary, military efficiency may have contributed to over-confidence and a failure to attend to social and political problems.

Essentially the failure is attributable to the Shangane's failure to resolve the problem facing all conquest states: how is the loyalty (or at least the acquiescence) of the conquered people to be assured? Assimilation failed, either becaue it was not attempted or because the numbers involved made it impossible. The Thonga did not learn to speak Nguni, and therefore language remained as a mark to distinguish conquerors from conquered. More seriously, the age-regiments did not contribute to a sense of single identity. Some Thonga were enrolled into the armies, but they were confined to their own regiments and did not serve alongside the descendents of the conquerors. Further, they were put under the authority of officers drawn exclusively from the ruling caste. It was even believed that, in time of battle, the most dangerous positions were given to the Thonga regiments. It followed that Thonga could not be promoted to important positions within either the army or the administration; and indeed the only eminent Thonga were chiefs who, by submitting easily, were permitted to remain in charge of their old areas.

A further complication arose from the mobile tendency of the Gaza state, with the capital shifting from place to place: Soshangane moved his headquarters twice during his reign; his son and successor, Mzila, shifted it after 1862; and Mzila's son, Gungunyane, moved it again in the 1890s. This frequent shifting of the centre of the Gaza state meant not only a failure by the rulers to establish a firm hold on the empire but also that the state itself remained rather unwieldy. For all these reasons, the Gaza state remained an empire; unlike the Ndebele state it did not develop into a nation. The conquerors behaved as if they were still an occupying army: their control over the area was loose and their failure to absorb the conquered people was striking. And to make matters worse, in his old age Soshangane believed that he was bewitched by Thonga, and accordingly massacred a few of them. When he died he bequeathed to his heirs a large variety of enemies – Portuguese, Swazi, Pedi, Zulu, Shona and especially Thonga.

If there had been only one claimant to the throne, the succession might have proceeded smoothly, and the state might have survived in reasonably good order. As it was, one son (Mzila) was supported by the Portuguese, and another (Mawewe) by the Swazi, and the succession war was greatly protracted to the advantage of the external allies of each contestant. Mzila's victory also gave the Portuguese a foothold in the country which they had previously lacked. The Gaza empire survived Mzila's reign, and even that of his successor Gungunyana, but its power steadily declined until there was a serious Thonga uprising towards the end of the century. The empire quickly collapsed into the hands of the Portuguese during the 1890s, leaving the Thonga (by now known as Shangane) disrupted but otherwise unaffected by their unwelcome masters.

The Makololo conquest of the Lozi kingdom

A similar case is to be found in the Makololo conquest of the Barotse in upper Zambesi. The conquest itself was achieved by a group of Sotho, displaced by the Mfecane, and led by Sebitwane. Moving northwards in search of security, they skirted the Kalahari desert and, avoiding the Ndebele, arrived at the Zambesi River during the early 1830s. So long as the Lozi state remained intact, it was impossible for the Kololo to move further north. However, a serious civil war broke out among the Lozi in 1833, and Sebitwane took the opportunity to invade the country and establish Kololo rule over all the factions. Immediately the problem of relations with conquered people came to the fore. Sebitwane realised that his minority of conquerors would have to come to some sort of compromise, and he resolved to allow equal status and opportunity to the aristocracy of the Lozi community. The aristocrats responded warmly to these opportunities, and in doing so they permanently adopted the language and customs and attitudes of the conquering Sotho people.

Like the Shangane, the Kololo had moved from a healthy to a very unhealthy climate, which affected them badly since they lacked immunity. With the passage of time, therefore, the power of the conquerors was bound to diminish, and although they did not realise this, it would have been expedient for them to come to terms while their numbers and strength were still sufficient for them to have a bargaining position. Age-regiments and equality of opportunity for the old aristocracy seemed a very promising way of dealing with this dangerous situation.

Unfortunately for the Kololo, Sebitwane was succeeded in the 1850s by Sekeletu, who lost sight of his father's political objectives. The founder of the conquest state enjoyed a charismatic aura which his successor could not inherit. As a leper, living in self-imposed isolation, he was unable to arouse any personal loyalties. Perhaps because of panic at the continued toll of diseases, which affected immigrants much more than indigenous grups, Sekeletu determined to recapture all power for the Kololo conquerors. His rule was much harsher than Sebitwane's, and discontent grew very quickly. Outside the area of Kololo control malcontents gathered around Sepopa, as representative of the pre-Kololo rulers. In 1864 Sepopa's army defeated Sekeletu's and all Kololo men who could be found were massacred: by that time the Kololo were too few and too weak – and too unpopular – to withstand a determined rising.

If empire-building was not the sole alternative available to the various refugee groups, but rather a very dangerous policy involving constant alert and perpetual risk of internal revolt, nevertheless it was an attractive option. Where empires were established, they had a local effect similar to that of the Zulu state. Neighbours were first attacked and if possible destroyed, but then attempted to reorganise themselves in order to resist further raiding. Small groups were dislodged, to roam the interior either as potential clients or as sub-imperialists on their own account. The dislocation and re-grouping affected – to differing degrees – every community from the Lozi state to the Cape frontiers, and from lake Malawi to the Kalahari desert. These movements and hostilities, in turn, profoundly affected the attitude of the communities involved towards the white farmers when they, in turn, flowed on to the interior plateau and spilled over into the eastern lowlands.

Chapter 5

Pastoral expansion and the formation of new societies

If the events in Zululand were the focus of the Mfecane, then Cape Town may be seen as the focus of another series of transformations, which altered human relationships throughout the sub-continent. Cape Town in 1800 was a prosperous little town inhabited by well-to-do administrators and merchants in the meat trade, sustained by a skilled population of slaves, and visited by inter-continental travellers. Its citizens took pride in their sophistication. Even during the Company period they had been in touch with republican and democratic opposition groups in the motherland, and they had no difficulty in accommodating the series of new and foreign administrators who held brief office at the turn of the century. They were inclined to sneer at the trekboers and their servants who brought herds of cattle and sheep from the countryside, unfashionably dressed, stumbling over the niceties of the Dutch language and entirely ignorant of English. They preferred to see themselves as part of a modern and highly civilised metropolitan community. They attended the Dutch Reformed Churches regularly, but with limited enthusiasm. Many of the slaves and the free blacks were Muslim, and that too set Cape Town apart from the interior.

The European wars were certainly a nuisance, since it was difficult to anticipate the next treaty or the next military victory, and the administration of the Cape might change hands yet again. But it was not difficult to satisfy the officials of Britain or of the Netherlands, who seemed mainly interested in preserving continuity; and anyway the increased numbers of troops, and of fleets rounding the Cape, were very good for trade.

When the Dutch East India Company monopoly was overthrown, and replaced by the much less strict monopoly of the London-based East India Company, there were even some new trading opportunities – though, to be sure, the limited range of rural products and the difficulties of transport made it difficult to respond to these offerings. The British authorities – mainly military men representing an anti-revolutionary government – were not inclined to upset existing relationships. Prices continued to be fixed by the Cape Town authorities. The slave trade was abolished in 1807, but the condition of slavery persisted, and the slave trade was no longer necessary to the well-being of the colonists, and in any case the British officials not only introduced strict laws governing master and servant, but even showed signs of enforcing them.

After a century and a half of Company administration, Cape Town was nominally a Christian town; but there had never been any serious attempt to convert Africans to Christianity, and those slaves from the East who wished to introduce and practise Islam were not prevented from doing so. The distinction between masters and servants coincided very closely with the more visible distinction between Europeans and everyone else. There were certainly free blacks – freed slaves and their descendants, and descendants of the Khoi – but few of these were prosperous artisans. In general, the civil status of burgher was confined to European colonists and a handful of exceptional blacks; and the terms 'Christian' and 'burgher' were freely interchanged in describing the most obvious distinction within urban society. The Dutch were consistent throughout their overseas adventures, dealing equally calmly with Buddhists in Sri Lanka, Muslims in the Indies, and Taoists in Japan – Dutch disinterest in evangelisation was one reason why the Japanese preferred to deal with them rather than the Portuguese. At any rate in Cape Town itself it was quite unnecessary to make hard and fast legal distinctions: the town was still small, the garrison often quite large, and slaves and free blacks had little choice but to accept whatever limitations were imposed upon them.

Affluent citizens of Cape Town liked to see themselves as sophisticated and metropolitan in their culture and conversations, but their affluence actually rested upon production by uneducated and unfashionable farmers of the interior. Close to Cape Town the distinction between urban and rural populations was not clearly marked. Wine was produced on estates which employed large numbers of slaves, and supported their owners in considerable comfort. The conditions of wheat farming were not very different. The more prosperous of the farmers were often visiting town, discussing international as well as local affairs, mixing socially with the officers of the garrison, and commanding attention whenever they commented on market prices or labour conditions or the state of the world. Some were involved in anti-Company agitation in the 1780s, but since that time they had been consistently loyal. The British annexation of the Cape meant that imported goods became cheaper and more plentiful; the new labour laws permitted a strict control over the agricultural labour force; the swollen garrisons meant lots of customers for the indifferent wine and brandy of the hinterland. Farmers realised that it would be foolish to throw away these substantial gains, by proving slow to transfer their loyalties to the new regime.

Farther away from Cape Town, the distinction between urban and rural colonists became much more noticeable. Instead of the well-established homesteads of the south-western Cape, roughly constructed houses and huts were more likely; instead of fashionable clothes in a European style, the pastoralists were more likely to wear clothes made from animal skins, at least for day-to-day working conditions; the few educational opportunities of Cape Town were absent from the interior, where children were lucky to be taught their letters by travelling ministers of religion. The advance into the interior was also a retreat from the high culture of the town. Pastoralists were living a life quite inconceivable to their western European ancestors, who practised intensive cultivation of small plots, not the herding of great numbers of animals over vast distances. Living in great isolation, the pastoral families had to be capable of a wide range of skills, including military skill to protect their herds (and from time to time to add to them at someone else's expense). Equally important, where the settled farmers of the south-west often employed slaves, very few of the pastoralists could afford to do so: instead they relied upon Khoi herdsmen and domestic servants. Until the arrival of a British garrison in 1795, the pastoralists were accustomed to making their own laws and enforcing them through locally elected leaders. In these circumstances the tensions between master and man were closer to the surface than in Cape Town, and the pastoralists knew that if they lost control, it would be a very long time before reinforcements would arrive from the capital.

On the face of it, then, Cape Town sophisticates were perfectly entitled to distinguish themselves from the rough frontiersmen: yet that distinction was less real than it seemed. Colonists and slaves and free blacks were all linked together in a single economic system whereby commodities were produced mainly in the interior, marketed in Cape Town, and the proceeds shared among the direct producers in the interior, the middlemen in Cape Town, and the colonial administration itself. Their society was also an expansionist one, persistently seeking fresh land and labour, systematically dispossessing its closest neighbours.

Frontier communities: Khoi

The colonial frontier attracted everyone who was dissatisfied with his or her conditions and prospects in the more settled core of the colony. Slaves, for example, had only the frontier to run to, though they were often ill-equipped to survive there, having neither the pastoral skills nor the cattle nor the languages with which to establish themselves. Slaves who were freed (manumitted) by their owners, found their opportunities rather limited: some of them, too, found their way to the frontier where they might hope to escape from social and economic inferiority. The largest single source of frontier recruitment, however, was displaced Khoi. Often they had acquired horses, firearms, and some familiarity with the language of the colonial community; and in addition they often possessed the herding and hunting skills of their forebears. This combination of qualities made them very effective in f rontier conditions. When they turned to guerilla methods of harassing the white pastoralists, they initiated a long and destructive series of 'Bushman' campaigns; when they acquired herds of their own, they could live as comfortably as the trekboers so long as they kept themselves on the frontier itself. They became, then, the cutting edge of the expansion of commercial pastoralism into the interior. As they moved steadily further from Cape Town, they took land and cattle from more settled communities – who in their turn became marauders. The process depended upon skill in frontier warfare conditions, and uninterrupted access to the horses and firearms and gunpowder supplied by the colony itself. The solid citizens of Cape Town might disapprove of these methods; but it was an intrinsic part of the colonial economy. Here, as in many other parts of the world, civilisation was the mother of barbarism.

The general features of cattle frontiers have been described in other parts of the world, and those descriptions fit southern African conditions quite well:

> Once the formation of a cattle frontier was far advanced, it tended to become a self-locking process. For one thing, the animals themselves modified their physical environment; heavy and hungry beasts made potential cropland marginal and reduced prairie to scrub . . . The expansion of cattle raising had the effect of uprooting the few settled Indians living in those areas. These Indians, as well as those who had been nomads before the European arrived, quickly learned the use of horses. The result was a native population capable of surviving and waging continuous warfare . . .

That passage describes the emergence of a gaucho population in the grasslands of South America, specialists in cattle management and violence, finding employment sometimes as cowboys, sometimes as bandits, occasionally as soldiers employed by the State. These words also describe the emergence of Coloured communities in the southern African interior.

As Khoi and slaves escaped into the interior, they needed to co-operate among themselves in order to acquire land and to protect it from its former owners; and it was also useful to form a united front against the encroachment of white pastoralists coming behind them. One instance of this process is the movement of Nama (Khoi communities) north towards the Orange River, and their alliance with Naoma already living in southern Namibia: led by Jonker Africaner, using horses and firearms, this combination was able to defeat the Herero who were attempting to colonise southern Namibia during the 1830s. Having achieved a decisive military victory, Jonker Africaner then established himself at the site of Windhoek as the overlord of both Nama and Herero. In a similar fashion, Kora communities formed further upstream in the Orange River valley, defending their territory from those Sotho and Tswana who attempted to recover it, and relying upon colonial firearms to maintain their supremacy.

These coloured communities were in a very ambiguous position. Many of them were refugees from discrimination and dispossession within the colony, seeking nothing more than land and cattle with which to live independently; but in order to preserve some measure of independence they needed weapons, and these could only be bought in exchange for cattle or ivory or sometimes slaves (or apprentices as they were more politely termed); so whatever their personal ambitions and wishes, the refugee communities were committed to hunting and marauding. On the one hand they depended upon sustained contact with colonial traders and merchants; on the other they sought their own autonomy, and the colonial authorities would not tolerate well-armed and disturbing communities in the colonial heartland. The only resolution of this dilemma was to stay on the frontier itself, directing their marauding and hunting activities outwards and turning a peaceful face towards the representatives of colonial order.

Among the more successful of these frontier communities were the Griqua. Mainly Khoi in origin, they were refugees who established themselves in the region where the Orange and the Vaal rivers, and several tributories, join: a well-watered region almost entirely surrounded by very arid karoo country. They were known as Bastards until a missionary encouraged them in 1813 to choose a politer term, and they selected Griqua probably because many were descendants of a Charigariqua community of Khoi which had earlier lived in the western Cape. A large number were direct descendants of Adam Kok I, a freed slave who had acquired burgher rights and grazing rights, but chose to exercise these as far from Cape Town as possible, since the legal position of a coloured man, even with burgher rights, was very precarious. When he died in 1795 he left a large and prosperous family of hunters and pastoralists, who kept drifting northwards into the Orange River valley, to stay ahead of the white pastoralists and inevitable conflicts over pastures and herds. His patriarchal authority was inherited by Cornelis Kok, his son, and then by Cornelis's son, Adam Kok II. Fresh adherents flowed to his nucleus of stability during the last years of the eighteenth century and the first of the nineteenth, including Khoi and San, runaway slaves, and people of mixed parentage.

As soon as missionaries found their way to the Orange River, Griquas were anxious to form Christian congregations. Christianity conferred a measure of respectability in colonial terms; and the congregational structure of the London Missionary Society strengthened the internal coherence of a very mixed community. The Griqua community split in 1820 between west Griqua led by Andries Waterboer, and east Griqua loyal to the Kok family; but each section evolved a stable political system, and each was recognised by the Cape colonial administration, which saw them as a source of order on a very turbulent frontier. Missionaries encouraged the Griqua to grow crops as well as to keep herds, and the Griqua dutifully accepted that advice, though the land was not very well suited to crop production. In all their efforts, the Griqua were seeking an elusive respectability, through agriculture, Christianity, loyalty to the British authorities, and a style of dress and of living which closely resembled that of the white pastoralists. Only through this strategy did it seem possible to escape a perpetual pioneering role one jump ahead of their white competitors. Unless they stayed ahead, they were likely to lose their land and their independence. Until the 1840s the strategy seemed to be working: the Cape Town authorities delegated power to Waterboer, and to Kok (as well as to Moshoeshoe) providing a small personal income and a guaranteed supply of arms and ammunition, in exchange for the preservation of order.

A similar process may be observed on the eastern fringe of colonial expansion, but there the process was much faster, and reached a climax much earlier. The cattle frontier expanded eastwards more vigorously than the northward movement: pastures were generally better, and they were not interrupted by great expanses of arid karoo. The Khoi and ex-slaves who chose to emigrate eastwards had to move more quickly, and were followed by larger numbers of white trekboers. They did not succeed in coalescing around leaders such as Jonker Africaner or Adam Kok. Some worked as herdsmen for the trekboers, others became clients of Xhosa chiefs, others again became San, prowling the frontier seeking opportunities to acquire cattle and land in order to become Khoi once again.

This was precisely the sort of unsettled and potentially violent community which could provide tough soldiers for the colonial militia, and the Dutch and British authorities did recruit many of them into the Cape Regiment, where their tracking skills and their intimate understanding of the dynamics of the frontier made them particularly useful. They were not the only unsettled people on the frontier: white adventurers, some escaping from justice and others from injustice, commonly acted as advisers to Xhosa chiefs on the border, performing a role rather like the missionaries on the northern frontier of the colony. A further, and decisive, distinction between the northern and eastern extension of the cattle frontier was that the Khoi could retreat no further on reaching the most westerly of Xhosa chieftaincies. Some resolution had to be reached.

The Xhosa themselves were far from united. In theory, there may have been a Xhosa paramount, but in practice the most likely paramount – Hintsa – was only a boy at the turn of the century. The strongest of the chieftaincies – the Rharhabe – was also weakened by their chief, Ngqika, being a minor in the 1790s, while his uncle Ndlambe acted as regent. Each of the chieftaincies comprised a royal as well as commoner clans, and it was in the interest of a great many Xhosa that the most powerful chieftaincies should be divided and weakened, lest the chiefs exert real authority over the people. This already confused situation was compounded by the adherence of Khoi clans as clients, since they also preferred that the Xhosa authorities be weak and disunited. In the persistent struggles between Ndlambe, Ngqika and Hintsa, the weakest could count on the support of some clans and individuals who did not want the feuds to die out. When Ndlambe defeated the Gqunukhwebe and chased them out of Xhosa territory, the Gqunukhwebe could recruit more numbers of the Khoi on the colonial side of the border, and return to take their revenge.

Frontier communities: trekboers

This confusion was all to the advantage of the trekboers. Faced by persistent San raiding in the northern sector of the eastern frontier, they had an easier task in the southern sector, selecting allies among the Khoi and the Xhosa, and using these reinforcements to drive their enemies out of the good grasslands of the Zuurveld. When warfare broke out again in 1799 however (the Third Frontier War), the trekboers were less fortunate. A combination of Khoi, Gqunukhwebe and some Xhosa defeated a commando of the trekboers, and forced the colonial detachment of troops to take refuge in a coastal garrison. White pastoralists had to abandon most of the frontier districts until such time as the colonial authorities could suppress the rebellion and expel the rebels from the contested territory. That was no easy task, and it required a political as well as a military solution. When British reinforcements reached the frontier, the military balance was changed; but more important was to persuade Khoi and Xhosa to dismantle their alliance. Some Khoi were won over by a reversal of normal procedure, allowing Klaas Stuurman and his followers to gain title to land within the colonial boundary.

Over the next few years the shaky alliance began to break up on its own, since the Khoi and the Xhosa were both so divided internally that it was difficult to prevent all factions from acting independently. The Xhosa were inclined to hold the land which the allies had recovered, and the Khoi were disposed to insist upon a large share of it. As the alliance crumbled, so individual Khoi were persuaded to go back to work for their former employers, or to join the Cape Regiment; trekboers slowly trickled back into the frontier districts; the Gqunukhwebe evacuated the frontier region altogether, moving back into the colony in search of empty land; other Khoi returned sadly to the patronage of Xhosa chiefs. Their moment had passed.

Although the Khoi certainly constituted a powerful challenge to the colonial structure in the years around the turn of the century, and were taken very seriously by trekboers and colonial officers alike, in the long run their prospects were bleak. They had enjoyed an intermediate position, either as the cutting edge of the expanding cattle frontier, or as warriors marauding the pastoralists, or as colonial troops defending the frontier. The expansion of trekboers, with better access to firearms and gunpowder, with better access to land registration mechanisms, and with closer contacts among the colonial bureaucracy, threatened the basis of the coloured frontier communities. Whenever the colonial authorities were faced with a choice between white pastoralists and black, they threw their weight behind the trekboers. The consequence on the eastern frontier was dramatic: on the northern frontier the Griqua survived for much longer, but their ultimate fate was already sealed.

In many ways the trekboers resembled the Khoi frontiersmen. They described themselves as Christian, and indeed objected to the missionaries whose work threatened the trekboer monopoly of Biblical knowledge and literacy. There was little literacy available, but it did permit the trekboers to make a permanent record of their land claims. They were equally realistic in their assessment of Cape Town, resenting the cartels of butchers who depressed meat prices, but recognising that their lifeline was securely tied to the town and its markets. On the few occasions when they were not in direct competition with the Khoi, they understood each other well enough: thus for almost a generation the trekkers across the Orange River co-existed peacefully with their Griqua neighbours. They also shared a hunger for pasture land, since there was no way of living honestly on the frontier without sufficient pasture for herds. At the turn of the century they were in a parlous condition, unable to protect their pastures simultaneously from San raids and Xhosa counter-attacks, relying upon unreliable reinforcements from whichever government ruled in Cape Town, unable to find new farms for themselves or for their constantly increasing families. The establishment of a substantial British garrison at Fort Frederick (later

Port Elizabeth) offered some security, but on the other hand it limited the opportunities for launching raids against the Xhosa. The trekboers were expecially infuriated by officials such as Maynier, who tried to keep the peace; and they believed (probably wrongly) that they could defeat the Xhosa and the Khoi by themselves – if only the colonial government would provide the firearms and the ammunition and permission to take the law into their own hands. In the declining years of the Company's rule, they had often enough formed their own commandos, elected their own leaders, and fought on their own account. Now that the Xhosa seemed to be consolidating under Ndlambe, military victory was much less secure.

Frustrated on the eastern frontier, many trekboers and adventurers turned to the northern regions. During the early 1820s the ravages of the Mfecane made life difficult across the Orange River, especially for pastoralists herding large numbers of stock. Even the Griqua had some difficulty in protecting themselves in these years. By the middle of the 1820s however, several trekboers had begun to use the sweet grass pastures of the Transorangia region for winter grazing, and by 1830 some began to see this as a permanent solution to the problem of winter grazing. These seasonal migrants began to establish themselves more permanently during the early 1830s: they might envy the Griquas their farms and grazing lands, but they had the sense not to provoke a well-armed rival in full possession. Instead, farms were leased from Griquas, and occasionally purchased from them. A precarious peace continued between the increasing numbers of trekboers, and the Griqua captains at Philippolis (Adam Kok II, then Adam Kok III from 1837 on the death of his father) and at Griquatown (Andries Waterboer). As late as 1840, the trekboers were willing to enter treaty relations with Adam Kok over the distribution of land between them: there was still room for both communities, and the colonial authorities still chose to rely upon Waterboer (in a treaty of 1835) and Adam Kok (in a treaty of 1843) to maintain law and order. However, that balance of power was shifting.

Trekboer was the term used by the semi-nomadic pastoral farmers of the colonial frontier. As they began to move beyond the colonial boundaries, they formalised their informal traditions of local self-government. Central to that tradition was the organisation of a commando, whereby adult males rallied with their horses and firearms to pursue a shared military purpose, and elected one of their member as commandant for the campaign. Across the border, it was necessary to define the membership of the community (and commonly that was done by asserting that all adult male trekboers were members, along with their wives and children), and the rights of the commandant in times of peace. The elected leaders naturally strove to become presidents, and to wield day-to-day authority:

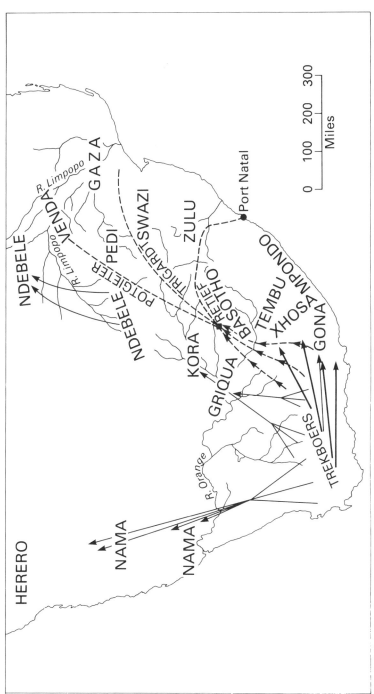

Map 5 Migration from the Cape, c. 1800–c. 1840: Trekboers moving east from the Cape peninsula; Nama, Griqua and Kora moving north from the Cape Colony; trekkers moving north from the eastern Cape

equally naturally, the followers were reluctant to concede more than the *ad hoc* authority of a commandant in a military campaign. The trekkers might aspire to a single and unified political system, but the realities of distance and poor communication and the absence of a paid bureaucracy meant that the real unit of government was a quite small geographical area. In all these respects they closely resembled the Griqua, which is not surprising when we remember the background they all shared, and the day-to-day difficulties which confronted them all.

From 1836 several parties of trekboers evacuated the eastern districts of the colony in concerted groups, following yet another disappointing campaign against the Xhosa, which had briefly seemed to be providing new pasture lands, but had then been reversed by colonial policy. The 'Great Trek', as this movement was termed, was not so much a single concerted migration, as a series of movements by distinct groups, each under its own leadership, and each trekking north in search of the elusive lands. Like all other extensions of the cattle frontier, this also proved disruptive. There was little enough peace and security on the high veld in the aftermath of the Mfecane, but the trekkers uprooted the settled communities which they did encounter, chasing them westwards to the fringe of the Kalahari, or eastwards to make their peace with Moshoeshoe, or (in the case of Mzilikazi) further north to spread fresh havoc beyond the Limpopo River. Apart from a common desire to find pasture land, the trekkers shared few assumptions. Some were determined to achieve complete independence from Britain; others saw the trek as a simple extension of the long tradition of colonial expansion. Some coveted the coastal lands cleared by the Zulu, others were content to travel a little beyond the Orange River, others again aimed to occupy lands across the Vaal River, and perhaps to link up with the Portuguese at Delagoa Bay. During the next ten years, some 14 000 trekkers left the colony, accompanied by herdsmen and domestic servants; but they moved in such an unorganised fashion that the full weight of their manpower and fire-power was rarely concentrated. In most respects the Trek is best seen as a reversion to the eighteenth-century practice of expanding the cattle frontier to cope with increased population and sustained market opportunities: it is the lull of forty years from the 1790s to the 1830s, when expansion was halted by San raids, by Khoi resistance, and by the density of the Xhosa population, which breaks the continuity of trekker history.

The nature of the frontiers

Some general features of the new frontier societies are worth noting, since they reveal the general pressures for change within the colonial community as a whole. First, the conditions of the frontier put a premium on the ability of a pastoralist to acquire stock (as often as not by expropriating someone else's), and then to defend it against all others: the frontiersman was first and foremost a warrior. Second, when political associations formed, they were associations of the warrior heads of pastoral households: whether in the Griqua or in the trekboer polities, adult males insisted on expressing their opinions, and deferred very little to the captains or commandants who led them in military campaigns. Robert Ross describes this administration as 'democratic oligarchy'. Peacetime administration was extremely difficult for a leader whose followers were so individualistic and stubborn. Third, the expansiveness of pastoralism meant that each political association was rather small in numbers. Fourth, mobility was an essential feature of these communities: when expansion was curtailed, tensions built up dangerously within the society, since the young men were unable to acquire the land which they saw as their birthright. At each frontier site, the frontier style was persistently eroded by the consolidation of private property rights, and the increasing control of the colonial administration. Fifth, the frontiersmen were tied tightly to the international market, through Cape Town, the only means of access to the market. When Port Elizabeth became the colony's second harbour, and when Port Natal began to receive regular shipping, the trekkers had alternative outlets to the sea and to the world market – but they simply transferred their ties from one mercantile centre to another.

Taking all these considerations together, it should be clear why the Griquas and Nama and trekboers were in such an ambiguous relationship with the colonial authorities. The commercial ties could not safely be broken, but the political controls were much less welcome, and yet it was not easy to see how the frontiersmen could enjoy the former without suffering the latter. Independence was an ideal to be cherished, but not an aim which could be realised. At any moment the colonial authorities could intervene to cancel the fragile independence of the captaincies or the trekker republics. As we shall see, the whole border of the colony, from southern Namibia through the high veld to the Natal coast, comprised fragmented states: some were the consequence of the Mfecane, and others offshoots of the cattle frontier. Their hostility towards each other made peace almost impossible; and the Cape authorities could pick and choose among them, recognising some as responsible for law and order, withdrawing recognition from others. The new communities were not the masters of their own destinies, but the consequence of commercial pastoralism in a great region where subsistence pastoralism had been the norm.

Chapter 6

Commerce and the extension of colonial law

The new communities in the region were all directly affected by world market conditions: those which expanded out of the Cape could not shake themselves free of their links to the coastal towns; and those which were created during the Mfecane began to enter into market relationships of much the same kind. Changes in external conditions therefore affected all of them to different degrees, so it may be appropriate to begin with some of the more important external conditions before we look at their southern African consequences.

The Dutch East India Company had been one of several merchant capitalist enterprises which conducted international trade by means of monopolistic control of imports and exports. During the wars of the French revolution and the Napoleonic wars (a period from 1791 to 1815) the Dutch Company was broken up, and so were many other European companies. The London-based East India Company survived, but after the wars even that powerful company had its privileges curtailed, and its monopoly was not an important limitation on Cape production and trading relationships. By the end of the generation of European warfare, British manufacturing industry was very much better developed than that of any other nation, and the British manufacturing capitalists needed no preferences. During the first half of the nineteenth century, therefore, the British Government responded to the new needs of the manufacturing industry, and lowered tariff barriers in Britain itself, and in other countries where British influence was powerful, moving gradually towards the condition of free trade. 'Free trade' was never perfectly achieved, but as far as the southern African societies were affected, the volume of trade increased very greatly, and competition was permitted in British markets. In 1815, at the end of the wars, British control was confirmed over the Cape (along with several other former Dutch and French colonial possessions). This involved not merely a change from Dutch to English as the language of government, but the exposure of the Cape especially –

and the other societies indirectly – to vigorous forces for economic change, resulting from the industrial revolution. The Cape remained strategically important, being now the half-way house to India rather than Indonesia, and the British authorities had more resources than the old Company, to impose their wishes on the hinterland of the vital port facilities.

Governors of the Cape for the first half of the nineteenth century were usually military officers, most of whom were authoritarian and conservative by instinct and training. This was appropriate for the office of Governor, representing the authority of the British Government which was equally authoritarian and conservative politically, seeing any political reform movement as potentially revolutionary, and always conscious of the revolution in France and the risk of a similar revolution breaking out elsewhere. At the same time, the nature of governments was being transformed by pressures from the industrialisation process. In Britain and in her colonies, government regulation of a new kind was necessary, to control the social forces generated by economic change. At the Cape then, we may see the paradox of conservative officials enacting legislation which had an almost revolutionary effect upon human relationships. The measures were as radical as was necessary, but the purpose was to change as little as possible.

Colonial boundaries

Undefined boundaries offended the military minds of the rulers at the Cape. If frontiersmen were beyond colonial control, they might provoke warfare which would affect the peace and order of the colony itself. Since the frontiersmen were an intrinsic part of the colonial economy and society, it was inconvenient to leave them outside the framework of colonial law. On the other hand the boundary could not easily be fixed, and it was not feasible to include regions which were used merely for seasonal grazing, and were not regularly inhabited by the colonial population. Occasionally a military governor would annex a great wedge of territory (as D'Urban did on the eastern frontier in 1835, incorporating land as far east as the Kei River; or as Sir Harry Smith did in Transorangia in 1848 and in Kaffraria the same year). Colonial officials in London would often take a much more conservative view, refusing to recognise these annexations, and turning the territory back to its inhabitants (as happened on the eastern frontier in 1836, the Transvaal in 1852, and the rest of Transorangia in 1854). Colonial boundaries did steadily expand, and military actions were occasionally fought, but the stabilisation of frontier conditions called for political and social engineering as well as annexation and conquest.

A common strategy for stabilising the pastoral frontier was to settle smallholder cultivators on it, hoping that agriculture would permit a closely-settled and peaceful population to grow up, law-abiding and willing to rally to the colonial authorities in a crisis. Those Griqua who had already moved into the Orange River valley region were seen by Cape Town officials as a possible buffer community if only they would concentrate on cultivation rather than herding, hunting and raiding. Sporadic attempts were made to settle Khoi in the same fashion on the eastern frontier, the Kat River settlement in 1829 being one of the more ambitious attempts. In 1861 the same strategy was applied to the land between the colonists of Natal and the Nguni communities south of the colonial border: Adam Kok III was encouraged to lead his Griqua followers to what became Griqualand East. Settlements of Khoi, however, seldom survived for very long, because the land which they occupied was coveted by white colonists, and the colonists could use their influence to seize control.

The same difficulty bedevilled the much larger settlement of Mfengu in 1835. Refugees from the wars of the Mfecane, the Mfengu were willing to take up colonial land on the conditions proposed, and 17 000 were settled on land conquered from the Xhosa, forming (for a generation or more) a dependable buttress to colonial authority in a much disputed area. In the long run they, too, were dispensable and their prosperity crumbled when the colonial administration no longer required their support. Attempts were also made to settle white colonists in this fashion. The most dramatic of these was the establishment of the '1820 Settlers', 4 000 British settlers planted west of the Fish River. The colonists were not very carefully selected for agricultural skills, but in any case this was an unpromising region for smallholder agricultural production, since pastoralism on the one hand, and urban jobs on the other, were more attractive financially.

In one sense then, these settlement schemes failed. By establishing new populations in land which was already in demand, they increased competition and warfare rather than suppressed it, and they did not save the colonial authorities from having to take direct political control over areas which were expensive to defend. Most of the settlers themselves did not survive as smallholders for more than a generation. However, if we look at the settlements in another perspective, the record is quite different. Wherever settlers were planted, property rights became better defined, and the turbulence of the pastoral frontier was shifted somewhere else. The settlement schemes steadily expanded the area within which rural commodity production was secure, and a population grew up which would be more attentive to the wishes and instructions of

Cape Town officials. If there had not been some benefits of this kind, it is unlikely that the colonial administration would have persisted in the smallholder settlement policy for most of the nineteenth century.

The pastoral and colonial frontiers were not merely regions for warfare, but the site of extensive interaction. Beyond each frontier for example, the chiefs were almost certain to be drawn into some kind of formal relationship with the colonial officials, receiving either recognition of their own authority, or a small annual stipend, or preferential access to colonial commodities. Equally important, individual young men were likely to cross the border and enter a period of wage employment, discovering for themselves how the colonial market economy worked, and returning home with ideas of how to produce marketable crops or beasts. Wherever frontier conditions prevailed, there were regular markets – including fairs on a regular basis, in an old European tradition – and regular markets encouraged people beyond the frontier to produce saleable goods. The effect of the fairs was strengthened by the activities of travelling traders both inside the border and beyond it.

Missionaries, too, were an important agency for interaction of people and ideas. As a rule, communities tolerated missionaries only if they were already committed to some kind of permanent relationship with the colony: missionaries might serve as channels for correspondence and even as quasi-diplomats. Those communities which were not (or not yet) persuaded that the colonial administration had to be recognised, were not very likely to accept evangelisation; but Griquas especially, other Khoi very often, the Mfengu and of course Moshoeshoe's Sotho, were very receptive to Christian evangelisation. The consequences often included changes in the property relationships within each community, in such a way as to consolidate individual wealth and to permit regular production for the market.

Colonial regulation of production

Within the colonial boundaries, increasing production for the market made it inefficient and unsatisfactory to rely upon earlier ways of mobilising labour. The random and uncontrolled coercion of Khoi into pastoral employment, for example, was neither a reliable nor a safe way of mobilising a labour force. Any colonial government at the Cape in the nineteenth century would probably have had to regulate labour conditions; but as it happened Britain had more experience of the regulation of a labour supply for capitalist production than any other nation at that time. The regulation of labour at the Cape was achieved by sweeping changes which sometimes annoyed employers, even though they would be the long-term gainers from a disciplined labour force. In 1806, for example, Britain outlawed the slave trade throughout the British empire – and therefore at the Cape as well. The condition of slavery continued (though the number of slaves declined) until 1834 when slavery was abolished.

However, in the interval before final abolition, a variety of laws were enacted which gave employers other means of recruiting and controlling labour. In 1809 for example, it was provided that all Khoi (now termed Hottentots), must have a fixed residence, and any Hottentot discovered outside that residence without a pass signed by an employer would be treated as a vagrant. The new regulations also provided for minimum standards of treatment for workers; but the main effect of the regulations was to give State support for settling all Khoi as wage labourers, treating as criminal anyone who was not securely in employment. Three years later, provision was made for the 'apprenticeship' of the children of farm labourers, for a period of ten years. Apprenticeship was in effect forced labour.

Early in the British occupation, in the aftermath of the frontier troubles at the turn of the century, colonial authorities had tried to expel Xhosa farm labourers from the colony; but during the next few years that policy was reversed, and attempts were made to settle refugees from outside the colony, again as a labour force for the colonists. There were even efforts to encourage the immigration of Europeans as indentured servants, obliged to work for a named employer for a fixed number of years. State coercion of reluctant labourers could not be a long-term policy. The steady decline in the Cape garrison, for example, made it desirable to find other techniques for controlling labour. Equally, the apprentices (if white) could often abscond; or (if black) could run away to the frontier rather than submit to humiliation and strict control. In either case the labour supply was threatened.

Newton King suggests that this is part of the explanation for Ordinances 49 and 50 of 1828, which conferred civil rights upon Khoi, scrapping the apprenticeship programme, and permitting Khoi to own property, including land. Khoi were becoming a straightforward working class, and their labour could be secured, mainly by means of economic pressures to drive individuals into employment. The harassment of labourers and their maltreatment by individual employers were now unnecessary and counter-productive. Some employers, especially in the frontier regions, were outraged at the regulation of their relationships with farm labourers, and undoubtedly the new ordinances made life difficult for the poorer employers who had relied on coercion more than wage payments; but for most employers the increasing regulation of master–servant relationships was a great advantage.

Colonial labour policy may also be seen in respect of those few areas where Khoi had gathered together under the protection of a mission organisation, preferring to become a poor but independent peasantry, than to remain at the mercy of employers. The London Missionary Society was often involved in these schemes, and some of the farmers imagined Dr Philip (the superintendent of the LMS in the Cape) to be an influential agitator on behalf of Khoi. Some missionaries also annoyed the colonists by taking Khoi wives. Nevertheless, within the colony the mission stations never became a viable alternative manner of development: their area and their numbers were strictly limited, and mission settlements were diverted towards the frontier where they served a strategic rather than a developmental purpose.

Colonial development

The colonial regulation of land and labour went hand in hand with a striking increase in the quantity of goods produced for the market. Some of this was provoked by the garrison at Cape Town and the other garrison at St Helena where Napoleon was exiled under guard; but much of the increased production resulted from improved market opportunities and the production of new kinds of commodities for sale. When the British Government lowered its import tariff for Cape wine for example, wine exports almost trebled between 1814 and 1824. Further changes in the British tariff structure removed much of that advantage, but the Cape wine industry survived.

The greatest source of increased exports was merino sheep. Unlike the indigenous sheep, merinos grew wool which commanded good prices in British markets, and during the 1840s and afterwards wool became the Cape's most important export. Merinos flourished especially in the eastern half of the colony, and the harbour at Port Elizabeth began to be busier than Cape Town itself; merino sheep were run in rather dry country, where they replaced the indigenous sheep and cattle. Wool was still a form of pastoral production, but merino sheep required more care than indigenous sheep and cattle. Wool was also a sufficiently profitable crop so that a farmer who could gain access to land and stock could become wealthier than anyone else in the colony. Merino sheep may therefore be seen as the means of bringing large areas of the southern African interior under more intensive production, and providing access to large and reliable sources of income. That is to say, that frontier conditions were destroyed when sheep were run; and those who were dispossessed by the new rural industry must leave the land, taking frontier turbulence with them. Sheep farmers were mostly white colonists (who were able to raise or borrow the capital to enter merino production), and the prosperity of their farms depended upon absolute security of property in land and in sheep. By the middle of the nineteenth century the colony was exporting about £500 000 worth of goods each year (more than half being wool), and it had become a modestly prosperous part of the empire.

Settler societies

So far we have been considering mainly the new society which began at Cape Town and spread into the interior. There is very little that is peculiar about this society at least until the middle of the nineteenth century: commercial pastoralism was common in other temperate parts of the world where population density was low. Argentina, parts of North America, southern Australia, parts of eastern Europe, all 'developed' on this basis. In the early days of pastoral expansion, labour was always difficult to obtain, and people often resorted to coercion in order to get work done at all. The convicts of Australia and North America, the slaves of the Cape and colonial South America and the southern States in North America, the apprenticeship schemes and the sheer individual coercion which so often occurred, were similar in all regions where land was cheap and labour expensive. The Cape then, is merely one instance of a pastoral settler society in sparsely inhabited parts of the world, remote from western Europe. After a century or more of pastoral expansion, however, this new settler society confronted a series of settled, mixed farming societies which could not simply be pushed away like Red Indians or Khoi or San or Aboriginals. We must now consider what happened to these communities when they confronted the settlers and their government.

The evolution of peasantries

The entry of African societies into regular market relationships had many and profound consequences; and much depended on the amount of power and autonomy which a society preserved in the encounter. Right on the frontier itself, for example, the disturbing influence of colonists, of Khoi refugees, and of adventurers of all colours, made it almost impossible for chieftaincies to remain in control of the changes which swept through them. The societies right on the frontier were in the most marginal arable land, which supported relatively small and weak chieftaincies, often the off-shoots of stronger societies further north and east. We have seen how the Gqunukhwebe were dispossessed and dispersed: the same fate rapidly overcame the Ntinde and other frontier communities. Ngqika, at one time the most powerful of the southern Xhosa chiefs, fared almost as badly, losing control over his followers in the course of a series of external and internal wars. His heir Sandile, and Sandile's junior (and more able) brother Maqoma, were beset by persistent internal divisions among the Rharhabe, and an erratic relationship with the colonial authorities. However, the influence of regular market relations stretched far into the Xhosa heartland, and in those areas which were safe from frontier violence, there were better prospects for controlled change.

The fairs and markets resulted from people's demands to buy cattle, and hides and ivory. In exchange, the merchants offered cloth and other trade goods, including horses and guns. Possession of these trade goods (and especially the guns and horses) could make an individual chief very much more powerful than he had been before; but near the frontier itself there were so many chiefs in rivalry with each other, that no single one of them could establish his supremacy (nor even lead a stable alliance of Xhosa chiefs, as Maqoma discovered in the 1820s and 1830s). In any case, it was most unlikely that any chief would accumulate as many guns and as much ammunition as the colonists on the other side of the border. A general consequence of this kind of trade was therefore to intensify intra-Xhosa rivalries.

Once market relationships began, they had farther-reaching consequences than the mere accumulation of some trade goods. The first batch of ivory and cattle could be accumulated simply by hunting, and by selling off surplus stock: but quite soon people discovered that they had to enter into the regular production of trading commodities in order to carry on acquiring the traders' offerings. On the frontier, again, that was particularly difficult because so much land had been lost to colonists and Khoi and Mfengu; but away from the frontier it was possible to combine continued subsistence production with the systematic breeding of sheep or cattle for sale. In the competition for additional land, however, not all families had an equal opportunity. Chiefly families were much more likely to get hold of sufficient land (and to mobilise sufficient labour) to benefit from market opportunities. The entry of a formerly self-sufficient community into regular market relationships is often referred to as peasantisation: what commonly happens at the same time, is a separation of the community into prosperous and poor families, the prosperous ones enjoying more land than they can use on their own, and the poor having access to much less. The peasantisation of Xhosa communities therefore was accompanied by a decided internal differentiation, creating a much wider gulf between chiefly and common families, than had been observed at any time in the past. But at the same time, at least for the first few years, markets presented irresistible opportunities, and some families did indeed become very affluent, while even the poor did not suffer immediately, since they could carry on producing subsistence foodstuffs, even though they lost the opportunity to produce surpluses for the market. The people most thoroughly involved in the peasantisation process were the Mfengu, who as refugees had little choice but to enter into market production, and who at the same time embraced the opportunities of Christianity and loyalty to the colonial administration. However, they were merely an early and striking example of a profound and widespread transformation of the Nguni throughout the eastern coastal belt in the early nineteenth century. Traders operated throughout this region, and wherever they traded they created opportunities for the generating of additional income, and unleashed internal competition.

Fragmented states and British hegemony

While the transformation of colonial and extra-colonial societies was proceeding, localised conflicts persisted. As the power which claimed responsibility for the whole region, Britain could decide which conflicts to ignore, which constituted a threat to colonial order, which local authorities to patronise and support, and which to suppress. At one extreme there were governors who wanted to impose colonial order on almost everyone, no matter what the cost: at the other were officials who were anxious to leave things alone: most commonly, colonial policy involved selective and limited intervention to adjust relationships rather than to revolutionise them. But with the expansion of the pastoral frontier in the interior, and the frontier of peasantisation along the coast, British direct responsibility tended steadily to expand. To the north, the British flag followed the trekboer; to the east, it followed the trader.

We have seen that the colonial authorities entered into treaty relations with some of the Khoi groups beyond the frontier, delegating responsibility for law and order. When trekboers moved on to the interior high veld in the 1830s some further measures were required to preserve the peace. The Cape of Good Hope Punishment Act in 1836 asserted that British colonial law operated in all areas south of 25° latitude, but did not suggest how that law was to be administered. Those trekboers who unwisely migrated into the eastern coastal belt were particularly troublesome. Piet Retief and his immediate followers secured a cession of land from King Dingane, but were killed before they left his kraal, and a concerted attempt to destroy the immigrant pastoralists was only narrowly defeated. The battle of Blood River in December 1838 gave the trekkers behind their wagon laager a complete victory over the Zulu regiments which attacked so bravely and recklessly; but the Republic of Natalia was soon confronted by other serious difficulties. Refugee Nguni groups seized the opportunity to return to their lands now that Dingane was no longer able to attack them, and soon the pastoral republic was flooded by people returning to resume mixed farming. An attempt to expel these refugees southwards, caused much alarm in the Cape where such large population movements might upset the whole frontier region. In

Laager method of defence used by trekkers to give them victory at the Battle of Blood River

particular, the colonial authorities were sensitive to the possibility of some other European power establishing a naval base on the south-eastern coast. During 1842 the Natal republic was formally annexed as a British colony. Once established in Natal, the British made it their policy to undertake as little as possible. The trekkers had overthrown Dingane and replaced him in 1840 by his more peaceable half-brother Mpande; so it required little effort to avoid further trouble for the next generation.

The trekkers who remained on the interior plateau (and who were joined by most of the trekkers from Natal when that republic was annexed) could safely be left alone. Few in number and widely dispersed, they could defend themselves even against Mzilikazi, who retreated north of the Limpopo following unsuccessful warfare against the trekkers during 1837. On the other hand they were strictly limited to those regions of the high veld which were clear of tsetse fly and anopheles mosquito, and which had no settled African population. An expedition which ignored these limitations was decimated on its way to the Delagoa Bay region, being harried by mosquitoes, tsetse fly and the coastal Thonga. In the persistent tussles with Moshoeshoe also, the trekkers were at a disadvantage, since Moshoeshoe was quite well armed, and possessed a series of defensible fortresses in the mountain ranges. The trekkers accordingly spread themselves throughout an expanse of flat and high country which favoured pastoralism, and were less successful in annexing arable farming land. Especially to the south of this region, many trekkers saw themselves as merely seasonal settlers; especially towards the north were a number of trekkers who sought a more explicit independence of the British authorities.

For a decade or more trekker administration was little more than local self-government on a patriarchal and semi-military basis, and it was unnecessary for colonial authorities to be alarmed. The trekkers – like the Griqua – were tied to the colony by the need for access to Cape markets, so they could safely be left alone to work out a series of relationships and accommodations with the African authorities who had survived the Mfecane. As in Natal, so on the high veld, the military defeat of the strongest post-Mfecane state (in this case Mzilikazi's Ndebele) encouraged earlier inhabitants (here the Sotho and Tswana groups) to filter back to their own lands. In this instance, however, the consequent disputes between Africans and trekkers were unlikely to damage any British interest.

So matters might have remained, but for the intervention of one of the more militarist and energetic (and simple-minded) of British colonial governors. Sir Harry Smith, arriving at the end of 1847, was outraged by the confusion of the region, and its fragmented polities. During his first year of office he extended the boundary of the colony to the Keiskamma River in the east (and annexed the adjacent region as British Kaffraria for good measure), and to the

Orange River in the north (and annexed Transorangia and the Transvaal as well). When several thousand trekkers resisted these annexations, Smith was able to defeat them at the battle of Boomplaats in August 1848. During the next few years however, it seemed to the colonial officials across the Orange River that the main challenge to orderly administration would be from the trekkers: and to pacify them, a number of measures were undertaken which accelerated their control over neighbouring African lands.

Warden, left in charge of Transorangia (or the Orange River Sovereignty as it was termed during the brief colonial era), demarcated a fresh boundary between Moshoeshoe and the trekkers, giving the trekkers a considerable area of arable land in the Caledon River and upper Orange River region. In the increasingly frequent disputes over Griqua land, the trekkers were able to consolidate their grip on land which they had previously rented. Matters reached a crisis in 1851 when Moshoeshoe and his African allies defeated Warden and his troops at the battle of Viervoet.

This defeat confirmed the belief of the Colonial Secretary in London, and his officials on the spot, that nothing was to be gained by formal British colonial control over the interior plateau. The Transvaal trekkers regained their formal independence through the Sand River Convention of 1852. At the time of independence, there were actually four trekker communities in the Transvaal, each with its own military leadership. One of these leaders – Andries Pretorius – led the Transvaal delegates at the independence negotiations, and he duly became President of the new republic – though his authority was not acknowledged by all trekkers, and he had no obvious means of enforcing his will over groups who chose to disregard him.

The colonial officials thought, however, that it might be feasible to retain direct control over Transorangia; but another battle lost to Moshoeshoe – Thaba Bosiu at the end of 1852 – suggested that British authority could be maintained only if a substantial (and expensive) garrison were permanently posted to the region. In fact the trekkers were not very anxious to see the last of the colonial troops, whose presence strengthened trekker security against Sotho, Tswana, San and Griqua and Kora rivals for the high veld lands. In the process of persuading the trekkers to accept a form of independence, colonial authorities withdrew their support from all African authorities north of the Orange River, with the sole exception of Adam Kok III. Even Adam Kok's people of course suffered from this abdication: it was during 1854 and 1855 (the year of the Bloemfontein Convention and the following year) that a great deal of Griqua farm land passed permanently into the hands of the trekkers. A general consequence of the British withdrawal and recognition of trekker independence was that the trekkers now had much better access to firearms and to gunpowder than their African neighbours. During the following generation, they steadily translated that military advantage, into a permanent advantage in access to pastoral and arable land.

In reality, whether the trekkers operated their own republics or accepted formal British administration, their relationship to the Cape was one of extreme dependency. As late as 1870, there were probably only about 45 000 trekkers in the interior republics. Having very little hard cash themselves, the pastoral farmers were reluctant to pay the taxes which would support effective republican

John Hendrick Brand, President of Orange Free State

administration. The republican states had little option but to give out land in lieu of official salaries. But the more land they gave away, the more it became necessary to conquer more African land for the trekkers themselves – and land was difficult to conquer, even with firearms and ammunition from the Cape.

Not surprisingly, then, political authority was extremely unstable on the high veld. Trekkers in the north were reluctant to assist their southern colleagues in warfare against Moshoeshoe; trekkers in the south were reluctant to assist in the northern campaigns against the Venda, Pedi and Tswana chiefs who defended their lands and herds. A *volksraad* (an assembly of the people) met from time to time, but there was no way to impose volksraad decisions on any group of trekkers who objected to them. From 1857 onwards, M. W. Pretorius (son of the first Transvaal president) struggled to unify all the republics under his own presidency. After much political manoeuvring and the threat of war among the trekkers, Pretorius reconciled himself to being the President only of the Transvaal from 1864 onwards, and the Orange Free State brought in a respected Cape colonist, J. H. Brand, as their President from 1864 onwards, a man who reflected the Orange Free State's close ties with the Cape, and who could also conduct a simple political system very competently. Brand would certainly not challenge British hegemony on the high veld; and Pretorius and the more anti-British Transvaalers had no opportunity to do so. Governor Sir George Grey played with the idea of re-annexation and the unification of the settler societies during 1858, but Grey was dismissed from office for having encouraged the settlers to think in terms of British annexation.

African peasant communites were annexed in much the same casual way as trekker republics, but they were less often restored to independence. Each frontier war involved land annexation at the expense of Xhosa communities. The annexation of Kaffraria by Smith in 1848 led not to retrocession of sovereignty, but (in 1865) to its incorporation into the Cape Colony. Xhosa resistance reached a climax in 1856, when Sarili the paramount chief instructed loyal Xhosa to destroy their herds and crops, to prepare for a return of the dead to aid the living. The appalling starvation and dispersion of Xhosa families which followed destroyed the possibility of concerted Xhosa resistance.

In the interior of the eastern Cape, Moshoeshoe's success in resisting trekker encroachment made colonial authorities nervous lest Sotho resistance might spill over to the eastern areas, undermining the authority of the magistrates and agents who represented colonial law in the conquered and still-to-be-annexed chieftaincies of the southern Nguni. One security measure of this period was the encouragement of Adam Kok III to bring his Griqua followers to what became Griqualand East centred upon Kokstad.

The migration was accomplished in 1861–2, and for a decade the Griqua remained nominally independent in their new lands until they were brusquely annexed in 1874. Their role in the east, as in the west, had been to buttress British authority; and as soon as colonial authority could be carried out in a more regular and conventional manner, Griqua claims fell away. The annexation of East Griqualand was only one of a series of annexations between the middle of the nineteenth century and the 1880s, which ultimately replaced British overlordship by formal colonial administration. The same officials also worked to hand over the new colonial responsibilities to an increasingly large and affluent Cape colonial administration. The sequence of formal annexations to the Crown, and of transfers to the Colony, do not seem to merit much discussion, since they were mainly the means of formalising a set of relationships set in train by traders and the adoption of cash crop production for the market, throughout the coastal belt during the middle of the nineteenth century.

There is one partial exception to the melancholy account of conquest and unsuccessful resistance. Despite the lengthening odds against their independence – or even autonomy under the Crown – the Sotho followers of Moshoeshoe persisted in repulsing the campaigns of the Orange Free State. Repeatedly, Moshoeshoe sought to gain the best terms which seemed feasible: namely, to be annexed directly to the British Crown rather than be swallowed up by the white colonists. The difficulty of pursuing a concerted policy was intensified by the continuing independence of Moshoeshoe's old rivals (such as Sekonyela, until the 1850s) and the increasing independence of his own grown-up sons. Nonetheless throughout the 1860s resistance to the trekkers continued, and the appeals continued to flow to the British Government.

Only in 1868 did the British authorities agree to annex his territory as Basutoland; and that event followed the last of the Orange Free State campaigns, which had at last been successful, and had deprived Moshoeshoe's people of most of their remaining arable land. What remained to be annexed was the defensible mountainous areas, which had little agricultural value.

Nevertheless the Sotho had made it clear that they were formidable enemies when provoked. When the dependency was transferred to the Cape Colony (in 1871), and the Cape Government rashly attempted to disarm the population, the Gun War broke out (1880–81), and was ended only by the abandonment of the Cape's ambition to break up the remaining Sotho community. In 1884 Basutoland was formally returned to the British Crown as a distinct dependency. Moshoeshoe had died in 1870, and the armed resistance was led by his grandson Lerothodi. Half a century of vigorous fighting, sustained and subtle diplomacy, and the slow formation of a new political association, had deflected the forces which overwhelmed many other southern African societies: but the most that could be accomplished was separate administration in a reduced area of land, very little of which was suited to agricultural or pastoral production.

The Cape assumes responsibility

Every government in Cape Town relied upon a measure of support from the colonists, whether or not power was formally shared with them. The second British annexation for example, was a military event: colonists enjoyed no formal political authority (and until the end of the 1820s they were not even guaranteed freedom of the press), but leading merchants and the more prosperous landowners were commonly consulted. Eventually in 1853 a system of representative government was conceded, in a more limited way than the Australian constitutions of the same period. Adult male citizens were enfranchised if they met a property qualification which tended to exclude coloured and African citizens, although there was no explicit colour bar in the legislation. The legislature which consisted mainly of elected members had a great deal of influence over the executive officers of the colonial states, but not control, since the heads of government departments were responsible to the Governor and to the Colonial Office in London, rather than to the elected colonists. This clumsy system was replaced in 1872 by responsible government, whereby the legislature did control the ministerial heads of departments, who formed their own cabinet.

It may seem odd that the colonial authorities were willing to allow the trekkers to be entirely independent (at least on paper), whereas citizens of the more prosperous and peaceful Cape colony were subject to so much more control. One important reason for the slow evolution of self-government at the Cape was the fact that most colonial governors did take the views of wealthy colonists into account very frequently: after the 1830s it was rare for a governor to face the opposition of large numbers of colonists. An equally effective reason for delay was tension between colonists in the eastern Cape (growing and exporting wool through Port Elizabeth and East London), and those in the western Cape (who were closely linked to Cape Town). Colonists were not sure that representatives from the other end of the colony would truly represent their immediate interests. Most important, however, was the reluctance of the colonists to assume responsibility for the (military) costs of self-government in addition to the (land and labour) benefits which might flow from it. Self-government would lead to the reduction of imperial garrisons, leaving the colonial government to cope out of its own meagre revenues with the ruinous costs of further frontier warfare.

The evolution of colonial self-government at the Cape, then, was not a classic struggle between autocracy and democracy, but rather a long and detailed bargaining process over the costs of long-term imperial commitment to southern Africa as a whole. Imperial hegemony in the region was not diminished by responsible government, and its achievement meant no revolutionary change within the colonial society. When self-government was formally achieved in 1872, the colonists were fully conscious of their dependence upon imperial support and they were in no condition to challenge it. For many years afterwards, imperial British authorities exercised their power to create and to destroy political systems throughout the region, whether they were trekker republics or African kingdoms of chieftaincies, or even – in the case of Natal's colonial administration in the 1870s – British colonies with representative institutions. As it happened, formal self-government for the Cape was followed by one of the more dramatic imperial interventions in the South African region: the imperial government clearly did not feel that it was on the way out. That intervention had much to do with the consequences of the discovery and mining of diamonds in border territory beyond the Orange River. That event brought quite new forces into operation throughout the region, and to that event we must now turn our attention.

Chapter 7

Diamonds: beginnii, mineral revolution

Colonial southern Africa was in deep depression in 1867. The major export staple was wool, on which the prosperity of colonists and peasants depended; but wool was not as profitable in southern Africa as in North America or Australia. The unprofitability of the region was reflected in the imperial government's reluctance to spend any more money there – whereas capital was pouring into the Australian colonies. It was also rather ominous that the Suez Canal would soon be completed, an event which might well reduce even the strategic value of the Cape, and discourage ships from calling at Cape ports. In this year, however, a diamond was found in Griqua territory near the Orange River. Hundreds, then thousands, of prospectors and small-scale fortune-hunters poured into the territory. The first diamond was not a fluke, and diamonds were discovered in larger numbers than ever before in human experience, making it possible for a large and permanent mining industry to grow up.

The first issue to be settled was the ownership of the diamond-bearing lands. Adam Kok had led the eastern Griqua out of the Orange River valley, but Nicholas Waterboer and the western Griqua were still in possession of the pastoral lands where diamonds were being dug. Waterboer and his followers were not able to prevent the influx of prospectors, nor to control them once they pitched their tents and began digging. His legal claims were strong, but his political power and influence were feeble. Stronger claimants to the area were the Transvaal Republic (which sought control over all lands north of the Vaal River) and the Orange Free State (which insisted upon all lands north of the Orange) and the Cape Colony itself (which controlled access to the diggings). It was not clear that any of these authorities would be able to preserve order on their own. In 1871 the British Crown annexed the diamond-bearing territory as the Crown Colony of Griqualand West, hoping to be able to pass that repsonsibility to the Cape Colony in much the same way as other troublesome frontier regions had been added to the Cape in previous years. From Kimberley a

Diamonds 85

Diamond mining in Kimberley fields, 1871

Lieutenant-Governor struggled to retain order over the new and very unruly population: at Cape Town the colonists reaped the benefits of new trade without assuming responsibility for governing the diamond diggers. In Bloemfontein, the Orange Free State Government resented its exclusion from the diamond-bearing lands, and continued to believe – perhaps romantically – that it had the capacity to control the new population. The imperial government was left with the expensive responsibility of keeping the peace in another land-locked territory, until such time as a general re-organisation of southern African affairs could occur.

Diamonds were first mined by each prospector pegging a claim to a particular piece of ground, digging up the earth, and running it through a sieve which would retain any diamonds in each shovelful. Prospectors needed little capital, and employed at most a few African labourers and perhaps a personal servant. This very casual system of diamond mining suffered three major difficulties. First, diamonds are small in size and often command spectacular prices, so they are ideal objects to steal. Labourers earning very small wages for very hard work were naturally tempted to pocket good diamonds – or to swallow them – and there was no difficulty in finding dealers who would buy these illicit diamonds. Equally naturally the prospectors were infuriated by the illicit diamond buying (IDB) network. Second, it soon became impractical to dig up diamonds from a large number of narrow holes, adjoining each other: pathways between the claims would cave in, and it became almost impossible to be sure whose claim was which, once the holes were deep. Third, although diamonds were (and remain) very expensive, they have little intrinsic value. Poor quality stones (industrial diamonds) are very useful for cutting, and are often used in the bits of drills; but high quality diamonds are essentially a luxury product. A large number of precious stones coming on to the world market at the same time tended to depress diamond prices generally. If diamonds were to retain a high value, then control had to be established over marketing arrangements, to ensure that not too many precious stones were being sold simultaneously. So long as diamond mining continued on the basis of many small producers, there was no way of resolving these difficulties, which indeed became worse all the time.

The problems were resolved in much the same way as similar problems have been resolved in mining fields throughout the world: consolidation of ownership. Diggers began to amalgamate their claims, and to exploit them jointly. But if a single company could take control over all mining claims, then the labour force could be disciplined, a single large mine could replace a multitude of small holes, and the flow of diamonds on to the market could also be restricted. In Kimberley this was not an easy problem, because the most profitable claims could only be bought up by paying very large

Cecil Rhodes, founder of 'Rhodesia', De Beers, Consolidated Goldfields and Prime Minister of the Cape, 1890–6

sums of money to the claim-holders. There was simply not enough money in the Cape or in Griqualand West to pay the cost of consolidation. Capital had to be imported from overseas.

The largest of these sums of capital was provided by a European company, Wernher, Beit and Company, which succeeded in purchasing all the necessary claims. The eventual market value of the company was more than £20 000 000. The local agent of this firm was Cecil John Rhodes, son of an English clergyman, who had been farming in southern Africa and had been attracted along with thousands of other adventurers to the new mining fields. The holding company for this enterprise was De Beers Consolidated Mines, which by 1890 had completed the task of consolidation. Rhodes was a successful and flamboyant and unscrupulous local manager; but the decisive advantage of De Beers in the struggle was the volume of capital it could draw upon. By the climax of the consolidation process, not only Wernher & Beit, but several local capitalists such as Rhodes and Rudd, and even the Rothschild banking empire, had been committed.

The consolidation of diamond mining meant that there was no further role for independent prospectors to play. If they were successful, they might be able to retire. If not, they must either go and prospect somewhere else, or accept employment as wage labourers. In 1881 there were 3 100 white miners employed in diamond mining; by 1889 when consolidation was nearly complete, there were only 1 272 white wage-earners in the diamond industry. They were mainly employed in jobs which required scarce technical skills, so those who survived in the industry were quite well paid. The reduction in their numbers also made De Beers willing and able to pay generous wages. The number of African mine-workers also declined very sharply, from about 17 000 in 1881 to 6 830 in 1889. For African workers, however, working conditions and wages did not improve at all. Employers certainly provided adequate accommodation and food, in order to be sure of a healthy and vigorous work force: but African workers were now recruited on contract for several months at a time, and for the whole of that contract period the miners had to live inside mining compounds. The compounds gave employers themselves control over the lives of labourers, preventing IDB, but also making it difficult for them to strike or to negotiate higher wages. White miners could not be forced into compound conditions, since they could threaten to go to some other country where their technical skills were needed; black miners were usually unskilled in mining techniques, so they had either to take the conditions offered them, or not come to Kimberley at all. As we shall see, the colonial government supported De Beers in insisting upon this division of the labour force, and in disciplining the Africans. In general, consolidation of the mining industry enabled diamond mining to be carried on with a much smaller labour force than before, and permitted the mine management very wide powers of control.

We may pause here to ask what happened to the people who had been living in the region before diamond mining began. Waterboer's Griquas had been under pressure from Orange Free State farmers to yield pastoral land; but they were still in occupation of much of that land in 1867. These claims were ignored by the diggers, and a Land Court established in 1875 dismissed much of Waterboer's claim. In 1880 Griqualand West was added to the Cape Province, and a certain amount of land was set aside for Griqua occupation. Under persistent pressure, the Griquas sold their remaining lands, their society was scattered, and they made a living as individuals mainly in wage-labouring jobs on much the same terms as other Africans. The claims of the Orange Free State had also been brushed aside, but in the aftermath of the Land Court hearings the OFS government was paid £90 000 in compensation – a very small sum, compared with the millions of pounds invested in the mining industry during this period. However, the OFS trekker government did at least survive as a sovereign and independent polity. Within the Griqualand West Colony, power was concentrated in the hands of the Crown, but exercised on behalf of the mine-owning companies. How that power was used, we should now consider.

A British magistrate went to the diamond diggings in 1870, and struggled to establish his authority against an informal republic of diamond prospectors. Even when Griqualand West became a Crown Colony in the following year, its administration was poverty-stricken and remote from possible reinforcement via Cape Town: to keep the peace at all, it was shrewd to heed the advice of the most boisterous claim holders. As claims were consolidated, the managers of capital became increasingly influential over the temporary Crown Colony administrators. Only in 1880, when the Cape colonists agreed to accept Griqualand West as a part of their own political system, could a coherent legislative programme come into being: by that time the division of the labour force had already been entrenched by practice. When the first Griqualand West members entered the Cape parliament in 1881, Rhodes was one of them, and he celebrated his arrival by assisting in the overthrow of the cabinet of J. G. Sprigg, whose unsuccessful attempt to disarm the Sotho had made him vulnerable. Until Rhodes's death twenty years later, he would be a major influence in Cape politics.

From the point of view of mine managers, an important issue was the control of illicit diamond buying. In 1874 diamond buyers were brought under a licence system, which certainly helped to restrict IDB; but the success of this legislation depended upon the vigour of police enforcement, and that in turn required persistent pressure upon the colonial state. In 1889, De Beers came to an agreement with a group of dealers who joined together in the Diamond Syndicate: De Beers would sell diamonds only to the Syndicate (which included many of the De Beers principals), and the problem of illicit diamond buying became a very small affair. Meanwhile the creation of a contract labour system, relying upon migrant labourers who lived in closed compounds, also required the endorsement of the colonial state. Cape politicians were not likely to object to restrictions upon African mine workers, but it was useful for the owners of De Beers to have Rhodes sitting in parliament to keep an eye on the issue. It was also useful to ensure that nobody attempted to tax the diamond exports of the colony, although occasional suggestions were made in that direction.

An equally important issue for mine managers was the long-term provision of a regular supply of migrant labourers. For the first few years of mining, it was not difficult to mobilise Africans, who were quite keen to come and earn enough money to buy firearms, with which to protect what land remained to them. Basutoland and the eastern Cape provided recruits to supplement the small numbers of labourers available within Griqualand West itself. As the sale of guns came under stricter control, however, there was some risk that the flow of migrant labour might disappear. Some general policy had to be laid down. The opportunity presented itself in 1892, when the Cape parliament turned its attention to Glen Grey in the eastern Cape, where a series of risings and migrations had confused the land claims of the Nguni living there.

The negotiations over Glen Grey, and the solution propounded, are worth some consideration since they formed the basis for a far-reaching land and labour policy. White farmers were anxious (as before) simply to clear the Nguni out of Glen Grey, and cut it up as white farms. The more liberal members were anxious to see a movement towards individual land ownership among Africans. Rhodes was by this time Prime Minister of the Cape, and the compromise which he allowed to come forward in 1894 was very much on the lines of the liberal members: Africans should acquire individual title to land in Glen Grey but (to satisfy the white farmers) this should not entitle African landowners to vote for Cape elections. The logic of the Glen Grey Act was to settle a limited number of African families on the land, and to make the others available as seasonal migrant workers either for farmers in the agricultural and pastoral regions, or for De Beers at Kimberley. The policy was neither very generous nor very liberal, but it was more subtle than the policy pursued by white farmers, and it was much better attuned to the long-term needs of the diamond-mining industry. Those who enacted the Glen Grey legislation described it as 'a Bill for Africa', not merely a piece of local legislation. The Glen Grey Act offered a model for control over other African populations, in the interest of all major employers in the region. The simple conquest and acquisition of land was no longer the main purpose of the colonial state.

Rhodes was able to influence the formulation of this new land and labour policy because he had achieved a solid and workable political alliance which gave him control of the Cape parliamentary institutions. The largest single political group in the parliament was the Afrikaner Bond led by J. H. Hofmeyr, an association of rural landowners which commonly controlled nearly half of the seats. The Bond was not keen to rule on its own, preferring to choose one of the many factions of English-speaking politicians who competed for Hofmeyr's favour. Rhodes's Kimberley supporters, sometimes in association with professional men from Cape Town, were sufficient to give Rhodes and Hofmeyr a workable majority of seats. However, this was more than a parliamentary alliance: the interests of Rhodes and the interests of the rural Afrikaners were highly compatible. Rhodes was anxious to expand his territorial interests northwards into Tswana country and across the Limpopo into Zambesia – and the rural Afrikaners were equally interested in the land which might become available through such expansion. The Bond sought improved extension services for agriculture, and better rural schools, and railway lines to link them to the market: Rhodes was willing to provide these services out of the revenue which diamond mining provided. De Beers and white farmers both sought cheap African labour – and the Glen Grey legislation was a satisfactory compromise between the needs of both kinds of employer. When Hofmeyr picked Rhodes as the next Prime Minister (in 1890), they were both already committed to colonial expansion northwards. For the next five years their alliance was profoundly harmonious, and from time to time Rhodes was able to advise his parliamentary allies of profitable developments on the stock exchange, and even occasionally to make small presents of shares in the companies which he managed. There was a certain symbolic appropriateness in the Rhodes-Hofmeyr alliance: the colonial economy rested upon diamonds and land – and so did the governing coalition.

It is important to notice a less dramatic transformation as well. The profits of diamond mining flowed not only to the investors of capital, but also to the Cape colonial economy. During the 1860s the Cape had struggled under a large burden of public debt incurred in fighting frontier wars: by the mid-1870s most of that debt had been paid off, and the Cape government was able to borrow money in London at quite reasonable interest rates, to pay for more productive investment. One product of this new flow of capital was the rapid construction of railway lines, first from Cape Town to Kimberley, then from Port Elizabeth, and then even from East London. (Even struggling little Natal began to build a railway towards the interior, in order to retain some share of the business with Kimberley.) These railway lines carried mining equipment and food and consumer goods inland – and they were also of some benefit to the farmers whose land they passed through.

A further consequence of increased revenue and capital at the Cape was an increasing military capacity at the disposal of the Cape government. Where the Cape had been reluctant to assume responsibility for troublesome areas, or areas densely settled by Africans, it became increasingly eager to assume these responsibilities. If chieftaincies objected to incorporation, the Cape had the police and paramilitary resources to suppress any such resistance. By 1885 the Cape borders had expanded eastwards and northwards as far as the borders of Natal, mopping up almost all the remaining outposts of African independence. Rhodes himself was anxious to expand north through the interior plateau: his companies, as well as the Cape government, placed increasing pressure upon the Colonial Office for authority to expand their operations into Zambesia through Tswana country. On occasions the Cape over-estimated its military capacity, and imperial troops had to be invited to assist; but these occasions were rare, and in any case they reflect an optimistic assessment of colonial strength, quite different from the pessimistic assessments of the 1860s.

Within the expanding colony, the government was increasingly able to provide for its (mainly white) voters a range of schools and governmental service which had been impossible during the impoverished 1860s. In the thirty years from 1870, the number of children attending Cape schools trebled, and the colonial state rather than the Churches provided the teachers. Such services were more easily supplied to urban populations, but attempts were also made to pay for one-teacher rural schools to serve the children on scattered pastoral holdings. By the end of the century, the racial segregation of schools was becoming normal even in areas where racially mixed schooling would have been more economical.

The Cape Colony expanded not merely in gross financial terms, and by the absorption of areas already inhabited by Africans – but also through immigration. Within ten years of the first diamond discovery, there were 18 000 people living in Kimberley. Some were migrants from Nguni and Sotho areas, and others white farmers who expected to do better for themselves in mining; but many came from overseas. By the 1870s there was a large population of miners drifting around the world from California through Victoria to southern Africa, wherever mining skills were in demand. They were supplemented by other Europeans seeking a better life outside western Europe, and settling in the Americas, Australasia and southern Africa. More whites travelled to Kimberley than had crossed the Orange River in the Great Trek, and they helped to bring the Cape's white population to nearly a quarter of a million by 1875, whereas the African population had increased at a slower pace, to nearly half a million. The Cape also boasted the only significant towns in the region: Cape Town with perhaps 45 000 people, Kimberley with perhaps 35 000, and Port Elizabeth with about 13 000. Whereas the Cape had been a rather limp colony, starved of funds and highly dependent upon a single crop, unable to provide much in the way of protection or services to the settler population, it was rapidly becoming a vigorous economy, attracting immigrants, and providing a wide range of services to them.

The rapid growth of urban settlements, especially Kimberley in the dry karoo area, might have been expected to provide great opportunities for agricultural producers. In reality they derived very little direct benefit from these new markets. Although wheat could be grown, it was not as cheap as the mass-produced grain of North America and Australia, which flooded the market through the new railway network. This would continue to be the case until farmers organised themselves to control the market, and to attract the capital needed to improve their production systems.

It might also be expected that the development of mining would create opportunities for increased manufacturing in the Cape. That also proved a very slow consequence. What the De Beers complex needed was heavy and sophisticated machinery, and explosives, which were not produced at the Cape for another generation. The diamond diggings were like a modern enclave, consuming great quantities of commodities, but bringing them cheaply from overseas rather than promoting their production within the Cape itself. Cape colonists and peasants gained almost no advantage directly from the mining operations: rather they benefited from the increased revenue which accrued to the government, and which could be re-distributed by the government. The distribution of benefits therefore depended upon the political influence of the colonists, rather than their ability to respond to new economic opportunities. This meant, of course, that benefits would flow strongly and dependably to enfranchised colonists, and less reliably to the peasant communities which were being incorporated into the Cape.

A revealing instance of this relationship is the fate of the wine farmers of the western Cape. One of the immediate causes of the formation of a strong Afrikaner political group, had been Sprigg's decision to impose an excise tax on brandy. Once the Afrikaner Bond became a powerful force in colonial politics, the brandy duty was lifted (in 1884) and was not re-imposed. During later negotiations between the Colony and the republics, the Cape government persistently requested the duty-free entry of brandy into the republics (though that pressure was not always successful). Without the political influence of the Afrikaner Bond in the colonial parliament, wine and brandy production might well have struggled to survive.

Though the Cape was transformed in the generation after 1867, there were limits to that transformation. Diamonds replaced wool, and diamond mining brought millions of pounds in capital investment, as well as creating millions of pounds of export value; but the economic development of the colony was very uneven indeed. Apart from diamonds, wool and wine, very little new production occurred at the Cape; agriculture was not particularly benefited by the intervention of mining capital; manufacturing was not stimulated. What did change was the size, the proportion, the wealth and the self-confidence of the white colonist community within the Cape. From the 1870s onwards (and especially from 1890 when Rhodes took control of the Cape government) the imperial government would have to cope with a colonial government which had its own policies for the region, and the means of carrying them out. The Cape was still highly dependent upon Great Britain – but Rhodes and the Afrikaner Bond could now use the colonial government in pursuit of their own ambitions, which might or might not coincide with those of the Colonial Office in London.

Chapter 8

Gold: the mineral revolution accomplished

The historian De Kiewiet (in *A History of South Africa: Social and Economic*) passed the judgment on southern African history, that 'South Africa has advanced politically by disasters and economically by windfalls'. He was referring particularly to the discovery of diamonds, but implicitly also to the discovery of gold-bearing ore along the Witwatersrand in the southern Transvaal. The discovery of mineral deposits is probably not quite as accidental as De Kiewiet suggested, but his judgment is a useful starting point in considering the prodigious results which have flowed from the development of a gold-mining industry in southern Africa. Even more than diamonds, gold has transformed human relationships throughout the sub-continent, and if the gold had not been present, southern Africa would have experienced a quite different kind of history during the past hundred years. As a matter of convenience, we may consider the gold-mining industry in terms of the same themes which arose in the chapter on diamonds. This approach may also allow us to grasp the dimensions of the mineral revolution as a whole.

Gold had been exploited in a small way for centuries, though not in the Witwatersrand area itself; small deposits had also been exploited for some years before the major 'find' of 1886. When the great deposits were finally unearthed, they were located in just as remote a region as Griqualand West, a part of the high veld which supported extensive pastoralism and a rather thin population. The Transvaal Republic, like Nicholas Waterboer's Griqua captaincy, was an area of little importance to Britain, or even to the Cape Colony. Its trekker citizens had rebelled against British rule in 1880, and their independence had been substantially restored in 1884, though with some provision for the vague British hegemony which still hung over the whole southern African region. The gold-bearing reef could at first be exploited as outcrop, and it was only over a period of a dozen years that the great extent of the deposits came to be appreciated: the outcrop was merely the rim of a saucer-shaped reef which sloped ever deeper under the land surface as it fell away to the south. It was created many thousands of years earlier as the bed of an inland lake, whose waters had long dried up. These ores have now been extracted with hardly an interruption for nearly a hundred years; and only a brave or foolish prophet would guess how many more decades will be required to exhaust them. More gold was located in the Witwatersrand than in any other gold-mining field in human history.

As in Griqualand, so in the Transvaal there was some doubt as to the capacity of the host government to preserve law and order over the new population which rushed to the gold fields from 1886 onwards, establishing the city of Johannesburg and several smaller mining towns east and west along the line of the reef. Citizenship was strictly confined to white families, whose total population was probably no more than 40 000 people: and that was barely sufficient to maintain a brittle control over perhaps two thirds of a million Africans living within the boundaries of the republic. The capacity of the republican administration to keep order, to assume responsibility for large volumes of mining capital, was from time to time questioned: but no attempt was made to overthrow that authority for the first decade of gold mining, and by the end of that period the republican officials had armed and secured themselves against such a challenge. There was no question of adding the Transvaal to the Cape, as had happened in Griqualand West. Rather the development of gold mining weakened the Cape's long-standing primacy among the colonies and protectorates of the southern African region, making the Transvaal an alternative centre of power and influence.

The first phase of mining operations, by individual prospectors, quickly came to an end. The gold might be plentiful, but it was embedded as a very small proportion of a very tough rock matrix: not much gold could be extracted by pick and shovel. The outcrop deposits were in any case quickly exhausted, and for the rest of the reef it was essential to dig main shafts into the earth, and then narow tunnels laterally, following the reef as it wound and looped its way under the ground. The cost of the machinery and of labour for these diggings excluded all but the very wealthy. Some consolidation was necessary almost from the inception of gold mining. Yet it was not necessary to achieve the complete consolidation that De Beers encompassed in Kimberley. In the late nineteenth century (and for many years in the twentieth) gold had a fixed price, which would not be depressed however much gold was poured on to the world market. It was never necessary for mine owners to combine in order to control the price of their product. Nor was there any serious risk of mine-workers stealing the gold: many tons of ore would have to be smuggled out of a mining compound in

Modernisation of the mining industry. Part of Wittersrand Gold Mining Company, known as 'Night's Battery', 1888

order to assemble a worthwhile mass of gold – and even then it would be almost impossible to extract the gold from the ore without the stamping machinery which only the mine-owners possessed. Instead of complete consolidation, mine-owners found that there were advantages in operating a series of mines under the same management, and co-operating with other groups of mines for a number of common purposes. A group of mines (or a 'house', as each group came to be called) could afford to recruit expert mining engineers, very sharp lawyers, and the best managerial talent in the world. By co-operating with other groups, it was possible sometimes to influence the republican government, or to control the level of wages being paid to mine labour.

By the early 1890s then, the characteristic long-term structure of the gold-mining industry had already been established. Almost every mine was part of a group of mines under common ownership; and almost all the groups came together as members of the Chamber of Mines in order to speak with a loud voice on those issues which affected them all.

The early development of Transvaal gold mining was strongly influenced by the experience of managers in Kimberley. Many of the early large investors in gold mining had first assembled their capital in Kimberley, before Rhodes and De Beers had bought them out: J. B. Robinson was one of these, and another was Barney Barnato, each of whom put together a group of gold mines along the Witwatersrand. Owners and managers knew from their Kimberley experience that it was very convenient to employ most of the labour force as fixed-term contract workers, living in mining compounds for the full duration of each contract. A labour force organised in this way could easily be regulated and disciplined, and was fairly regular in turning up to work. They also knew, however, that skilled white miners would not tolerate such constraints, but would rather leave the gold fields for some other country where their mining or engineering or organisational talents were better rewarded. The gold-mining labour force was deeply divided right from the start into a majority of migrants from African rural areas, bringing little relevant skill, and a minority of overseas migrants, bringing a great deal of skill and demanding high wages. Kimberley also taught the mine-owners and managers that they need not tackle white workers directly: with the passage of time it would be possible to thin out their numbers and to develop production techniques which reduced the amount of skilled labour needed.

The first entrepreneurs to acquire mining claims were able to select the easiest ores to exploit, and they could raise most of the initial capital from within southern Africa. Those who came later to the mining fields had to face more difficult and expensive technical difficulties, and were unable to raise much of their capital within the region. Among the late-comers were Rhodes himself, and the

Wernher & Beit interests. Rhodes missed the easiest opportunities, as he was preoccupied in the late 1880s with assembling De Beers, participating in Cape colonial politics, and expanding into Zambesia. Once these major interests did decide to enter the gold-mining industry, they had to move fast and vigorously to catch up. Rhodes became the most conspicuous principal in Consolidated Gold Fields; Wernher & Beit assembled a group of mines in the name of H. Eckstein & Co., and in the early 1890s they organised another group – Rand Mines – to exploit deeper-level gold deposits than had been exploited until that point. Some of the capital raised by the late-comers was British, but a great deal was German and French.

After nearly ten years of mining, the structure of the gold-mining industry was roughly as follows: nearly £40 000 000 had been invested in gold-mining ventures by 1895, financing 79 producing mines while several new deep-level mines were about to come into production. The leading houses were Rand Mines, Ecksteins, Consolidated Gold Fields (Rhodes), J. B. Robinson, Johannesburg Consolidated (Barnato), Albu, Goerz, and Anglo-French, which together accounted for almost all the producing or promising mining ventures. Many small investors in western Europe had invested their capital in these groups, but the principals of the finance houses made sure that they held on to the most lucrative shares themselves, offering less promising shares in dubious ventures to the small investors.

Each mine had a divided labour force. A total of some 100 000 African contract workers, mainly from the eastern half of southern Africa, performed most of the hard work; a tenth of that number were whites, including Cornishmen experienced in hard-rock mining, American and Australian mechanics and engineers, and a host of artisans and supervisors of the African workers. In order to make sustained profits, the groups were obliged to use the most up-to-date techniques, and to employ highly skilled chemists; in order to afford the services of the highly skilled, the groups struggled to hold down the wages of the majority of workers in each mine. Repeatedly the groups reached agreements to place a low ceiling on African wage levels, so as to prevent competition for scarce labour; and repeatedly the agreements would be broken as particular mines were desperate to keep the mining compounds full. They were therefore only partially successful in restricting African wages: but no such attempt was made to restrict the wage levels of whites, which were determined by the need to compete with wages paid in Australia or North America. Since about three tons of ore had to be crushed, for each ounce of gold to be separated, and as the price of gold was very stable, the managers of gold mines were acutely conscious of all the elements of their cost structure. By the end of the century they were producing over £15 000 000 worth of gold each year, which represented virtually all the Transvaal's exports, and was the largest single source of gold in the world market.

Whereas Waterboer's Griquas were swept away by the influx of miners, the Transvaal – under the title, South African Republic – was more successful in siyphoning off some of the profits of mining to its own advantage. Before gold mining began, the Republic had virtually no revenue at all, and was obliged to hand over land titles in lieu of cash payments. Within three years of gold being mined, annual revenue had reached £1 500 000, and before long the Transvaal had the largest regular revenue of any southern African state. Much of this revenue was devoted to strengthening the armed forces; providing firearms for the militia, and equipping a small but effective professional artillery detachment. By the 1890s the republicans held a decisive military advantage over those African societies which had managed to retain some autonomy until that time.

The gold-mining industry also attracted the railway lines which had been impossible to pay for in the 1870s: not only did the Cape Government seek to extend its railway system to Johannesburg, but so did Natal, while a German railway company (NZASM) built the shortest line to the coast, from Delagoa Bay in Mozambique. The Transvaal Government was in the happy position of choosing which of these lines to favour with its heavy traffic, and by manipulating freight rates over the Transvaal sections of these lines, it could determine exactly what proportion of traffic would travel over each of the rival railway systems. Even after military and railway expenditure, there was revenue available to begin a system of public education for the children of the farmers – though that was slow to get going. Just as important was the ability of the Transvaal now to attract first-class public servants such as J. C. Smuts from the Cape who became Attorney-General in the late 1890s, and W. J. Leyds from the Netherlands who served as Secretary of State. The powers and privileges of a 'modern' state were now becoming available on a pastoral frontier which had lacked such amenities. In these respects the Transvaal not only emulated the 'modernisation' and strengthening of the Cape colonial state – in many respects it surpassed the Cape.

In one decisive respect the experience of a mineral revolution differed in the Transvaal from the earlier pattern in the Cape colony. The Transvaal Republic imposed stringent conditions upon citizenship and the franchise. The miners and capitalists who migrated from Britain to Kimberley were soon and easily assimilated into the Cape political system. In the Transvaal it was not enough to be an adult male of European descent: most of the white immigrants remained legally foreigners – Uitlanders – having neither the responsibilities nor the privileges of citizenship. Most of the time,

Paul Kruger, President of the Transvaal Republic, 1883–1902

most of the Uitlanders were not bothered by this restriction. Few intended to spend the rest of their lives in Johannesburg, and Transvaal citizenship offered few of the advantages of British or United States citizenship which most of them already enjoyed.

However, this restriction did mean that representatives of the mining community were unable to find their way into the volksraad through parliamentary elections. Rather they tried to influence government policy through back-door methods. J. B. Robinson was an old crony of President Kruger, and probably wielded more influence over him than any other Transvaal resident. Major groups kept a lobbyist living permanently in Pretoria, the capital, to keep an eye on legislation, and the administration of the laws, and where necessary to give small (or sometimes quite large) gifts to influential public servants and politicians. Naturally, it was mine-owners and managers who were best able to use these clandestine methods – the workers of any colour had no such access to decision-makers. In some respects, then, a good working relationship did develop with the Afrikaner landowners (who controlled the mining economy), and this was rather similar to the alliance between De Beers and Rhodes on the one hand, and Hofmeyr and the Afrikaner Bond on the other, in the Cape.

Much of the legislation and the public administration of the Republic reflected this harmony of interests between landowners and mining capitalists. The legislation covering gold mining made it possible for the original landowners to gain some financial benefit from the transformation of their farms into mines; but in general the mining capitalists were content with the provisions of that law, which guaranteed their property and protected the groups against small prospectors and stubborn claim holders. The law was imperfect, but when a move was made to change it in the early 1900s, the Chamber of Mines judged that it was 'the most capitalist law in the world' and preferred to leave it alone. The Republic was also rather generous in framing taxation policy. Again, the taxation structure was imperfect, but in general it imposed a much lighter burden upon the mining industry than could be found in many other mining fields. Republican officials were also willing to assist in the recruitment of labour (provided that there was no direct competition with farmers for pastoral labour), and in the administration of Pass Laws to restrict the free movement of Africans from one employer to another – though there were limits to the officials' competence to administer such laws. A few leading Afrikaners became share-holders in the mining industry; conversely several mining companies became major landowners, holding land in the hope that some precious minerals or stones might later be discovered there. The relationship between mining capitalists and the republican state was very informal, but it was harmonious for the first few years of the mining industry. If it had not been for divisions among mining capitalists (unlike the totally united De Beers), and the irregularity of communication between mining and landed interests, they might have co-operated just as happily as Rhodes and Hofmeyr in the Cape during the same period.

As in the Cape, so in the Transvaal, the earlier inhabitants derived very little direct benefit. The 1896 census counted over 50 000 whites living in and around Johannesburg: they, and at least twice that number of Africans, had to be fed. However, the pastoral farmers of the high veld could only respond very slowly to these market opportunities, since they lacked capital, and the extension services to guide them towards market gardening or successful grain production. Most of the food consumed in the new urban centres was imported from outside the Republic. Again, very little advantage could be taken of the manufacturing opportunities presented by the rapid growth of Johannesburg. Mines constantly required new machinery but it was cheaper and more efficient for them to import it from overseas and transport it by rail from the coast than to promote engineering works on the Witwatersrand. The mines also needed explosives, and a clever entrepreneur was granted a monopoly concession to produce it: however, it soon turned out that he was importing fully manufactured explosives, re-packing them, and adding a substantial mark-up to the price. No real manufacturing was going on in that factory. Similarly, the mainly male population of the mining district was chronically thirsty, and soon enough there were entrepreneurs claiming to be distilling alcohol for Johannesburg consumption. Much of it proved to be lethal combinations of chemicals, often fatal to those who drank it. The new industry did not lead to a rapid diversification of the Republic's economy. On the contrary, the mining industry in Johannesburg was as much an enclave as that in Kimberley, with very few links to local producers of consumer goods.

The Republic in the 1890s may therefore be seen as a classic 'banana republic'. One product accounted for 97% of all exports; the export sector of the economy was entirely controlled by foreign capital; government was in the hands of a very small (but very well-armed) minority of landowners; government business was surrounded by a cloud of speculators using more or less corrupt means to secure privileges for themselves and the interests they represented; and the managers of the foreign-owned industry were free to conduct their operations much as they pleased, in the absence of an effective administration; and despite the Republic's sovereign independence, its freedom of manoeuvre was hampered by irksome treaty relations with Britain. In these circumstances it would be the Transvaal, rather than the Cape, which was not only unstable in itself, but a source of instability throughout the region.

One major source of instability was the dissatisfaction of some of the mining capitalists. Although the Republic made generous provisions for the growth of the mining industry in its first years, its fiscal arrangements were not helpful to those capitalists who were developing deep-level mines. Their profit margins were very narrow indeed, and they resented the high costs of railway freight, the unnecessarily high cost of dynamite and the prevalence of illicit liquor which paralysed much of the labour force. When they approached the government, they found the President surrounded by financial sharks, already benefiting from the eccentric fashion in which the Transvaal economy was being administered. Given the general instability of the political system, it was not too difficult for Rhodes and his financial allies to mobilise a protest movement among white Uitlanders in and around Johannesburg, and to plan an armed revolution to replace the Afrikaner republic with a republic of miners. Confident that such a rising had been organised, Rhodes's lieutenant L. S. Jameson rode into the Transvaal at the head of a detachment of Bechuanaland police in the last days of 1895, hoping that the invasion would coincide with an Uitlander rising. As it happened, Rhodes had over-estimated the anger of the Uitlanders: the rising failed to occur, and Jameson's police were easily surrounded at Doornkop, where they surrendered. However, although the armed rising had failed, the grievances of some of the mining capitalists remained, and they simply sought some more effective way of bringing influence to bear on Kruger's Republic.

Another major source of instability was the Transvaal's determination to make a reality of its flag independence. The old ties of dependence upon the Cape were steadily broken, as railways provided access to non-British ports, and prosperity attracted bankers and speculators from all over Europe, proposing to link the Transvaal's economy to other metropolitan countries than Britain. An important constraint was the Transvaal's landlocked condition, and its inability to expand in any direction. Rhodes occupied Zambesia in 1890, in search of new gold fields; and that move almost encircled the Transvaal. After a long diplomatic struggle, the Transvaal gained entry to Swaziland but not to the Indian Ocean, since Portuguese Mozambique and British Zululand and Natal occupied the whole of the relevant coastal strip. Frustrated in all these directions, Kruger's government turned its attention to the possibility of gaining a more sympathetic metropolitan ally: Germany, already catching up with British industrial production, and by the late nineteenth century a growing naval and colonial power. However, the more the Transvaal courted Germany, the less tolerant was Britain. A Transvaal which remained linked to Britain represented no threat; but if the wealthiest state of the region fell under German influence, then it was likely that British hegemony would be destroyed throughout the sub-continent. In brief, the

Transvaal threatened British supremacy, whereas the mineral revolution in the Cape had merely entrenched British interests in the region.

These diplomatic and financial manoeuvres took place at a very high level, beyond the vision of most of the people affected by the mineral revolution directly. There is one very general and very important trend which is becoming clearer as more research is conducted on the subject. The growth of towns and of new industries at first offered splendid opportunities to some African societies. Rhodes's expansion to the north meant that there was a great demand for food supplies and for transport facilities along the old 'missionary road' through Tswana country. Khama's Ngwato were well placed to seize these opportunities, providing meat to the travellers, and even to Kimberley, and assembling teams of oxen to transport goods by wagon. By the end of the century however, the extension of the railway line brought cheaper foodstuffs and cheaper transport facilities, so that the brief prosperity of the Tswana was brought to a close. The outbreak of rinderpest which in 1896-7 swept right through southern Africa, also caused particular havoc to those (like the Tswana) who relied heavily upon cattle for their income. In the eastern Cape too, a period of prosperity can be observed among the peasant societies in the last years of the nineteenth century. It became increasingly easy to sell goods on the market as well as to grow food for self-subsistence. Here again though, rinderpest was a major disaster.

Even more of a disaster was the process of peasantisation itself. As population grew, the land area became crowded; and as the strength of the chiefs was reinforced by colonial administration, so commoners lost their access to sufficient land for subsistence and the earning of annual taxes. The only recourse for poor families was to send young men as contract workers to the diamond mines or to the rapidly growing compounds of the Witwatersrand. As the gold-mining industry grew, it could count upon regular supplies of cheap labour from the eastern Cape, from Lesotho, to a limited extent from Natal and Zululand, and especially from Mozambique as Portuguese authority became more effective. At first, young men had gone to Kimberley to earn the money to buy guns, and to protect their lands. With the slow decline of the African peasant economies, it was no longer a matter of choice but of necessity; no longer a question of gaining additional wealth, but rather an urgent matter of earning enough to keep the family alive. The growth of the mining industry contributed very directly to the impoverishment of the peasantries of the region. In a sense, the peasantries were subsidising mineral development. It was much cheaper for mine managers to employ migrant labourers – who were paid as if they were bachelors and took home a pitiable quantity of money and trade goods at the end of a contract – than to allow African families to settle around Johannesburg, where the employers would have been responsible for supporting the families as well as the male workers. By growing their own food when they could, and sending only the strong and healthy members of the family out of work, the peasant families made possible the development of a mining industry which relied upon very cheap labour. If there had been no mineral revolution, the African areas in southern Africa might not have become as hopelessly impoverished as they have during the last hundred years.

Chapter 9

Imperial control re-asserted

Britain's supremacy as a world power lasted throughout the nineteenth century until 1914, despite the transformation of much of the world during that period. Naval supremacy, established by sailing ships during the Napoleonic wars, still lay with Britain in the age of steamships – though the German and United States and even Japanese navies began to challenge it. British leadership in world trade, another pillar of world dominance, was beginning to be challenged in the late nineteenth century by the other North Atlantic powers. And British leadership in industrial production – perhaps the single most important measure of power – was also threatened by rapid industrialisation in France, Belgium, Germany, the United States and Japan. The doctrine of free trade had become almost a religious creed in Britain during the nineteenth century, supporting the entry of British goods into every market in the world. But as other industrial and trading nations began to capture markets which had long been British preserves, there were moves by the British government to protect her gains – a pessimistic and defensive view which Robinson and Gallagher (in *Africa and the Victorians*) have contrasted with the confidence and aggressiveness of the mid-nineteenth century. Tropical colonies were integrated more closely into British financial and economic networks; but there was also anxiety about economic links with temperate regions of the world, where partial industrialisation had begun, and where the rivalry of Germany was especially dangerous. In general, towards the end of the nineteenth century British authorities were increasingly nervous and intolerant of German rivalry, which was seen as the most dangerous immediate threat and which required a determined defence of long-established British interests. Rulers of remote regions of the world, previously linked to Britain by informal and loose diplomatic associations, found themselves drawn more tightly into relations of dependency, prescribed by treaties, and enforced by naval strength.

The defence of British interests in southern Africa became especially difficult towards the end of the nineteenth century. It was no longer sufficient to hold on to the Cape peninsula and the more obvious harbours, leaving the interior to a variety of petty clients. The rapid expansion of the regional capitalist economy, the rapid growth of population, and the increasing strength and self-confidence of the states, complicated the affairs of the region. The general purpose of British policy – the maintenance of British interests and the peaceful expansion of trading links – remained the same; but the administration of that policy required ever-increasing intelligence and determination. At the beginning of the nineteenth century, the governorship of the Cape required merely the talents which almost any senior army officer would possess: by the end of the nineteenth century the post required the most talented minds in British public life. Similarly, the administration of the Colonial Office was not seen as a difficult job in 1815, but by the 1890s it required the attention of some of the leading politicians of the day.

Imperial confederation

Relationships throughout the region might, perhaps, have been placed on a more solid footing during the 1870s – if anyone in Britain or in southern Africa had been able to predict the problems of the 1880s. There were three British colonies – the Cape, Griqualand West and Natal – and border lands, like Basutoland and the Nguni chiefdoms along the east coast, were in a rather precarious relationship to the Cape. There were at least two trekker republics – the Transvaal and the Orange Free State – and sometimes more when the Transvaalers disagreed among themselves. Several African societies were partially under British influence, and substantially autonomous – Basutoland of course, the two Griqua captaincies which were breaking down, Zululand, Swaziland, the Tswana societies of the Kalahari fringe, and the Pedi and Venda, nominally within the Transvaal political system but practically autonomous. It occurred to British officials during this decade that a more rational system could and should be devised than this patchwork of small and quarrelsome states. However, it was already too late to bring them together by means of persuasion alone: the Cape was self-governing, and reluctant to assume costly responsibilities; the Orange Free State and the Transvaal were irate at their exclusion from the diamond-bearing lands of Griqualand West; the whites in general were nervous in the face of continued African independence and self-assertion; until African societies were generally disarmed, their opinions could not safely be ignored. The Colonial Secretary, Lord Kimberley, tried to talk the settlers into closer association and self-reliance, but his appeals were simply ignored.

The imperial factor in southern Africa clearly meant different things to different people. In Basutoland, the imperial government was seen as a restraining influence upon white settlers, and the same view was seemingly shared by other African leaders confronted by white-settler land hunger. For the white settlers, the imperial government was the ultimate guarantor of the safety of the white minorities – a source of military support if all else failed. None of the small societies of the interior was willing to see the imperial authorities depart from the region, lest stronger neighbours overwhelm them. These confused perceptions created an intractable dilemma. So long as African chiefdoms and kingdoms remained powerful, the whites would not accept responsibility for their own defence. However, if the African societies were crushed, the whites would accept autonomy, but they might not care to maintain the British connection at all. Southern Africa's internal divisions were the essential reason for imperial strength and influence in the region: although imperial officials saw these divisions as a problem to be solved, there was no solution available. Certainly a confederation of states would be tidier, and would permit the imperial government to withdraw its expensive troops – but that was a solution which no significant group in the region would willingly accept.

Kimberley was succeeded at the Colonial Office by Lord Carnarvon, who persisted in seeking to persuade the colonists and republicans to accept confederation, but never achieved sufficient agreement among them to make it possible to proceed. By 1877 he had lost patience, and resolved upon stronger methods. Griqualand West and Natal and perhaps Basutoland could be coerced into unification with the Cape; the President of the Orange Free State, J. H. Brand, was willing to contemplate some such proposal; the stumbling block seemed to be the Transvaal and its President, T. F. Burgers. As it happened, the Transvaal was especially vulnerable. In the far north, the Venda were still preventing trekkers from occupying their lands. In the east, the Pedi under Sekhukhune were as successful against the Transvaal, as Moshoeshoe had been against the Orange Free State. A joint Afrikaner-Swazi campaign against Sekhukhune failed in 1876, and a fragile peace had emerged between them. Farther south the Swazi were willing to co-operate with the Afrikaners against the common threat of a resurgent Zulu kingdom; but Cetshwayo (who succeeded Mpande as king of the Zulu in 1872) was an unknown quantity. The Transvaal Afrikaners could hold their own just so long as they could play one African chiefdom off against the others; but this was a very risky strategy. In its financial and military weakness, the Republic was in no position to resist British demands.

During 1877 then, Theophilus Shepstone, the Natal Secretary for Native Affairs, was instructed to enter the Transvaal at the head of a police escort, and to annex the republic to the Crown. There was no more than verbal resistance to the restoration of direct imperial control, and for a moment it seemed as if Carnarvon had found the

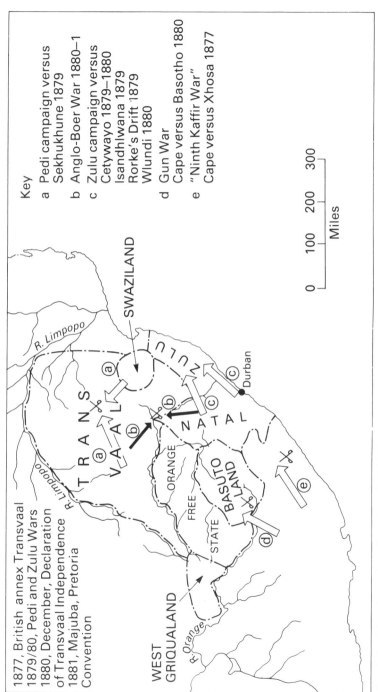

1877, British annex Transvaal
1879/80, Pedi and Zulu Wars
1880, December, Declaration
of Transvaal Independence
1881, Majuba, Pretoria
Convention

WEST
GRIQUALAND

R. Limpopo

R. Limpopo

SWAZILAND

T R A N S V A A L

Z U L U

N A T A L

Durban

ORANGE

FREE

STATE

BASUTO
LAND

R. Orange

Key
a Pedi campaign versus
   Sekhukhune 1879
b Anglo-Boer War 1880–1
c Zulu campaign versus
   Cetywayo 1879–1880
   Isandhlwana 1879
   Rorke's Drift 1879
   Wlundi 1880
d Gun War
   Cape versus Basotho 1880
e "Ninth Kaffir War"
   Cape versus Xhosa 1877

0	100	200	300

Miles

Map 6 Confederation and conflagration, 1877–1884

111

short cut to the federation of all the settler societies of the region, together with the African states which would ultimately be handed over to them.

Carnarvon's chosen agent for accomplishing confederation was Sir Bartle Frere, Governor of the Cape and High Commissioner for South Africa. Frere's view of the problem was simpler, and probably more accurate, than Carnarvon's: African independence must be suppressed before the settlers would accept responsibility for defending themselves and the imperial link in the region. On every hand continued African independence threatened the settler minority, except in the heartland of the western Cape. Among the Xhosa, war broke out in 1877, and the Xhosa were finally conquered only during 1878, when imperial as well as colonial troops and their African allies combined against them. The Cape Government followed up this campaign by enacting that the Sotho should be disarmed: when an attempt was made to enforce this legislation, the Cape colonial forces failed to conquer the Sotho, and resistance spread from the mountain strongholds into the coastal regions of East Griqualand and much of the Transkei. During 1880 and early 1881 the coastal resistance was suppressed, but the Sotho remained undefeated, and in 1884 the imperial government had to resume direct control over Basutoland, recognising that the people simply could not be administered by the Cape. There had been violence too in Griqualand West during 1877 and 1878, instigated by the surviving Griqua, and by Tswana and Khoi whose lives had been disrupted by the rapid evolution of a mining industry and an entirely new community around Kimberley.

The most serious threat to settler security, however, seemed to stem from Zululand. During Mpande's lifetime, Natal colonists and Transvaal trekkers were fairly sure that the Zulu regiments would not be despatched against them. Mpande had become king with the assistance of trekker allies, and he was careful to avoid any pretext for hostilities breaking out against his white neighbours. During his long reign (1840 to 1872) the Zulu economy recovered from the cattle losses of the 1830s and from the serious loss of manpower during the civil wars. Even so, Mpande resisted the temptation to expand his territories, and even tolerated the continued encroachment of Afrikaner pastoralists on Zululand's western border. He was also the first Zulu king to live to old age, and even by the 1850s his sons had become adults, potential foci of discontent and opposition within the kingdom. The more ambitious and energetic sons became the leaders of powerful factions, and then began to mobilise their own regiments, until 1856 when the most astute of these sons – Cetshwayo – defeated his chief rival, Mbulazi, and became Mpande's heir.

After 1856 it became increasingly difficult to restrain the young men, since their energies could no longer be channelled into internal

Cetshwayo, King of Zululand, with Major Poole, the custodian during his exile and detention in Cape Town

civil campaigns. Nevertheless Cetshwayo had sixteen years in which to observe his father's policies, and to share responsibility for them. Although the colonists and trekkers were alarmed at the prospect of Cetshwayo's inheriting the Zulu kingdom, their fears were unfounded. Cetshwayo took care to cultivate the friendship of Shepstone (who was even invited to crown him in 1873) as an ally if trouble broke out with the Transvaal; missionaries lived in peace in the kingdom, though they made very few converts; trade with Natal was encouraged, though again it was small in scale, and was largely concerned with attempts to acquire firearms. By 1877 Cetshwayo ruled over the largest and most formidable African society in the southern African region, and he and his regiments looked with much interest at the Transvaal's inability to cope with the resistance of the Venda and especially the Pedi. When Shepstone marched into the Transvaal in that year, Cetshwayo offered him military support which, however, Shepstone politely declined.

The economic and military recovery of the Zulu caused alarm in Swaziland. King Mswati (1840–68) and his successor Ludvonga (to 1874) and then Mbandzeni (1874–89) all noticed that the Zulu tolerance of white settlers did not extend to the Swazi, who continued to suffer occasional cattle raids from the south. Naturally, then, the Swazi regarded the Afrikaners as the most promising allies against continued Zulu aggression. White farmers were encouraged to take up land in the buffer zone between the two kingdoms, and Swazi regiments assisted the Transvaal commandos in many of their campaigns. In particular, the Swazi were involved in the Transvaal's persistent campaigns against Sekhukhune's Pedi: and in exchange the Swazi rulers expected the Afrikaners to assist in the event of a major invasion from Zululand.

Frere identified Zululand as the key to the politics of the Transvaal and Natal. In December 1878 he presented Cetshwayo with an insulting ultimatum, demanding that he disband his army within a month. Cetshwayo recognised that this was merely a pretext for war, and he duly assembled his regiments: but he continued to hope for peace, and determined to fight merely a defensive campaign, so that peaceful relations might be restored thereafter. His regiments were on no account to cross the border into colonial Natal. In January the British expeditionary force marched confidently into Zululand, led by one of many charming and ineffectual generals who flourished in the Victorian empire. Cetshwayo's generals were probably less charming, and certainly better prepared for this kind of campaign. At Isandhlwana on January 22 they surprised Lord Chelmsford's column, and destroyed it. However, winning a battle was not decisive: British troops regrouped, and proceeding with much more caution, defeated the Zulu army at Cetshwayo's headquarters in Ulundi in July of the same year. Cetshwayo was captured and sent into exile at

Cape Town; the kingdom was divided into thirteen potentially quarrelsome chieftaincies under as many Zulu leaders of anti-Cetshwayo factions as could be identified. In this manner, Zululand was neutralised without having to be annexed.

With the Zululand 'problem' dealt with, British troops were next sent against Sekhukhune in November 1879, who was duly captured and replaced by his half-brother (and rival) Mampuru as paramount chief of the Pedi. The Venda in the north and the Tswana to the west of the Transvaal could safely be disregarded, now that the most obvious threats of the Transvaal had been violently removed.

Ironically, the Zulu remained the key to southern African politics, even after their defeat. The settlers had been willing to tolerate direct imperial rule so long as this was necessary for the defence of settler security; but with the Zulu temporarily disarmed, there was no further reason to tolerate imperial control. The Cape politicians were reluctant to be mere pawns in imperial tactics for the region, and were unwilling to assume long-term responsibility for a turbulent region. While the imperial government waited for the Cape politicians to co-operate, the Afrikaners of the Transvaal grew impatient with the Crown Colony administration. Confederation seemed no closer in 1880 than it had been when the Transvaal was annexed three years earlier, and there was no sign of the British restoring self-government to the white citizens of the new colony. In December 1880 the Transvaal Afrikaners rose in rebellion: in February 1881 another British general was defeated (and killed) in a skirmish at Majuba: and in March negotiations began which led to the restoration of the Transvaal's independence by the Pretoria Convention (1881) which was confirmed and amplified in the London Convention (1884). The intervention of imperial forces had certainly succeeded in suppressing most of the autonomous African societies of the region; but in doing so the troops had weakened the case for the confederation of the South African settler societies. The continued fragmentation of southern Africa into settler colonies, African dependencies, Afrikaner republics and African chieftaincies, guaranteed friction between them and British hegemony over all of them.

Another piece was added to the jigsaw puzzle in 1884 when Chancellor Bismarck announced a reversal in German policy with the annexation of territory in the Pacific Islands and in Africa. Every German dependency shared a border with a British sphere of influence. German South West Africa surrounded the little British territory of Walvis Bay (given to the Cape as part of the tidying up process after confederation failed) and made it necessary for Britain to define the geographical limits of its Cape colony and the Tswana country which intervened between the Germans and the Transvaal. For the moment, German intervention in South West Africa caused little alarm: the territory was partly desert and almost entirely arid, it seemed to possess no great natural resources, and it had long been a refuge for those who found colonial control disagreeable. So long as the Transvaal was unable to link up with German territory, no crucial British interest was challenged: and in due course Transvaal claims over Stellaland and Goshen (two little trekker republics on the western border of the Transvaal) were added to the Transvaal but in such a way as to leave the 'missionary road' to the northern interior securely under British control.

Colonialism

The development of the diamond-mining industry, which strengthened the Cape economy, enabled the Cape Government to pursue policies which were not identical to those of Britain. During the late 1870s Afrikaner opinion in the Cape was shaken by the sight of Britain's imperial policies in action, and by the financial consequences of frontier warfare. The Afrikaner Bond, founded in 1879, looked forward to the unification of the settler states under Afrikaner control; but a congress in 1883 made the Bond more directly a political party within the Cape political structure, emphasising the economic interests of Afrikaner farmers rather than any long-term ambition for the sub-continent. The Afrikaner Bond strove to dominate the political institutions which already existed, by political techniques which were already widely ' practised. Hofmeyr and his followers were willing to form coalitions with non-Afrikaner politicians in order to dominate the parliament securely; and they had no objection either to the small numbers of coloured voters who held the franchise qualifications in the western Cape, nor to the equally small numbers of Africans who qualified to vote in the eastern electorates. Rather than becoming a distinct and independent political movement, the Bond formed the backbone of a wider movement, which was termed 'colonialism', and which implied the supremacy within southern Africa of enfranchised colonists, preferably in harmony with imperial policy, and seeking no revolutionary transformation of society as it was.

When the Bond formed its alliance with Rhodes, the resources of De Beers and of Rhodes's other economic and governmental companies were added to the numerical strength of Bond parliamentarians, and colonialism became a very powerful force. Even before the alliance was established, Rhodes was influential in steering British policy among the Tswana towards the annexation of the southernmost Tswana as British Bechuanaland (1885), which was transferred to the Cape in 1895. At the same time the northern Tswana chiefs – Khama of the Ngwato, Sechele of the Kwena, and Gaseitsiwe of the Ngwaketse, all under the influence of LMS missionaries – came under imperial protection in the Bechuanaland

Protectorate, and remained outside the scope of Rhodes's or the Cape Colony's immediate control. That region became the object of intense dispute, once Rhodes began to mobilise his northward expansion.

As Rhodes observed the consolidation of the Witwatersrand mining industry, he regretted his slowness in staking out claims in it; but it also occurred to him that if one gold-bearing reef had been discovered, there might well be others of equal value. He was quite right in that suspicion, but he hoped to find the 'second Rand' to the north, in Zambesia, whereas it proved to be further south, in the Orange Free State. Reports of gold exports from the Shona societies of Zambesia no doubt strengthened his enthusiasm for northward expansion, but the Shona had been exploiting very small gold deposits, nowhere comparable with the Rand itself. Until Rhodes was ready to take a direct part in northward expansion, it was important to encourage the imperial government to advance some kind of claim against the Germans, the Transvaalers, or the Portuguese, all of whom might be able to establish strong claims. Lobengula, the Ndebele king in succession to Mzilikazi, actually signed a treaty with an agent of the Transvaal Republic in 1887: immediately Rhodes persuaded the High Commissioner to send another agent (Moffat) to persuade Lobengula to sign another treaty which gave the British authorities control over Lobengula's foreign policies. Also in 1888 Rhodes sent one of his own colleagues (Rudd) to extract from Lobengula a third treaty yielding to Rudd and to Rhodes a monopoly over all mineral deposits within Lobengula's kingdom.

The 'Rudd concession' was the basis of the British South Africa Company which Rhodes now launched, and for which he gained a royal charter conferring authority to govern Zambesia. In 1890, the first detachment of settlers was sent north from the Cape – the Pioneers. Taking care to avoid direct conflict with Lobengula, they conquered several Shona chieftaincies further east. Only in 1893 was Lobengula directly challenged and defeated. In retrospect Lobengula's willingness to sign treaties seems almost suicidal, but there is a case to be made for the rationality of his actions. His neighbour Khama did not seem to suffer as a consquence of having accepted Queen Victoria's protection. Either the Transvaalers or the British imperialists or Rhodes's colonialists or perhaps the Germans or the Portuguese were almost certain to enter the kingdom and to make non-negotiable demands. In his treaties, Lobengula attempted to acquire the capital, and the trading contacts, with which to arm his regiments for future battles; and battles of some kind were absolutely inevitable, because the Ndebele were on friendly terms with none of their immediate neighbours. Finally, his strategy did seem to be working until 1893, since it was the Shona rather than the Ndebele themselves who first suffered the shock of conquest. Nevertheless that strategy did fail, and the immediate consequence was to make Rhodes (through the BSA Company) the effective ruler of both Mashonaland and Matabeleland. From an imperial point of view, this was satisfactory: the British flag now flew over a large new region, for which the British Crown had no financial responsibility whatever.

The Transvaal had consented, reluctantly, to this expansion of Rhodes's authority – but used it as an argument for republican expansion to the east. There was no possibility of expansion through Zululand itself (which had been formally annexed to Britain in 1887), but some advantage might be obtained by expansion into Swaziland. The Afrikaner-Swazi alliance had become increasingly unequal over time, especially after the conquest of Cetshwayo's kingdom removed any urgent need for close co-operation between the two parties. During the middle and late 1880s Swaziland was over-run not only by Afrikaner pastoralists, but also by fortune-hunters who had been disappointed at the Transvaal mining fields. The nominal independence of Swaziland became almost a myth, as Mbandzeni signed concessions to these newcomers, granting them land, minerals and exclusive trading and manufacturing rights. Briefly in 1890 the Transvaal was offered not only Swaziland but also access to the Indian Ocean – provided that the Transvaal entered the Cape-dominated Customs Union – but the price was too high. Eventually in 1895 the Transvaal took full control over Swaziland, but this time with no access to the sea. There was little that the Swazi could do about it, since by the 1890s British interest in land-locked Swaziland had faded away entirely. The Transvaal's only other prospect for access to the sea lay through Mozambique, where the Portuguese administration seemed always on the brink of collapse; however, with Rhodes's encouragement the British Government negotiated with other European powers and staved off any possibility of the Transvaal inheriting the ramshackle dependency and its vital harbour facilities at Delagoa Bay. By 1895 Kruger's Republic was encircled.

From peace to war

By 1895 then, Afrikaners did not seem to threaten British interests in southern Africa. In the Cape, the Bond was reconciled to a colonial parliamentary system; Afrikaners in the Orange Free State had no particular quarrel, and no means of imposing their will in any case; and if President Kruger attracted the more enthusiastic Afrikaner republicans to his administration, the Transvaal Government seemed to have little option but to accept imperial hegemony over the region. Potentially more serious was the risk of African resistance to the settler societies, but for the moment that posed no threat to the established order. In Bechuanaland and Basutoland,

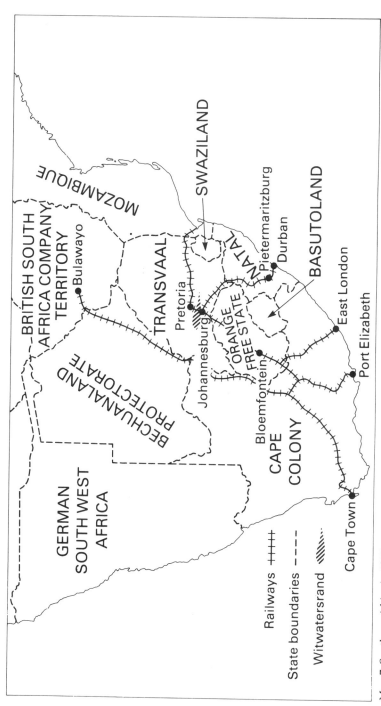

Map 7 Southern Africa in 1897

Railways +++++
State boundaries −−−
Witwatersrand ///

GERMAN SOUTH WEST AFRICA

BECHUANALAND PROTECTORATE

BRITISH SOUTH AFRICA COMPANY TERRITORY

Bulawayo

MOZAMBIQUE

TRANSVAAL

SWAZILAND

Pretoria

Johannesburg

ORANGE FREE STATE

Bloemfontein

NATAL

Pietermaritzburg

Durban

BASUTOLAND

East London

CAPE COLONY

Port Elizabeth

Cape Town

119

the chiefs demanded no more than the retention of imperial administration, in preference to being handed over to the settler states. In the Transkei generally, a minority of prosperous cash-cropping peasants held chiefly offices, making it unlikely that there would be any concerted resistance to Cape colonial control. The small African and Coloured elite who were enfranchised in the colonial political system were willing to prove their loyalty and respectability in European terms. The Zulu were a different matter, but for the moment the divisions fostered within the Zulu political system were sufficient to paralyse any Zulu initiative in the affairs of the region.

Around the fringe of the British sphere, African independence was steadily being crushed. Not only had the Shona been conquered by Rhodes's pioneer column, but also the Ndebele; and even in Mozambique the Portuguese were beginning to assert their authority over the long-independent kingdom of Gaza. The two processes of peasantisation and migrant labour for the mining industries were tying rural Africans ever more tightly into economic relationships from which they would derive little benefit. And this peaceful transformation of southern Africa was taking place without increased expenditure by the British Government; republicans and colonialists were equally determined to stamp out any African resistance within their respective territories.

But all was not well in Rhodes's increasingly complex financial empire. The Shona and Ndebele might be pacified, but the 'second Rand' had failed to appear in the conquered territories, and the conquest and administration of Chartered Company territory proved expensive. Massive sums of money had been invested in Consolidated Goldfields, mining ventures in the Transvaal, but these were proving much less lucrative than Rhodes had expected. His closest financial allies – Wernher & Beit – were equally irritated at the disappointing rate of return on moneys invested in Rand Mines. Witwatersrand investments were supposed to be funding other projects in the region, but instead they tied up a lot of capital. De Beers was flourishing, and Rhodes's position in Cape politics was secure – but continued disappointment in the Witwatersrand threatened the whole interlocking edifice of Rhodes's empire. He was not the man to accept this reverse quietly.

What followed was precisely the sort of phoney revolution which stood a fair chance of success in overthrowing an unstable and isolated government. Uitlanders in and around Johannesburg had a variety of grievances against the republican administration, though not sufficient to make them abandon their jobs and investments. Rhodes encouraged the agitation among Uitlanders, and secretly sent arms to the 'Reform Committee' which orchestrated the agitation. Meanwhile he prepared for the armed invasion of the Republic, persuading the imperial government to

Scene outside the goldfield offices in Johannesburg during the Jameson Raid, 1895

annex British Bechuanaland to the Cape, and to lease a strip of land along the Transvaal border of the Bechuanaland Protectorate to the BSA Company. These measures were plausible as devices to improve communications between Cape Town and the Chartered territories, but their real purpose was quite different. The imperial government itself suspected that some kind of revolution was in the air, but the Secretary of State, Chamberlain, chose to have no official knowledge of what was being planned. The essence of the plan was that the Uitlanders should rise and create just sufficient disorder to justify an invasion from the Protectorate whose alleged purpose would be the restoration of peace. Similar plans have worked quite well in overthrowing governments in other poor countries in the nineteenth and twentieth centuries; but the Uitlander rising was too flimsy to be plausible in this case, and when Jameson grew impatient and led his detachment of police across the border at the end of December 1895, there was no persuasive pretext for his action, and he was quickly surrounded and forced to surrender to republican forces. Rhodes had to resign as Prime Minister and devote his full attention to the protection of his BSA Company Charter. Jameson and the leaders of the Reform Committee were tried, found guilty of treason, sentenced to death – but soon released on condition that they played no part in Transvaal politics.

At one level, the Jameson Raid and the politics surrounding it were quite trivial. In 1896, for example, Shona rose in rebellion against the Chartered Company, and were shortly joined by equally angry Ndebele, all hoping to benefit from the crisis in the affairs of the Chartered Company. Military measures were not enough on their own, and Rhodes himself travelled north to supervise pacification. In this crisis the Transvaal Government took no steps to prevent Rhodes from reaching his destination; and their neutrality in this dispute suggests how shallow were the divisions within white South Africa by comparison with the profound division between white and black. Neither Rhodes nor Kruger would treat African opponents as gently as they treated each other – even though Jameson and the Reform Committee were quite clearly guilty of invasion and treason, there was no question of carrying out the sentence.

Nevertheless the Raid did influence the nature of white politics decisively. Afrikaners in the Cape felt that Rhodes had betrayed their trust in him, and it was several years before another similar political alliance could be patched together. Afrikaners in the two republics had all their anti-British suspicions confirmed, especially when they realised that Chamberlain had known that some crisis was developing, and had neglected to warn them against it. The German emperor cabled to Kruger, congratulating him on defeating the invasion – and suddenly there were bright prospects for bringing Germany into southern African affairs to outweigh the influence of Britain. Southern Africa by the 1890s was a significant market for British goods, and the loss of this market was in itself an alarming prospect, which would have the further effect of loosening the ties between Britain and its other settler colonies. The outbreak of a major war was by no means inevitable, but it was now much more likely than it had been since the first annexation of the Transvaal in 1877.

Through Rhodes's initiative, the whole British position in southern Africa was very much weaker than before the Raid. The support of Cape Afrikaners could no longer be relied upon; and the hostility of the republicans was deep-seated. It had been sufficient before the Raid for British High Commissioners to keep a watching brief: now some kind of action was essential in order to arrest the erosion of British authority. Joseph Chamberlain, Colonial Secretary from 1895 to 1903, was a more important (and more forceful) politician than any previous holder of that office: he sent to Cape Town in 1897 a more important public figure than had ever held the office of High Commissioner – Alfred Milner. After a few months of investigation and consultation, Milner resolved upon forcing matters to a crisis: Kruger must either give the vote to the white Uitlanders (and risk losing control over the republican state machinery) or fight to protect his independence. Cetshwayo would have recognised these tactics at once, and it did not take Kruger very long to realise that he was being forced to a decision. Late in 1899 the South African War broke out. Again, Cetshwayo would not have been surprised that the British army lost the first few battles, until competent generals were brought to the war, and tactics were developed to suit the conditions of great open grasslands. He would not have been surprised either, to discover that the British armies were reinforced, and advanced to capture the republican capitals of Bloemfontein and Pretoria by the middle of 1900.

There were some curious features of this war though, which distinguish it from the many frontier wars which broke out throughout the Victorian era. For one thing, both sides chose to fight without arming Africans, though there were small-scale incidents when African scouts and spies were used. The Afrikaners might well have feared to arm Africans, since more Africans supported the British than those who hoped for a republican victory – and some might even begin to fight on their own account. The British decision to wage an all-white war is more striking. East and West African troops, Indian soldiers, and even Maoris were available to fight under the Union Jack: several offers of assistance were received from within southern Africa itself. None was accepted, since the purpose of the war was not to establish complete British authority throughout the region, but rather to assist the forces of colonialism to gain an ascendancy over the Afrikaners, within a society which would rest upon cheap African labour, and a powerless African majorority, after the war as much as ever before. It was restraint of this kind which earned the South African War the title of 'Last of the Gentlemen's Wars'. A second striking feature of the war was that Afrikaners did not seriously expect to win. In the early weeks of warfare, when victories had opened the railway routes to the sea, republican generals failed to seize the initiative, and instead settled down to casual and unsuccessful sieges of small British garrisons in Ladysmith, Kimberley and Mafeking. Once the capitals had been lost to the British, and President Kruger had left for exile in Europe, the younger generals decided to continue a guerilla campaign which lasted for a further two years. They decided not to blow up the gold mines as the British approached but rather to harry the extended lines of communication of the invaders. It was not anticipated that these tactics would achieve victory – but rather that they would prolong the war and give Germany an opportunity to intervene. By 1902, however, it was clear that Germany would not intervene. It was also becoming clear that Africans would. The last republican armies gathered in May 1902, and decided that the bitter end had now come. On 31st May 1902 they surrendered and signed the Peace of Vereeniging with the victorious British. Apart from Portuguese Mozambique and German South West Africa, the Union Jack flew over all territory south of the Zambesi. The high point of Victorian imperialism had been reached, and Afrikaner nationalism defeated as a military factor.

Chapter 10

The formation of Union and new regional divisions

Southern Africa in 1902

The Union Jack fluttering over most of the region was almost the only common feature in 1902. A century of commercial pastoralism, localised commercial crop production, and a generation or more of capitalist mining enterprise, had affected the region very unequally. Many observers thought of the Africans as living in the remote past, Afrikaners living in the late middle ages, and only the British whites feeling at home in the twentieth century. That notion was of course inaccurate – everyone was living in 1902 whether they liked it or not – but it reflects the extreme inequality of ways of life and standards of living. We need an overview of the region at the beginning of a period of reconstruction and reorganisation; and perhaps the most convenient way of looking at the region is to observe the different impact of these three transforming processes – pastoralism, agriculture and mining.

Cattle were still the most valued form of wealth in most parts of southern Africa – the hardy indigenous cattle which could survive drought, produced little milk and terribly tough and sinewy meat. In other countries in the late nineteenth century, pedigree cattle were being bred either for fat and tender meat to be chilled and exported to Britain, or for creamy milk to be made into butter and cheese for the same market. Southern African cattle had none of the qualities required for this lucrative market, and commercial pastoralists relied upon the local market. During the war, the importation of frozen and canned meat had begun, and South African cattle-farmers had to struggle even to hold on to the domestic market. To compete at all, pastoralists needed large herds, occupying extensive pastures, and the capital with which to cross-breed and improve the quality of their animals. Most Africans found it impossible to compete on even terms: the loss of much of their land, the human over-crowding of what remained, and the impossibility of raising large volumes of capital, all worked against them. In German South West Africa, where Herero possessed great herds, they were steadily losing them to the new German settlers who acquired cattle by trade if possible and by coercion if necessary. Only in the Beçhuanaland Protectorate were there Africans – Ngwato particularly – who had sufficient pasture and herds to engage in successful commercial production, supplying the markets of Johannesburg and Kimberley. Elsewhere, Africans kept small numbers of stock mainly for home consumption and for bride-wealth payments. In 1897 all cattle-keepers had been struck down by the invasion of rinderpest from the north, which literally decimated the cattle of the region. The constant movement of soldiers and animals during the guerilla war had made it impossible to control the spread of animal diseases. After the war, the more prosperous white pastoralists – and Afrikaners in the republics who received money as compensation for war-losses – could begin to re-build their herds, using some of the tough Texan and Australian cattle imported by British officials for this purpose. It was much more difficult for Africans to re-stock. From this time onwards, commercial beef or dairy production would be mainly a white-owned enterprise, with the single exception of some individual African pastoralists in Bechuanaland.

It was more profitable to raise merino sheep than to keep cattle, and the dry grasslands of the central Cape and much of the Orange Free State were well suited to this activity. In the Americas and in New Zealand especially, the breeding of sheep which would give wool as well as mutton was a great advantage to farmers: in southern Africa the pastures were usually too dry to permit this strategy, and merino sheep continued to dominate. Again, it had become mainly a white-owned enterprise, well suited to the flat interior plateau and to the karoo, from which Khoi and San had been expelled, and where Sotho and Tswana had no natural protection against land-hungry trekkers. Few Africans possessed the wide lands and the ready capital to engage in commercial wool-growing.

Where Africans did retain advantages was in agriculture. There was still no capital available for agricultural investment such as irrigation, and Africans were much more knowledgable than Europeans about dry-land cultivation in this environment. Sotho had supplied grain to Kimberley until the wars of the 1870s and 1880s interrupted production, and American grain had invaded the region. Wheat could be grown in a few favoured areas, but the hardiest and most reliable grain crop was maize, which African peasants cultivated successfully for their own consumption, and on a small scale for the market. Although trekkers and colonists could conquer the land, they could not make it yield good crops; and the result was a variety of schemes whereby white landowners either employed African farm labour, or rented the land back to its original owners in exchange for a share of the crop or a regular and fixed rental. White landowners tended to concentrate on pastoralism, leaving cultivation to Africans: and as a result, a few African families were accumulating capital, and offering to purchase the land outright. In the Transvaal and Zambesia especially, there was some risk that Afrikaners might be driven off the land entirely. On the one side there were land companies buying large areas of land for mineral exploitation or leasing it to African tenants; on the other side were some of the more efficient tenants wanting outright possession; and in the middle were Afrikaners who still lacked the agricultural skills to exploit the land themselves. And the land must be very efficiently exploited, otherwise urban consumers would choose to buy imported wheat rather than locally-grown mealies.

There were two areas where white-owned agricultural enterprises were quite successful. One was the western Cape, where wheat and especially wine could be grown profitably. Here were the most prosperous Afrikaners, often very Anglicised in their culture and living standards, employing coloured labour in large numbers. Here was Hofmeyr's constituency, and here also were Rhodes's experimental fruit farms; and from this region there would eventually be a lucrative export trade in grapes, wine, brandy, citrus and stoned fruit to London. The other area of profitable white agriculture was the coastal belt of Natal and (from the 1890s) Zululand, where plantation production of sugar had been established. Since the Zulu were not yet so impoverished that they would work for low wages offered by the sugar farmers, indentured labour was imported from British India. Some African peasants were growing a bit of sugar as well, but the structure of sugar production and processing favoured much larger enterprises which could control the production processes as well as the cane fields. In brief, those forms of agricultural production which required capital and a large labour force, could support white ownership: but the small-scale production of grain was still much better conducted by Africans.

By 1902 the diamond industry had settled down to regular and profitable production. De Beers owned the mines, the Diamond Syndicate had a monopsony on sales, the Cape Government tolerated De Beers' compound system, a small number of skilled white technicians were well paid, and most of the work was carried out by African contract labourers from the eastern Cape and Basutoland. A few of the mission-schooled Africans from the Cape, such as Solomon Plaatje, were beginning to hold clerical and semi-skilled jobs in the industry; but the bulk of the labour force was unskilled in mining techniques, comprising workers who returned to their rural homes at the end of their contracts. The profits of the enterprise were divided (though unequally) between De Beers itself, the labour aristocracy of whites, and the colonial government which redistributed these profits among the electors (who were mainly white). The diamond-mining industry and the colonial political system reinforced each other. The public disgrace of Rhodes, and even his death by 1902, made no great difference to the harmony between mining capital and the colonial state.

The influence of gold mining in the region was more dynamic. By the time war broke out, there were over 10 000 white and 100 000 black miners employed along the Witwatersrand. Johannesburg was by far the largest and wealthiest city in the region, attracting rich and poor, adventurous and timid, from throughout southern Africa. Almost everything and everyone depended upon the mining industry: wages paid in mining determined the level of wages paid in other enterprises; railway construction and coal mining rested upon traffic generated by the gold mines. Without gold, the Transvaal would enjoy almost no cash revenue at all. The Premier Diamond Mining Company began operations after the war, and caused acute alarm to De Beers by flooding the world market – but even that was a small enterprise in comparison with gold.

Yet different groups were affected in quite different ways by the expansion of gold mining. The owners of the mines, the managers of the enterprises, and the bankers and share-market speculators all took their profits directly from the industry. The skilled white working class took their income in the form of wages. Until the war, mine-owners had relied upon the white working class – the core of the Uitlander population – not only for its technical skills, but also for political support against Kruger's republican administration. Wages had been high, and the white miners had not bothered to form unions. After the war the mine-owners took a more critical view of a very expensive labour aristocracy. The war had hardly finished, when members of the Chamber of Mines began to reduce wage levels for skilled men, and to seek ways of employing a higher proportion of cheap black labour. The labour aristocracy responded by forming unions to protect their interests, and from 1902 there were five years of persistent strike action and political agitation as the old Uitlander coalition broke up into the mine-owners and their professional allies and merchants on the one hand, and the wage-earning whites on the other. Where white politics had looked like a two-sided struggle between Afrikaners and Uitlanders, it became more of a triangle, involving landowners, white workers, and the magnates and managers themselves.

The impact of animal disease, warfare, and the systematic destruction of rural property during the campaign against the republican guerillas, speeded up the changes taking place among rural Afrikaners. When the war began, all Afrikaner adult males had rallied to the flag; by the end of the war a significant minority were fighting on the side of the British, and these collaborators included a high proportion of the poorest rural whites, who had little land of their own and no other means of livelihood. After the war Afrikaner landowners were the acknowledged political leaders of the volk: poor *bijwoners* – tenants at will – were steadily squeezed off the land, and drifted to the urban areas to seek work either as labourers, or more often as supervisors of African labour. As the mine-owners attacked the living standards of the labour aristocracy, so landless Afrikaners began to replace ex-Uitlanders in urban and especially mining employment. Here again, the simple division between urban British and rural Afrikaners was beginning to break down into a more complex pattern.

But the bulk of productive labour continued to be done by Africans. Landowners were not pleased to see their tenants go off to work in Johannesburg, leaving their families to live on the farms: they preferred to see mining labour recruited from further away. Few farmers could afford to pay their workers (or tenants) anything like the cash wages which the mines could afford (even though these levels were also low, at £1.5 to £2 per month, plus compound accommodation and rations). Mine-owners had preferred migrant labour to a stabilised labour force, and during the 1890s there had been attempts to recruit regular labour supplies from the eastern Cape, Basutoland, and Mozambique especially.

After the war the mine-owners organised themselves more efficiently, setting up the Witwatersrand Native Labour Association (WNLA) as a single recruiting agency which would distribute recruits among all the mines which belonged to the Association. When British troops entered Johannesburg, the African workers celebrated wildly, expecting that the coercion and pass laws and the low wage levels of the republican era would be overthrown. In practice, pass laws were reinforced, wage levels were actually reduced, and the State control over African compound labourers became very much more stringent. Those Africans who had any choice therefore chose to stay at home or to work on railway construction, rather than return to the mines. In this crisis the mine-owners quickly arranged to recruit 50 000 Chinese to replace the reluctant African workers – and wage levels fell again, after a period in which labour shortages had led to a steady increase in wages.

As the mining industry settled down, it drew the bulk of its labour requirements southwards from tropical Africa. White farmers in Nyasaland resented the loss of local labour; and the small mines in Rhodesia were jealous of the Witwatersrand mines which could attract labour from the whole of the region. If the Witwatersrand mines had a free hand, other white employers would suffer acutely. These rivalries had to be resolved, and they were resolved by the informal partition of the region into labour reservoirs for different employers. The Witwatersrand mines, through the Witwatersrand Native Labour Association, recruited mainly from the Transkei and Basutoland, and through the chartered companies which governed most of Portuguese East Africa. These companies, and the Portuguese administration, won most of their incomes from recruiting fees paid for migrant workers. Meanwhile the smaller gold mines of Rhodesia gained control over the labour migrants travelling south from Northern Rhodesia, and there was a struggle over access to workers from Nyasaland. Nyasaland and Mozambique became highly specialised economies, exporting little besides the labour of their people.

By oversimplifying the general picture, we may perhaps summarise it as follows. Around Cape Town (and to a smaller extent around Durban) there was an area of large-scale and successful agricultural production owned and controlled by whites. Behind Cape Town, much of the rest of the dry interior was devoted to wool-growing. Further into the interior, from South West Africa through Bechuanaland into the Transvaal and Rhodesia, cattle production was struggling to overcome disease and the competition of imported beef. Only in the eastern half of the region, and in the far north, was small-scale peasant production of grain being practised; and this great belt of territory – from eastern Rhodesia through Mozambique, Zululand, Natal, Basutoland and the eastern Cape – was being squeezed to yield migrant labourers for the mining industry on the high veld. In this great region, grain production was being slowly destroyed in favour of labour-production on a regular and humiliating basis. Another way of describing this process is to contrast the development of mining with the underdevelopment of cultivation.

Creating a successor state

For at least a generation, British policy-makers had considered southern Africa to be a settler society similar to Canada or to the Australasian colonies. Though Africans were manifestly the majority, southern Africa was not to be administered in the fashion of tropical African or Indian dependencies. Carnarvon's federation, if it had come into existence, would have been a white political system responsible for keeping order among subject Africans. If southern Africa were only a settler society (admittedly one with special features) then the normal imperial policy was to federate all the separate dependencies and grant the federal structure a great measure of self-government. Canada had been a federated Dominion since the 1860s, and the Australian Commonwealth had come into existence in 1901: in each case the settlers had drafted their constitutions, which had then been enacted at Westminister. Before such a development could occur in southern Africa however, several measures had to be taken to ensure that British capital would be secure, British strategic interests guaranteed, and a stable political system created which would not require persistent imperial garrisons and expensive warfare. To grant self-government to the ex-republics, without modifying their constitutions and their administrative systems, would merely re-create the unstable conditions which had provoked war in 1899. Since the Transvaal had been the storm centre, and might become so again, High Commissioner Milner transferred his office from Cape Town to Pretoria, to supervise the transformation of an unstable republic into a stable colonial society.

As in the 1870s, so in the 1900s, the most urgent governmental task was to disarm Africans and get them back to work. The Cape Government would handle the Transkei, and Natal (which had incorporated Zululand in 1897) might perhaps do the same for the Zulu. In the ex-republics, a rural police force was established, under the energetic command of Baden-Powell (who then went on to found the Boy Scouts), whose clear purpose was to disarm those Africans who had acquired rifles during the fighting, and to protect Afrikaner farmers as they returned to their burnt-out homesteads. Whenever a rumour of an African rising was heard, arms were quickly distributed to the white farmers.

In brief, pre-war rural relationships between black and white were quickly and ruthlessly restored in what has been described as a counter-revolution. The Shona and Ndebele had been disarmed following the rising of 1896-97, so they posed no immediate problem. In Mozambique there was some African resistance to the chartered companies which were set over them, but that too was suppressed during the first years of the century. A much more serious problem was provoked by the Germans in South West Africa, where Herero (in the centre of the country near the capital Windhoek) and Nama (in the southern sector) rebelled in the years from 1905. It took several years for the Germans to exterminate this resistence, but in the end they were thoroughly successful. The majority of the Herero died, and some others emigrated to Bechuanaland.

There remained the Zulu. Neither Dinuzulu, the paramount chief, nor any other Zulu leader contemplated a rebellion, but the small white settlement at Natal could not feel secure until every trace of Zulu independence was destroyed. The intensification of taxation of the Zulu and the high-handed behaviour of officials eventually forced some of them into the 'Reluctant Rebellion' of 1906–08; a savage and punitive campaign was fought against them. Dinuzulu was put on trial in 1907; and then even the Natal settlers felt safe.

Military coercion was one thing: getting a reliable labour force was something else. In the Transkei, Basutoland and eventually Zululand the related problems of land-shortage, regular taxation in cash, and the separation of the societies into a prosperous minority of peasants and a land-short majority, all combined to guarantee a flow of migrant labour to urban and mining centres. In Mozambique, it was necessary for the mines (and the imperial authorities) to negotiate a treaty with Portugal, fixing the recruitment fees for labour (to be paid to Portugal, not to the labourers), and the numbers to be recruited each year, and the volume of railway traffic which should flow through Delagoa Bay. This agreement was reached in 1903, and as soon as the Portuguese and the chartered companies had restored their authority, a reliable volume of labour began to flow once again to Johannesburg.

Within the ex-republics themselves, something of a crisis blew up when Africans began trying to purchase the land which they had been cultivating as tenants and share-croppers. Here again, the old republican custom of refusing to register individual African landowners was ultimately reinforced by legislation: Transvaal Africans would not escape into independent agricultural production, but must remain forever wage labourers or tenant-farmers.

Finally, those Africans who did come to work in Johannesburg were now protected more successfully by the urban police from illicit liquor. More work would now be extracted from black miners and labourers than had been possible before the war. They would also receive rather lower wages, and it was expected they would have to spend more time in wage labour to earn the same target amount of money, further impoverishing agricultural production. And if these measures failed to induce a sufficient number of labourers, then the imperial officials permitted mine-owners to import even cheaper labour from the most impoverished regions of China.

The next major concern was to place gold mining on a more secure basis, since gold was by now the chief export staple of the whole region. Railway rates were slashed, protective tariffs were dismantled, the expensive dynamite concession and liquor concessions were abolished, and therefore the working costs of the mines were significantly reduced. The colonial state encouraged the formation of WNLA which, by taking control of foreign labour recruiting for all mines, reduced labour costs to all employers. The state also observed with some sympathy the mine-owners' reductions in the proportion and the wage levels of the labour aristocracy. The increased mechanisation of mining enabled managers to employ a larger proportion of unskilled machine-operators, and a lower proportion of skilled technicians.

These measures all required a more professional and modern public service than Kruger's Republic or the Orange Free State had been able to recruit. The new bureaucracies were rather larger than the republican public services, and much improved by the recruitment of graduates (mainly from Britain) to staff them. The new bureaucracy was not solely concerned with the regulation of mining and taxation (though these departments were overhauled and expanded), but also with agricultural extension services, the education of white children, the regular administration of rural Africans, and the administration of justice by professional magistrates and judges. When mining revenue was collected, it could now be redistributed within the society in a more coherent manner than before. As in the Cape, of course, so in the new colonies: the enfranchised white population, rather than Africans, benefited most from public expenditure. In this way, the whole white population of the Transvaal (and later of the other settler societies as well) could see direct benefits to themselves from the expansion and prosperity of the gold-mining industry.

These reforms inevitably provoked increased political agitation. The Afrikaner leaders – generals left over from the war, such as Louis Botha, J. C. Smuts, J. B. M. Hertzog and Christian de Wet of the Orange Free State, and J. H. de la Rey from the western Transvaal – welcomed many of the reforms, especially agricultural extension and Baden-Powell's para-military police force. On the other hand they could see no good reason for leaving the state under the control of imperialists and mining capitalists. From 1904 onwards they mobilised Afrikaner political parties to contest elections whenever these should be held. Curiously, they won some support also from two kinds of ex-Uitlanders. One group were old mining magnates like J. B. Robinson, who had done very well for himself through his personal relationship with Kruger, and the new diamond-mining magnates who feared the influence of De Beers. Another group comprised migrants from the Cape, who sought to re-create the relationship between the Afrikaner Bond and English-speaking professionals.

The leaders of the mining industry hoped to hold together the old coalition of Uitlanders which had been so successful as a pressure group before the war. However the mine-owners' determination to crush the white trade unions, and the unpopular policy of importing Chinese indentured labourers, made it difficult to hold that coalition together. When elections were held, there was a united Afrikaner party in each of the major colonies, with a few English-speaking allies: against them were the mining magnates, deserted by some of their employees. The first post-war election in the Transvaal in 1907 returned Afrikaners to power (as the Het Volk political party), led by Botha and Smuts. In the Orange Free State there were very few non-Afrikaner voters and it was not surprising that Hertzog's Orangia Unie won an overwhelming majority in 1908. In the Cape, many Afrikaner rebels had been disfranchised after the war, and it was only in 1908 that a test of political strength could be staged. Jameson's Progressives lost power, to J. X. Merriman's coalition of Afrikaners and some English-speakers,

General Louis Botha, J. X. Merriman and General J. C. Smuts

while African and coloured voters were unable to have a decisive influence on the results. Self-governing Natal and Chartered Company Rhodesia hardly mattered, since neither government was capable of leading the movement towards closer union of the British colonies. On the face of it, it seemed as if Britain had won the war only to lose the peace, since non-British political parties dominated the administration of three powerful states within six years of the Peace of Vereeniging.

The newly elected governments at once proceeded to negotiate the terms of closer union – a policy which was popular not only among imperial officials but also among Afrikaners. The five settler societies sent delegates to conferences in 1908 and 1909, drafted an Act of Union which the imperial government passed into law, and formed the Union of South Africa in 1910. Botha led the new government, closely assisted by Smuts: it seemed as if the result of the war had been reversed, since both were Transvaal generals. Appearances were deceptive. Careful research into this era of southern Africa history – especially that of Martin Chanock in *Unconsummated Union* – enables us to see these proceedings as an early instance of the building of a successor state to uphold the substance of imperial interests, and harmonise them with the wishes of the local electorate. It is in this light that we can best understand what happened in the negotiations leading to Union.

For one thing, Britain retained control over three significant territories in the region – Basutoland, Bechuanaland and Swaziland (which had been split from the Transvaal immediately after the war). Britain was also responsible for the Rhodesias, although power was actually delegated to the British South Africa Company. For these reasons alone, imperial opinion was bound to be influential in the new Union government. The Act of Union provided for the eventual incorporation of these areas into South Africa – and that provision was intended to encourage the South African Government to prove worthy of increased responsibilities. It is also true, however, that Britain could not administer these territories without South African co-operation. A second source of continued British influence upon the new South African Government was its control over foreign policy (at least until the 1920s), since South Africa (like the other British self-governing dominions) was not recognised as a fully sovereign nation. More importantly, Britain had the power in international affairs to be very useful, especially if the Union government needed the co-operation of Portugal (Britain's oldest ally) or Germany (her most dangerous rival).

A major British interest in the region was the security of mining capital, of which a large proportion was invested by British capitalists and small investors. While Botha and Smuts and their followers were acutely suspicious of individual mine-owners and group managers, they were now entirely reconciled to the gold-mining industry as the backbone of the whole southern African economy. The mines provided the revenue which financed agricultural extension, rural credit, and markets; the mines provided jobs for dispossessed Afrikaners from the rural areas; and the large bureaucracy which the mines also paid for provided the means of employing yet more Afrikaners, and for the administration and strict control of a potentially mutinous African majority.

Once these relationships had been established and understood, then British investment in gold-mining ventures was just as safe under an Afrikaner government as it had been under a British Crown Colony administration. When white miners went on strike in 1907, Botha and Smuts called in British troops to keep order: they relied on British forces for the same general purpose until the eve of the Great War. Mine-managers themselves were startled to see how rapidly the Afrikaner generals had reconciled themselves to the logic of the situation, and its implication that imperial links were a source of southern African stability. In some ways, the processes leading to Union simply repeated on a large scale the coalition between Rhodes and Hofmeyr in the 1890s. Afrikaners now held office as the government of the Union, but they relied upon the mining industry for revenue, and on mine managers for economic advice.

As they steered Uitlanders and Afrikaners towards a successor state, imperial officers disappointed those Africans and Indians and coloureds who hoped for better prospects under imperial auspices. At the talks at Vereeniging, Afrikaner generals had asked for an assurance that Britain would not enfranchise non-white voters: the British were only too happy to give such a promise. As Milner had put it already, there would only be a few Africans and coloureds qualified to vote if the Cape qualifications were extended, and 'for the sake of principle' it was foolish to provoke the anger of the whites. The imperial connection rested upon the co-operation of the settlers. The Union constitution prevented Africans and coloureds from being members of parliament, and permitted them to vote only in the Cape where they had long exercised that right. There were liberal objections to this provision, both in the Cape and in London, but once again it seemed inexpedient to antagonise the colonists. The fate of the African and Indian and coloured elites was a matter of almost complete official indifference in London.

Only four British colonies entered the Union. The fate of the three protectorates – or High Commission territories as they came to be known – was thought to be their eventual inclusion in the Union. Meanwhile the imperial government was exempted from the need to think about them seriously. Shorn of their arable lands, the Sotho in Basutoland became increasingly dependent upon wage labour on Free State farms and especially in Johannesburg gold fields. In

Swaziland the royal family and the leading chiefs tried to mobilise capital to buy back the pastoral and arable land owned by white farmers, in order to stave off the complete dependency which had overcome Basutoland. The chiefly families in the Bechuanaland Protectorate developed their herds, and resisted offers by the chartered company and by individual white pastoralists to take over the usable land. All three territories were linked to South Africa by a customs agreement (initiated in 1903) and by common currency and a unified railway system. They were intrinsic parts of the growing South African economy, but they successfully resisted attempts to incorporate them into the Union political system.

British Central Africa posed problems of a different kind. The settlers in Southern Rhodesia were predominantly British rather than Afrikaner, and although they attended the negotiations towards Union as observers, they preferred to remain outside a political system governed by Afrikaners, especially as incorporation would require them to learn Dutch, and perhaps to share the conquered land with an influx of poor Afrikaner farmers. In any case, the chartered company was still responsible for the administration of the region, and a small white population – a little over 20 000 at the time of Union – could not afford to buy out the land and mineral rights of the company. Neither the imperial government nor the chartered company was willing to push the settlers into the Union, and the settlers preferred to be part of separate political system, in which they could exert powerful influence through their elected majority in the Legislative Council, but were not directly responsible for keeping law and order. When the charter expired in 1914 (after the initial 25 years) it was renewed. Meanwhile the prospect of ultimate incorporation into the Union encouraged law-makers in Salisbury to keep the law and its administration as much as possible in harmony with South African precedents. Southern Rhodesia began to become a poor imitation of the south.

The BSA Company held a variety of land and mineral claims in Bechuanaland (which did not prosper) and in Northern Rhodesia. Northern Rhodesia stood in an uneasy relationship with the rest of the region. The BSA Company represented an important link to South Africa, and much labour travelled south to Southern Rhodesia. The small numbers of white settlers tended to look to the south for support and advice. At the same time the African communities were large and the settlers few, so that an administrative style like that of tropical Africa had some attractions for British officials. The Lozi kingdom in the west lent itself to the theory and practice of indirect rule through the king; elsewhere the settlers were too few to aspire to the status of a self-governing settler society. For the next sixty years the fate of Northern Rhodesia veered between closer association with the settler states to the south, internal division into North-Western and North-Eastern Rhodesia, and closer association with the predominantly African dependencies of East Africa. Nyasaland suffered much the same ambiguity, although the BSA Company had no particular claim on it. The unusually thorough western education system which grew up in Nyasaland enabled the dependency to export not only unskilled labour to Rhodesian and South African mining compounds, but also clerical workers wherever Africans were allowed to occupy such jobs.

Although Mozambique had no constitutional links with the Union, in practice the colonial economy was very closely geared to the demand for mining labour. Without such a demand (and the capitation fees which WNLA paid to the Portuguese for each recruit), and without the railway link to Johannesburg, it is difficult to imagine how the Portuguese authorities would have extracted any benefit from the region. German South West Africa, on the other hand, was developed quite separately from the Union. There was no surplus of population to export as labourers – after the disastrous mortality of the Herero during the 1905 campaign – and no easy access for goods across the Kalahari desert and Bechuanaland. After the bad publicity attending the Herero and Nama campaigns, the German imperial authorities delegated a great deal of power to the local settlers (as indeed they did in German East Africa in the same period and for much the same reason), but the settlers were content to exploit the pastoral resources of the country without assistance or intervention from the Union. The densely populated northern border lands of South West Africa were not effectively administered by the time German colonial administration was violently overthrown on the outbreak of the Great War.

What emerged by 1910 was a powerful settler state, wedged between Portuguese territory on the east, and German territory on the west, with an unclear northern limit. The settler state itself was dependent upon Great Britain for naval and military defence as well as foreign policy support and access to capital markets; and the British presence was strengthened by her retention of enclaves of land and people within southern Africa. The possibility of incorporating these territories, and of expanding northwards in an African version of 'manifest destiny' would also bind the South African governments to imperial Britain. But more important than any of these considerations was the fact that the leaders of Afrikaner nationalism in the region were reconciled to exercising power through institutions designed in Britain, and to manage an economy which resulted very largely from British capital investment.

Chapter 11

Agricultural development and rural underdevelopment

A year after Union, a census of South Africa found that about half of all whites, coloureds and Indians lived outside the towns, and so did seven out of eight Africans. They added up to about 75 per cent of the total population of six million. Not until the 1960s did the rural population fall below half of the total – and the rural population was still overwhelmingly black at that time. Rural production was a matter of central importance for the society as a whole, and for Africans especially. That would be a good enough reason for examining the history of rural areas. But there is an even more compelling reason for such an examination. Southern Africa is the only region in the continent which has established capitalist agricultural production on a large scale, and it has been able to grow sufficient food for its own needs and to export rural produce as well. Even more extraordinary than that achievement is the increasing poverty of most rural people: the successful evolution of capitalist agriculture has had extremely unequal consequences for different sections of the rural population. Perhaps the most astounding dimension of this transformation is that it involved the systematic destruction of the agricultural and pastoral skills of the African population, the concentration of resources on the least efficient landowners in the region, and some success in overcoming some enormous environmental difficulties. This unusual combination of efficient production and miserable poverty has attracted a great deal of attention in recent years, precisely because it is so different from most of the rest of the continent's experience.

Central to all discussions of southern African production is the notion of 'peasants', and this is a difficult concept to use. For one thing, very few people like to be called peasants – probably nobody reading this book would like to be called a peasant, because peasants are often thought to be somehow backward. Another problem is the very vague definition which is usually attached to the term. It is clear that people who produce crops and herd animals mainly for their own consumption should not be described as peasants, especially if the household, or the lineage, or the clan, makes all the important decisions about what crops to grow, and how to organise production. The term peasant always involves some external force upon the rural population, usually from a state and from an urban area, to ensure regular rural production: and peasants exist only if there is some social class in the society which does not produce food, but nevertheless gets quite enough to eat. The common definition is (in Shanin's words) 'small agricultural producers who, with the help of simple equipment and the labour of their families, produce mainly for their own consumption and for the fulfilment of obligations to the holders of political and economic power'. We should add to that definition that peasants are people who produce in this way for a long period of time, from one generation to the next. Most of the population of the world, for the last few centuries, have been peasants – from China to Peru, and from Uganda to Yugoslavia. There are so many different ways of being peasants that the term tells us very little about the nature of day-to-day life among any particular peasant population. Most people in southern Africa began to be peasants in the nineteenth century, and stopped being peasants at some time in the twentieth century: but that is just the beginning of any kind of explanation of rural change.

In Chapters 5 and 6 we saw that the effect of the expanding pastoral frontier was to break up settled rural communities, except in those areas where their sheer weight of numbers made that difficult (in the eastern Cape) or where mountains gave them some military protection (in Lesotho and for a while in the mountains held by the Pedi) or where very dry conditions made life difficult for commercial pastoralists (around the fringe of the Kalahari desert). But we also saw (in Chapter 7) that the colonists developed a new strategy for dealing with African rural populations, once diamond mining became the chief export-producer of the Cape economy: the Glen Grey system did not simply sweep Africans off the good land, but rather left them in possession, with a quite new system of individual land tenure. This strategy was then applied throughout the eastern Cape Colony, to the benefit of some African families who could control enough land and sell produce to the market – but to the disadvantage of those who had little or no access to land. The old policy of simple confiscation had been amended. Naturally, this did not abolish the pressures upon African rural societies, but imposed a fresh set of constraints. Through poll tax payments, school fees, church contributions, and the need to purchase manufactured commodities, rural groups were linked into the cash economy; and in order to survive in it families must either produce commodities on a regular basis or sell their labour for wages.

The consequences for rural societies were not evenly spread, nor were they immediately disastrous. Families which had enjoyed access to markets continued to prosper: in the eastern Cape they could send their children to mission schools where they received a formal education as good as anyone else's in the colony, often with the children of missionaries and administrators. Education and a regular income – either by cash crop production or through bureaucratic or professional employment – often won them the vote and a measure of acceptance within colonial society. Descendants of the Mfengu refugees were prominent in this group. Essentially this prosperous and respectable group was a small minority, committed to non-racial assimilation, and relying upon the favour of the state for their continued acceptance and continued market opportunites. By the turn of the century the crisis in production throughout the African areas was eroding the position of even the partially assimilated minority: but in their heyday the Jabavu family and the Soga family and several others seemed to be pioneering a path towards the ultimate assimilation of the whole of Cape society, in which social class alone, rather than colour, would be the essential division.

The nature of the crisis in African rural production is complex. At one level it was provoked by the rinderpest epidemic which swept through southern Africa in the mid-1890s, and which was especially damaging for families with few cattle, since they were unlikely to be able to breed up another herd. The disruption of the South African War, when animal diseases spread unchecked, intensified this crisis. But the problem was more profound than that. Africans could not expand the area of land available to them, whereas the population was steadily increasing, and production could not be intensified without great risk. Fallow periods became shorter, as families could no longer afford to let land rest; and as a result the quantity and the quality of rural production tended to decline. The state was either unwilling or unable to come to the rescue with the land distribution or the large rural credits which might have arrested the decline. Periods of wage labour on white farms or in mining or on public works programmes became increasingly common – an essential part of most family incomes, rather than simply a means of accumulating capital for investment in firearms or in agricultural machinery or livestock.

Outside the eastern Cape the same kind of development can be seen, though on many different time-scales. Market opportunities were grasped eagerly throughout the region, and a period of prosperity ensued, which only slowly gave way to depression. In Natal and Zululand the authorities were nervous about overt interference in Zulu politics between the battle of Ulundi and the arrest of Dinuzulu: it was safer (if less convenient) to import indentured Indian labour for the sugar plantations, than to squeeze the African rural communities for labour migrants. In the trekker republics, it remained official policy to dispossess Africans of their land, rather than attempt the sophistication of the Glen Grey strategy. In the Orange Free State that strategy was almost entirely successful, but in the Transvaal the military difficulty of disarming and then dispossessing Africans was much greater. In either case, most of the land which was cultivated at all, was cultivated by Africans, whose slow decline into poverty kept pace with the increasing military strength of the rural white population. The old policy of simple dispossession was halted only during the period of British colonial administration from 1900 to 1907, when the boundaries of African land were demarcated and further encroachment on that land became much slower and smaller.

African rural production faced a battery of difficulties. One of these was the near impossibility of purchasing more land for an expanding population, either because of legal obstacles (in the republics and in Natal) or because of rising land prices. Another was the difficulty of obtaining credit for intensifying production. Yet another was the unequal availability of agricultural extension services (in the Transvaal, for example, the British administration prohibited extension officers from entering African areas). Perhaps the most formidable difficulty was that African peasant producers were in direct competition with white farmers who were beginning to learn how to grow crops on a commercial scale: and the white farmers had access to state facilities to help them in this competition, as we shall see. Even these difficuties might have been overcome by some energetic families, if not for a further general problem: the mining industry was more interested in harvesting labour than crops, from the peasant communities. As the mining industry increased in political influence, so state policy reflected the interests of mining capital in respect of rural production.

A very general change in policy may be observed if we compare the two British occupations of the Transvaal, from 1877 and again from 1900. On the first occasion, as we have seen, British troops were used to crush the most dangerous African rural communities which threatened the livelihood of rural whites. Conquest permitted the dispossession of Africans throughout the Transvaal. On the second occasion Africans were disarmed, but were not dispossessed. From 1903 onwards Afrikaner leaders demanded the break-up of African lands (on the argument that this strategy would yield more African labour for the mines and white farms), but on this occasion the strategy was not adopted. Certainly Africans were prevented from purchasing significantly more land, and a little African land passed into white ownership; but in general the

African societies were not to be dispossessed outright. Labour was brought from China to resolve the labour shortage; the recruitment of African labourers from Mozambique was placed on a solid treaty relationship with Portugal; starved of credit and extension services and access to fresh land, Transvaal Africans were left to decline gently into poverty and labour migrancy. All these measures served the interests of the mining industry, and they added up to a very different rural development strategy than the republican government had attempted. When Afrikaners returned to political power in 1907, they mainly allowed that strategy to continue.

The other side of the political coin was an energetic policy of promoting white agricultural and pastoral production. The new bureaucracy encouraged the building of fences to control the movement, breeding, and diseases of cattle. An expensive and ultimately successful veterinary institute was built at Onderstepoort, training skilled veterinarians for the new department of Agriculture, whose brief was to give all possible assistance to white landowners. Road and railway construction gave access to Johannesburg markets; rural credit (and eventually a Land Bank) enabled white landowners to respond to new market opportunities. The agricultural services of the Transvaal were extended to the whole of white South Africa, after Union in 1910. But perhaps the most decisive measure was taken not by the state directly, but by informal agreement between mine managements and white cultivators: the mines agreed to purchase the bulk of the white farmers' maize crop. The political relationship between mining managers and Afrikaners was cemented by (in Trapido's elegant term) an alliance between maize and gold. This agreement, which meant that mine managers abandoned the possibility of importing cheap bulk food from overseas, eventually placed white cultivation on a secure and prosperous footing.

Many of the problems of white agriculture in the interior, in the late nineteenth century, were consequences of attempting capitalist production without capital. Lack of capital made it impossible to fence properties or to improve the quality of either soil or cattle – so pastoralism was extensive and inefficient, and cultivation mainly a side-line. Without a substantial cash income, it was impossible to employ paid labour since the wages which would attract Africans away from their own land were too high for white farmers to pay – so instead coercion was sometimes used, and a great deal of land was leased back to African smallholders who paid for the privilege through providing labour or a share of the crop. The remarkable emergence of white farmers during the twentieth century is therefore very largely the story of efforts to make capitalist relations of production work in the rural areas. These efforts were successful mainly because the state provided assistance in critical areas and at critical moments.

A central feature of the transformation of white rural production has been the abolition of non-wage labour and its replacement by a wage-earning rural working class. Among the first people to be removed from the land were white bijwoners, many of whom claimed kinship with the landowners, but many of whom had fought on the British side towards the end of the South African War, and were not very welcome afterwards. From 1902 onwards the British colonial authorities tried to settle bijwoners on the land as smallholders growing crops, but this strategy was not very successful, and a more common solution after 1907 was to create public service jobs or to reserve mining jobs for rural whites who lacked their own land. However, African tenants on white land were also under pressure from the beginning of the century. A few prosperous white farmers began to dispense with labour tenants, and to employ wage labourers instead – which meant that the landowner had much more control over the processes of agricultural production.

Then in 1913 the new Union Government enacted the Native Land Act, which made it illegal for white landowners to lease land to Africans for a half share of the crop. The same purpose had been attempted through earlier republican Squatters' Laws – but by 1913 the law could be enforced, since there was now a large and effective bureaucracy and police force to carry out government policy in the rural areas. The consequence of the Act was to destroy the relative prosperity of a large number of African families, who had accumulated farm machinery and their own herds of animals. They were forced either to migrate to the reserves (which were already full of people) or to sell their animals and machinery and become wage labourers. Furthermore it had been the practice in the northern republics that Africans could not register individual land titles: instead, Africans sometimes nominated friendly whites as the legal owners of land. As the first generation of nominal landowners died off, their heirs and successors began to insist upon real property rights. In this way, white landowners were able not only to increase the proportion of land which they actually controlled, but even to expand the area of land which they could legally claim. Again, the distribution of new road and feeder railway systems in the twentieth century makes a lot of sense in terms of the needs of the rural majority. White and black farmers were locked in competition, and in that contest the influence of the state was crucial in promoting white farming. Through subsidies for exportable crops, through tariff protection against overseas competition, through state coercion of the labour force, and through the provision of credit and extension services and educational institutions for white farmers, they were enabled to become a prosperous rural bourgeoisie.

Throughout the rest of the southern African region there were important differences, distinguishing them from South Africa itself.

Basutoland had no white settler problem – but neither did it have sufficient arable land for self-sufficiency, and under the British protectorate the country languished as a labour reservoir. In Swaziland, attention was focused on the attempt to buy back land which was alienated by concessions in the nineteenth century, but although the strategy enjoyed some success, the long-term trend was towards dependency upon the South African economy, since rural capital was not avaiable on a sufficient scale to make the country self-sufficient.

In Bechuanaland an era of great prosperity came to an end with the completion of the railway line to Rhodesia, but the chiefs did succeed in limiting the amount of land alienated to settlers, so that the basis for rural prosperity did not entirely disappear. Among the Ndebele mixed farmers, the loss of cattle in the wars of the 1890s and the rinderpest epidemic required a sharp re-orientation towards cultivation; whereas the Shona responded vigorously and successfully to the opportunities of the new markets; and for both communities there was continued market opportunity until at least 1908 when the BSA Company decided to promote settler agriculture. It took several more years before white farmers were successfully growing maize and tobacco, and driving African producers out of the market.

In Northern Rhodesia, the Lozi kingdom at first benefited from market opportunities. King Lewanika initiated capital works which irrigated large areas of flood-plain (one of the few areas of the region where such capital works were attempted before the Great War). It was not until the impact of cattle disease in the 1920s, and the collapse of the royal capital works programme in the same period, that local self-sufficiency gave way to dependence upon wage labour by migrants who travelled to mining areas outside their homeland.

Even in South West Africa, in the generation after the appalling wars of the years 1905–08, Herero and Nama began to build up their herds once more. In the northern parts of the German colony, however (and across the border in Angola), the gradual imposition of colonial administration over Ovambo-speaking people in the first years of this century brought an end to trading and cattle-raiding. By the outbreak of the Great War the Ovambo too had been reduced to a migrant labour reservoir.

In Mozambique, the equally slow imposition of colonial authority tended to transform relatively autonomous societies into labour reserves, administered by a series of chartered companies.

With very few exceptions (and the exceptional cases were mainly cattle-keepers who managed to retain land), Africans throughout the southern African region had lost their economic autonomy by the 1900s, or by the 1920s at the latest. The slowness of that process outside South Africa itself has much to do with the relatively weaker pressures of colonial administration, and of land alienation for white settlement. African resistance to pauperisation was therefore more successful in delaying the process of under-development.

The development of agricultural capitalism throughout southern Africa was exceptionally ruthless. At one level this may be seen in the brutal treatment of the land itself. South African authorities often point to African areas, criticising land use practices which exhaust the soil and transform arable land into eroded and bare countryside. In view of the increasing overcrowding of African land, and the very low nutrition levels which have become such an alarming feature in them, the abuse of the land is hardly surprising. (When more land was available, and fallow periods were possible, that criticism could not be made.) Less defensible is the extent of land abuse and soil erosion in white-owned land, where farmers were encouraged to grow maize on land which would not support cultivation for long, in response to guaranteed high prices for grain crops. The Kalahari desert is very much larger now than it was before commercial agricultural production began in the nineteenth century. Only in the 1950s were soil protection and restoration measures begun, which halted the steady extension of semi-desert conditions into the western regions of the Cape, the Orange Free State and the Transvaal.

Ruthless measures may also be seen in the manner whereby the white rural population itself has been thinned out. Afrikaners see themselves as an essentially rural society – but Afrikaner landlords have been just as determined as English-speakers to squeeze landless whites off the land, and to move away from kinship towards wages as the basis of rural relations of production. But these measures are less significant than the systematic destruction of the African peasantries throughout the region. Cooper sums up the literature on the subject by saying that 'The South African peasant was murdered'. Unlike the situation in most of colonial Africa, throughout this century African rural cultivators have been discouraged from growing cash crops either for export or for the regional markets. Neither credit, nor marketing facilities, nor extension services, nor even land itself, have been made available to promote African rural production. Two crucial groups of people ensured that the African peasantry would be destroyed throughout the region. One of these groups was the white landowning population, which required ultra-cheap labour in order to establish themselves on the market at all. The other group was the management of mining operations, which needed cheap migrant labour even more than they needed cheap food for the compound labourers. Wherever these two forces combined – in South Africa itself, in Chartered Rhodesia, in British or German or Portuguese dependencies – African agricultural production was strangled.

African responses to sustained pressure of this kind have had further effects upon the capacity of the land to sustain its people. Outside the 'reserve' areas, people commonly preferred forms of tenure which gave them control over the cultivation of their own crops and the disposition of their own herds – only with extreme reluctance would people accept wage labour instead of share-cropping or a fixed rental. In the aftermath of the 1913 Native Land Act, therefore, there was a huge and tragic wave of ex-tenants herding their cattle and carrying their machinery around the countryside in search of farmers who would continue the old system of share-cropping – until the truth dawned that there were almost no such farmers to be found. From the early years of this century onwards, individual Africans fought through the courts for the right to purchase land – again in vain. The Land Act and its implementation limited African land to some 13 per cent of the South African land area, and the development of white farming in the rest of the countryside steadily eliminated any other choice except the reserves or wage labouring. With the development of mining, and later of manufacturing, many families preferred to send young men to work as migrant labourers rather than accept rural employment. Resistance of this kind was heroic – but in vain.

A further response was less heroic, though understandable in the circumstances. It became clear that African-grown crops were increasingly difficult to market – but that cattle (and to some extent other livestock) did not face such severe marketing problems. Wherever it was possible to switch away from grain to livestock therefore, favoured families adopted that option. In Namibia and in Botswana this has emphasised a sharp economic distinction between cattle-keepers (who have often preserved their autonomy, and even occasionally enjoyed prosperity) and cultivators (who are much more likely to be drawn into seasonal wage labour). Within South African reserves themselves, the same trend can also be observed.

However, the allocation of land for grazing, instead of cultivation, is not the most efficient way of feeding the rural population; and the emphasis upon pastoralism has exaggerated the difficulties which cultivators would face in any case. Peasants – in the sense of small-scale cultivators of the soil – have been almost eliminated, not only by the obvious non-African forces of land-grabbing and labour-recruiting, but also through the internal division of many rural African societies into a very small minority of pastoralists who require a disproportionate amount of land, and a very large majority of cultivators who have too little land (and land of too poor a quality) for independent subsistence. This process has led to a very strange reversal. In the nineteenth century, almost all white landowners made their living through pastoral production on a large and inefficient scale: African societies enjoyed the advantage mainly in their skills as cultivators. By the late twentieth century, almost all cultivation is conducted on white-owned farms; and the only rural Africans to have any serious prospect of an independent livelihood are those who can accumulate land and livestock for pastoral production. As prosperous cultivators, African families enjoyed only a very brief golden age, before they became the chief victims of the process of agricultural capitalist development.

Chapter 12

Mining and industrial growth

It is very tempting to imagine that the development of a massive mining industry *naturally* leads to the development of manufacturing of a wide range of goods. If we look at Africa as a whole, mining and manufacturing have usually occurred in close association with each other: where there is mining there is some manufacturing. However, the connection between these two economic activities is not a simple one. In this chaper we will trace the growth of mining from the nineteenth century into the mid-twentieth century in southern Africa, and look at the manufacturing industries, before drawing some conclusions about the relationship between them.

The expansion of mining

The De Beers diamond-mining complex was securely based by the 1890s, having complete control over Kimberley production, and control also over marketing of diamonds through the Diamond Syndicate. This security was threatened immediately after the South African War when a large volume of diamond production began at the Premier Mine in the Transvaal, whose owners would neither sell to De Beers nor agree to a fixed share of production. The difficulty was intensified when a German company began producing diamonds through the Diamond Regie Company in South West Africa; and it was not until 1914 that all three producers reached agreement about their shares of diamond production. Until that agreement was reached, it was difficult to control the world price of diamonds – which was necessary in view of the luxury nature of most diamond sales, and the likelihood that over-production would undercut prices. During this unsettled period De Beers sensibly diversified their investments as widely as they could. They acquired half a million acres of land, and used some of it for pastoral and for fruit production; they invested in the mining of coal, gold and copper; and money was invested in railways, telegraphs and newspapers. Innes calculates that De Beers was responsible for half of the Cape Colony's exports by 1900, with diamonds providing half of that amount. By investing in the British South Africa Company De Beers had access to Bechuanaland and the Rhodesias; through Rhodes's and Werher & Beit's gold-mining ventures, De Beers was linked to the Transvaal as well. By the turn of the century the De Beers complex was much larger and more powerful, economically and politically, than the small merchant companies and banking operations which controlled the rest of non-agricultural capital in southern Africa.

There had, of course, been some manufacturing in the Cape even before the diamond-mining development: wagon-making, house-construction, the processing of grapes into wine and brandy, and similar small-scale enterprises. The clothiers, hat-makers, wagon-makers and others also required banking facilities, and small locally-incorporated banks had sprung up to meet their needs as well as the needs of wool-farmers and wine-growers. During the last years of the nineteenth century many of these processes were either consolidated into larger enterprises, or else they dwindled under the impact of overseas competition. Banking facilities were consolidated into a handful of banking companies, the largest of which were extensions of London banking houses: the service industries had to compete with the mass-produced goods of the North Atlantic, which spread wherever railway services brought them. The effect of De Beers' diversification into the rest of the colonial economy was not to diversify that economy, but rather to promote those economic acitivities which served the mining interests, or at least were not in conflict with those interests. Apart from dynamite production at the turn of the century, there was nothing which could be described as heavy industry – except perhaps the repairing of railway stock. In brief, the growth of diamond mining did not lead directly or naturally to a similar growth in industry: rather, capital came to be concentrated in a small number of productive activities, clustered around diamond mining itself.

Matters were slightly different in the Transvaal Republic. For all practical purposes, we may say that capital was invested almost exclusively in the gold-mining ventures and activities very closely related to them. However, the gold-mining industry was not itself a united and consolidated activity, and not all capitalists were committed to serious mining. An important point to notice at once is this, that the individuals who promoted mining investment were reluctant to put their own personal fortunes in such risky ventures. A successful promoter was one who could persuade thousands of small investors (or a handful of large investors) in Europe to buy shares. The discoverer, or the promoter, would often receive a parcel of these shares for nothing or for a very low price, as a reward for starting the company – but the bulk of the money did not come from these enterprising promoters themselves.

A second crucial point to notice is that investment in gold mining was seldom very profitable. In almost every mining field in the world, investors would have won better returns by leaving their money in a bank. The reason why a lot of people did invest in gold mining was not the prospect of a *safe* return on their capital, but the small chance of making a fortune. More than other forms of capital investment, this was essentially a gamble, and it attracted some very unscrupulous characters to the share market. As one unhappy investor said, 'a gold mine is a hole in the ground owned by a liar'. Of course that was an exaggeration; but the fact of the matter is that gold-mining capital is attracted by risk rather than by regular profit. A typical gold-mining investor puts his money in for a short period, hoping that a rise in share prices will provide a profit in the very short term. Naturally, the managers of the mining companies had the best opportunities to play with the stock market, to make their fortunes, and to leave overseas investors in possession of useless mining property.

Although the Witwatersrand attracted a great many sharks and swindlers, it was necessary to attempt the serious development of mining property, once large sums of money had been committed. From 1895 onwards, deep-level gold mines were coming into operation, which involved the investment of capital on a very long-term basis, and only a slow movement towards profitability: meanwhile, the shallow mines along the outcrop began to be exhausted, so that the nature of the capital invested changed over time away from largely speculative ventures towards serious and carefully-thought-out developments. By the turn of the century, when perhaps £100 000 000 had been invested, it was no longer possible to think of the gold mines as merely a windfall. Major investors, the managers and engineering experts, and the British colonial officials who took over the Transvaal at this time, began a massive restructuring of the industry. As we have seen, recruitment of contract labour was placed on a regular and reliable footing: at the same time labour compound conditions were made subject to law, and serious efforts were made to control the liquor trade. Careful economic calculations led not only to the more systematic exploitation of African migrant labour, but also to squeezing more work out of a smaller proportion of white labour supervisors and technicians. The price of gold was fixed, and the mines were constantly becoming deeper and more expensive to run; so constant technical improvement and more careful labour management were needed if the mines were to make regular profits. At the same time Afrikaners were mollified by the way in which profits from mining operations were diverted towards rural credit, and by the manner in which the mines could absorb at least some landless Afrikaners into a regular working population. The Afrikaner political leaders were now willing to listen to the advice and demands of major mining

151

investors – whereas President Kruger had been more attentive to the interests of speculative capitalists seeking short-term profits.

President Kruger and his administration had also thought of using the mines in order to diversify the economy of the landlocked republic. German capital, for example, was encouraged to build railway systems connecting Pretoria and Johannesburg to the coast, offering an alternative to the Cape and Natal railway systems. Again, a concession was granted to some speculative investors who were permitted to distill alcohol – since it was obvious that a large male population of miners would be willing to buy a great quantity of liquor. Eerste Fabrieken – the First Factory of the Republic – was actually a distillery. Van Onselen has described this venture vividly, noting how poisonous were many of the drinks which were produced, and how a mafia of illicit liquor suppliers grew up in Johannesburg. The distillery was not a great success, but it was clearly an attempt at some kind of economic diversification and small-scale industry.

A similar enterprise was the dynamite concession, whereby speculative businessmen were allowed to manufacture dynamite for sale to the mines. Here again, profits were made but dynamite was not in fact produced: instead, the concession holder imported dynamite, repacked it in new boxes, and simply sold it at an increased price. Both these ventures may be seen as incompetent attempts at diversification – and both were abolished when the British took control of the Transvaal after the war.

If republican officials had been trying, ineffectually, to diversify the republican economy, then colonial officials were not keen on diversification at all. They attached supreme importance to cheap factors of production, to enable the mines to make profits and expand their operations. Accordingly, railway rates were reduced, the dynamite and liquor monopolies abolished, and customs barriers lowered, all to improve the profitability of gold mining. In that political climate, it was unlikely that the mine-owners would invest outside the mining industry at all, except in a very few kinds of activity which were directly beneficial to the mines. Machinery was imported rather than manufactured at Johannesburg, although some repairs were done on the spot. Similarly, the government railways system had locomotive repair yards, but did not attempt to manufacture rails or engines or carriages. Mine-owners did put some money into brewing of beer (a very profitable investment, and less dangerous than the 'whisky' and 'gin' of the republican era); but most of their investment outside mining went into land for future prospecting and possible mining development.

Cape Town and Johannesburg were the major manufacturing centres: not much manufacturing went on there, but even less occurred elsewhere. The 'second Rand' failed to appear in Zambesia, and the very small-scale mining operations of the 1890s and 1900s did not require an industrial infrastructure to maintain them. The other settler societies were equally backward in attempting any industrial process except the processing of agricultural items like sugar; and in any event the southern African market was both small and easily accessible from Britain.

It is this state of affairs which some scholars describe as 'dependency': the southern African colonies produced mainly those exports which could readily be sold in western Europe; they made little attempt to process any goods which could be imported from industrial economies; and control over the means of production, over banking facilities, and over transportation, rested in the hands of overseas capitalists. During the first years of this century, when British colonial authorities were in direct control of most of the region, many more links were forged between southern African primary producers and British manufacturers and investors – German competition for southern African markets was now at a great disadvantage. That kind of dependency was not modified by the grant of self-government in the ex-republics, nor by the formation of Union. Generals Botha and Smuts were content to leave the structure of the economy in much the same condition as they found it, relying heavily upon Britain for capital, markets, and shipping and banking services. When the Great War broke out therefore, more than half of all southern African imports came from Britain, and almost 90 per cent of all exports went there. So little industrial development had taken place that South Africa ranked with New Zealand in terms of the value of industrial production – six million South Africans manufactured only as much as one million New Zealanders, and New Zealand was certainly not a major industrial economy. The beginning of industrialisation in southern Africa was a much later event.

Gold mining was no longer an enclave activity, unrelated to the rest of the southern African economy; and yet for many years from the beginning of this century there were very few links between gold mining and the rest of the South African economy. Skilled labour at the beginning of the century was almost always performed by first-generation white immigrants, few of whom intended to live and die in the country: unskilled labour was performed largely by migrants from Mozambique, Lesotho and other territories: but that situation changed as Afrikaners and Union Africans were also drawn into the mining industry. More strikingly, for the first forty years of gold mining, little industrial activity flowed from it. The mining industry itself remained rather stable until the end of the Great War, in the sense that the numbers of workers, and the amount of gold produced, remained the same from 1910 to 1920 – and the proportion of white to black labour also remained fairly constant at about one to eight. During the Great War however, the London price of gold increased by 50 per cent, and more generous

One of 1300 armed policeman employed in Johannesburg to keep order during the 1922 strikes is seen here protecting a 'blackleg' tramcar driver

terms of employment could be offered to white workers – although black workers made hardly any gains, and the increased cost of living made them relatively poorer than before the war.

When the Great War came to an end, and the price of gold returned to its pre-war level, there were serious difficulties among mine labourers. Black miners were the worst off, and the first to strike (in 1920). That strike was suppressed by armed force. In the following year, the continued decline of the gold price encouraged the Chamber of Mines (on behalf of mine-owners and managers) to propose a lower proportion of white workers in the mining work force. When negotiations between the Chamber and the white miners' unions failed, violence broke out, reaching a climax in a rebellion by white miners in the first weeks of 1922. That insurrection – the Rand Revolt – was also suppressed by military force, and the mine managers did reduce the proportion of whites (and the wage rates of many of them), and deployed black miners in more responsible positions. The 1924 election, however, brought to power a coalition of Afrikaner nationalists and white workers, which modified the mine-owners' success, protecting white workers from some of the consequences of their unsuccessful insurrection.

Manufacturing

More important perhaps than the new government's intervention in the mining industry, was its attempt to promote industrial diversification. The difficulty of war-time transport had meant that manufacturing had expanded in order to replace scarce imported goods. At the end of the war, however, this trend had not been encouraged. Most manufacturing was of a very simple nature, putting the finishing touches to goods processed overseas. If the new government's white supporters were to be found jobs, energetic measures were needed. Protective tariffs were made higher, in spite of the risk of upsetting British and other western European governments; and in 1928 the state established the Iron and Steel Corporation (ISCOR), to produce heavy industrial goods which private capital had been unable to make. The finance for this investment – and for the increased numbers of whites employed in government institutions – was drawn from the taxes paid by the gold-mining industry, whose owners were not at all pleased to support local industrial development. The existence of the mining industry had created very little industrial diversification; it was state intervention which lay at the basis of the industrialisation process.

Meanwhile the structure of the mining industry itself had changed quite drastically. Diamond mining was beset by rivalry among De Beers, Premier, and the South West African producers (as well as smaller producers elsewhere in Africa), and this rivalry had led to a truce in 1914, but there was always a risk that competition would break out again, leading to lower diamond prices on the world market. In 1917 the Anglo-American Corporation was established, under the direction of Ernest Oppenheimer. During the next dozen years the Corporation steadily bought diamond-mining shares, until 1929 when Oppenheimer became chairman of De Beers, as well as controller of South West African diamond mining and an influential share-holder in every other major diamond-mining company. By that time Oppenheimer enjoyed the kind of control over diamonds which Rhodes had enjoyed in the 1890s, except that diamond mining was by now a much larger and more complex industry. Oppenheimer outdid Rhodes in the other dimension of Anglo-American expansion. Beginning with parcels of shares in the eastern end of the Witwatersrand, the Corporation steadily bought further shares until it became, during the 1920s, the single largest and most powerful gold-mining corporation. Oppenheimer was not only the new Rhodes of diamonds, he was also the new Wernher & Beit of gold mining. As these two sets of interests were integrated with each other during the 1940s, an unprecedented degree of control over mining capital was achieved. Naturally, this consolidation required colossal sums of money. Just as Rhodes had relied upon western European finance for the creation of De Beers, so Oppenheimer relied upon capital from the United States as well as London, and enjoyed the backing of some of the most famous and powerful capitalist firms in the world, including J. P. Morgan and the Guaranty Trust.

The consolidation of mining capital, and the clear dominance enjoyed by Anglo-American, had decided consequences throughout southern Africa and beyond. Diamond mining in Angola, Zaire and Tanzania, for example, was affected by Anglo-American control over marketing. The beginning of large-scale copper mining in what is now Zambia, during the late 1920s and 1930s, was financed by Anglo-American. Diamonds were the leading export from Namibia – and Namibian diamonds were Anglo-American. Outside South Africa itself, there was little risk that the state would tax mining in order to promote manufacturing. Colonial administrations were only too pleased to attract foreign investment, and extremely unwilling to antagonise foreign investors by using them as stepping stones towards other kinds of economic development.

By the 1930s, then, the South African gold-mining industry had become the centre-piece of mining operations throughout southern Africa, setting wage rates for black and for white workers, determining the proportion of each to be employed, and therefore having a profound influence upon employment practices throughout the regional economy. The gold mines themselves, however, were languishing. The price was once again fixed, the volume of production and the numbers of labourers employed were increasing only at a very slow pace. When the world-wide depression began in 1929, not only were luxury goods like diamonds affected, but at first the gold mines were badly affected as well. Only in 1931, when the South African Government (later than most other governments, including Britain) left the gold standard (and therefore allowed currency to devalue against gold), was this situation arrested. The price of gold nearly doubled in the next ten years, the volume of production increased by a third, and the number of workers employed almost doubled. Even more dramatic was the expansion of manufacturing activity, especially as ISCOR came into production and made possible a variety of other industrial processes which required steel. By the end of the 1930s the social category of 'poor white' had been effectively abolished: 21 000 new jobs in mining, and 56 000 new jobs in manufacturing, had taken care of almost all the Afrikaners ejected from the countryside and unemployed in the towns.

The early 1930s gave evidence of a decided transformation of the southern African economy as a whole. As gold mining expanded, so white employment was assured, and the remaining privileges of the labour aristocracy survived. The expansion of gold mining in the early 1930s has continued to the present day, with few interruptions. The rapid growth of manufacturing, which also dates from the mid-1930s, has also persisted with few interruptions. Some scholars regard the early 1930s therefore as the date of the 'take-off' into sustained economic growth. More realistically, we should notice that the growth of industry (including heavy industry) was a consequence of deliberate state intervention, in spite of the preference of mining capitalists for concentration upon mining alone. Mining did lead to manufacturing, but only after more than half a century, and only because the state insisted on diverting revenue. Indeed some mining enterprises were promoted by manufacturing, rather than the other way round: as industry developed, and as railway and shipping services expanded, there was an increased demand for coal throughout southern Africa; and coal mining in northern Natal, the Transvaal and Rhodesia expanded to meet this demand.

In the 1930s other drastic economic trends were observed, which would also affect the whole sub-continent. For nearly a generation, the mines had been prohibited from recruiting labour from tropical Africa. The depression, and the sheer difficulty of raising revenue in the tropical African colonies, helped to persuade colonial authorities to permit labour recruiting as far north as Malawi, northern Mozambique, and throughout the Rhodesias. The availability of fresh sources of labour averted problems in southern Africa itself, where the shortage of African labour was so

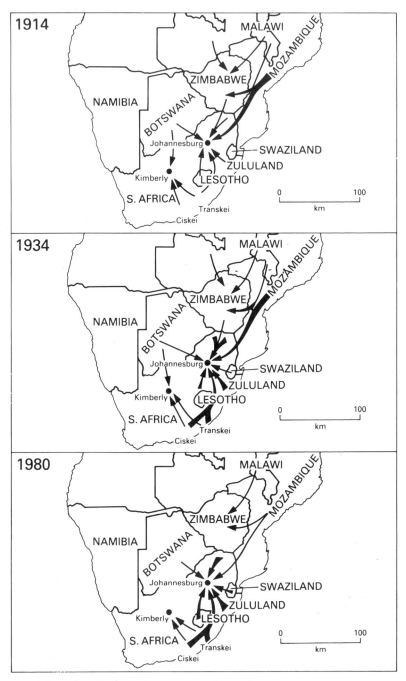

Map 8 Patterns of labour migration in southern Africa in 1914, 1939 and 1980

severe that African wage levels actually improved relative to white wages. During the 1930s and 1940s then, the regional division of labour became entrenched: white farmers did not have to compete directly with the mines, and the bulk of mining labour was drawn from well beyond South Africa's borders. In this way, the steady evolution of capitalist agriculture on white land was able to continue without having to cope with landless whites (absorbed into mining and manufacturing) or with competition for black labour.

Meanwhile some of South Africa's neighbours – notably Mozambique, Malawi and Lesotho – based their whole economic strategies upon regular labour migration. Offices of labour recruiting organisations could be found everywhere from the Zaire border to the eastern Cape, creating a regional dependence upon the South African mining industry which has proved very difficult to break. Copper mining in Northern Rhodesia, gold and coal mining in Southern Rhodesia, and diamond mining on the Skeleton Coast of Namibia, represented the only extensive opportunities for wage labour throughout the whole of British central and southern Africa or Mozambique.

Through the development of manufacturing and the proliferation of state employment, which workers had a measure of choice in whether or not to work in the mines. Through the expansion of the labour reservoir for black labour, the possible bargaining position of Africans was undermined, and in any case black workers suffered legal disabilities which will be considered in the next chapter. The consequences of this unequal leverage may be seen in the evolution of wage rates. In cash terms, for example, white average wages rose from £333 in 1911 to £800 in 1951 – and in real terms, taking account of the depreciating value of money, white workers were perhaps 10 per cent better off. In cash terms, African average wages were £29 in 1911, and £55 in 1951 – and in real terms they were perhaps 10 per cent worse off. Now this is important not only for miners themselves, but also because of the pervasive influence which miners' wages have had on every other sector of the labour market. It was the model of the mines' wage rates which came to be adopted by manufacturers, and therefore the ratio of at least 10 to 1 in white to black wages was entrenched in manufacturing just as it was in the mining industry.

In the second half of the nineteenth century, manufacturing scarcely existed in southern Africa, and mining investment was often a matter of gambling. Once the mining industry became a permanent feature of the regional economy, and a framework of legislation and employment patterns was laid down, the state was able to divert mining revenue towards the sponsorship of manufacturing. By the time that industrial development began, however, the mining industry had shown that it was possible to organise an extremely modern and large-scale productive enterprise on the basis of a sharply divided labour force. The vast majority were recruited on humiliating terms at derisory wage levels, transforming their rural homelands into dependencies whose main export was labour itself. Once this had been shown to be possible, manufacturing investors and industrialists insisted on substantially the same social relations of production in their own new enterprises. We have also suggested that mining 'led' to manufacturing only through the determination of the state that this should happen. In some ways the 1924 Pact government seemed to be a threat to mining capital, since it represented Afrikaners on the land, white workers in urban and mining areas, and the white unemployed, none of whom had a high opinion of mining capitalists. As it happened, the aggression of the Pact government was deflected from the mining industry. The gains made by employers before and during the Rand Revolt of 1922 were not entirely eroded (though the security and conditions of employment of white miners who survived that attack were indeed entrenched). Rather the need to find employment for the government's supporters involved the promotion of manufacturing as an alternative source of employment.

At no stage were Africans able to take advantage of the crises in mining and manufacturing. Their strikes – in 1920 and again on a massive scale in 1946 – were suppressed even more abruptly than the white miners' revolt of 1922; and when direct industrial action failed, they were unable to influence the political processes. Since the evolution of mining, and of manufacturing, as well as the victory of white capitalist agriculture over peasant producers, all seem to flow from state action, it is now time that we turned our attention to the South African state, and its internal evolution, and the relationships between the South African state and other political institutions in southern Africa.

Chapter 13

Entrenching the post-colonial state

The centre piece of southern African history in the twentieth century has been the South African state, the Union of four British colonies which assumed the status of a British Dominion from 1910 until 1961, and has been a Republic since that time. That state has caused astonishment throughout its life. In Europe there was amazement from 1910 onwards that Afrikaner generals behaved as loyal ministers of the British Crown. Among Africans at the time, and ever since then, there has been disbelief that a racially-defined minority should be permitted (and should be able) to exercise power over a disfranchised majority for generation after generation. By the 1960s a large number of people throughout the world found it difficult to recognise the South African state as at all legitimate.

The Afrikaner generals who held the centre of the political stage in the early years of this century were not simply opportunists: in their different ways they expressed a genuine commitment to the welfare of the Afrikaner people. By the time they came to power, however – in 1907 and 1908 in the ex-republics, 1910 in the Union itself – the structure of the colonial states had already been cemented by colonial officials, and the simplest way of bringing the four colonies together was to emphasise features shared in common between them, which is to say mainly the institutions which they had all acquired from the colonial past. As practical politicians, Botha and Smuts and Hertzog accepted the world more or less as they found it, and were willing to believe that institutions which permitted them to win elections could not be entirely bad. They were not visionaries (visionaries would hardly have been able to win elections), so they had no very clear idea of how a state could be run better than by British colonial institutions.

In the new constitution, the link with the British Crown was symbolised by a Governor-General – usually a British politician or a junior member of the Royal family – whose job was largely ceremonial, but who also kept the British and the Union Governments in regular communication with each other. Since the Governor-General was also (until the 1930s) High Commissioner responsible for the territories of Lesotho, Botswana and Swaziland, and indirectly responsible for Rhodesia as well, his office constantly reminded the South African ministers of the imperial context in which they also operated. Britain retained responsibility for the Union's foreign affairs, not only by constitutional right, but more importantly through being the great power most closely connected to the Union. The Union Jack which fluttered over the Union's official buildings was a further reminder of the limits of South African sovereignty; and so perhaps were the pounds, shillings and pence which served as currency. The Union cabinet could have modified many of these symbols and some of the substance of the imperial relationship, but in general the advantages of that link were seen to outweigh the disabilities. As soon as Botha and Smuts came to power in 1907 they were faced by an interruption of gold mining because of a strike among white miners. They chose to keep the mines in operation by breaking the strike, and therefore they called upon the British Army garrison. For the next six years that British garrison proved its worth to the South African authorities, assisting in the devastation of Zululand for the Natal colonial government, and in suppressing further strikes in the Transvaal. It was not until after the 1913 strike that the Union initiated its own Defence Force to replace the British garrison: and even then the Union relied upon reinforcements from the British Army, and upon the Royal Navy to protect the sea-routes around the Cape. The ministers, conscious of these links and their potential value, were in no hurry to move towards military and naval self-reliance.

The substance of political institutions was not, however, the representative of the King, but rather the representatives of the electors, sitting in two houses of parliament, and by majority vote in the lower house deciding which party should hold office. Of the two houses, the Senate was of little significance. It was merely a pale reflection of the lower House of Assembly, where most of the ministers had their seats. None of the features of the parliamentary system was peculiar to South Africa. Throughout the self-governing colonies of the empire, a cabinet held office only so long as it commanded a majority of votes in the lower house, and the powers of the upper house were everywhere inferior to those of the lower house, where all financial bills had to be initiated and passed. Even the most famous feature of the South African parliament – its reservation for members of European descent – was very similar to Australian constitutional practice at that time. Whereas Aboriginals and Torres Strait Islanders were only a small minority within Australia, however, it was the whites who were a decided minority within the South African political community. Those African and coloured voters who had been enfranchised in the Cape retained the right to vote for members of the Union House of Assembly, though they could not be elected themselves.

It was widely assumed that the Cape electoral provisions would spread to the other provinces, after Union. Instead, the Cape tradition has itself been eliminated. The Cape franchise was the product of a long evolution during colonial days. It was supported not only by those Africans and coloureds who were enfranchised, but also by a variety of white politicians described rather vaguely as 'liberal' – professional men and merchants for the most part, who saw the Cape franchise as symbolising the gradual assimilation of coloured and African citizens towards a full equality. These men were on the way out in politics by the beginning of the twentieth century: some were appointed judges, and a few went into exile overseas, and when they left parliament they were not replaced by men with similar enthusiasms. Instead, the powerful drive towards white capitalist farming, and towards the discovery of urban and mining jobs for landless whites, brought men of quite different enthusiasms into parliament. The most famous Cape liberal (and perhaps the last of political significance) was John X. Merriman, Prime Minister of the Cape at the time of Union, passed over when the first Union Prime Minister was being selected, and spending the last years of his political career on the back benches. In brief, the Cape franchise soon ceased to be seen as an 'advanced' institution which other provinces could adopt, and instead began to seem like a relic of some forgotten era.

The state included not only the holders of political office, but also a very elaborate bureaucracy drawn from the four colonial bureaucracies which had developed before Union: teachers, lawyers, police, engineers, agronomists and economists staffing the specialised departments, each department the responsibility of a cabinet minister. Botha was very appreciative of some of the Transvaal bureaucrats – especially the agricultural experts – and brought them into the Union public service to perform their old functions on a much larger scale. A high proportion of this mainly white bureaucracy were English-speakers; and opinion in the cabinet was divided on how far and how fast to introduce Afrikaners into these careers; but the politicians agreed that this inherited bureaucracy needed only a little modification. In the separate colonies the bureaucrats had proved their ability to carry out political instructions and their willingness to adapt to new political masters. There seemed no particular urgency in overhauling the machinery of the state.

To describe the institutions of the state is not to explain how it worked, since that depended mainly on political forces outside the state itself. Members of the lower house were elected by the adult, male, white population (except in the Cape where a minority of electors were coloured or African); and the constitution allowed rural constituencies to be 15 per cent smaller than average, while urban constituencies could be 15 per cent larger. The effect of this provision (which was common in many other British colonies) was to give a marginal advantage to rural voters. When the first elected lower house convened in Cape Town, a majority of members adhered to the new South African Party, a coalition of all the Afrikaner parties from the separate colonies. Most of the Natal members had no strong party affiliation, and were content to support the SAP. Against the government stood the Unionist Party – a coalition of non-Afrikaner politicians, led by leaders of the mining industry – and the small Labour Party representing the organised white working class. No Afrikaners sat on the opposition benches: only a few English-speakers sat on the government side. Yet this arrangement did not accurately reflect the linkages within the political community. Mine-owners and managers might sit on the opposition side, but they were confident that the Prime Minister would listen to their demands with sympathy; there were better relationships between mine-owners and the state, for example, than between Unionists and leaders of the Labour Party. At least as important were divisions within the SAP. Botha's political experience had taught him that the Progressives were not to be feared, and that the imperial connection could be very convenient. The hope of incorporating Swaziland or Rhodesia, and placing on that land some of the landless Afrikaners of the rural Transvaal, reinforced his attachment to the imperial factor; and his experience with the colonial bureaucracy made him reluctant to tamper with it. By contrast, Hertzog's political experience in the Orange Free State led him to emphasise the need to assist impoverished Afriakaners, and to underestimate the value of imperial relations. Within the SAP were also Cape politicians whose experience of the qualified franchise, and whose personal relations with some African political leaders, made them uncomfortable with the more explicit racism of the northern Afrikaners. However, perhaps the most urgent disagreement within the SAP cabinet was between those who considered that electoral victory was merely a stepping stone towards a new Afrikaner republic with fewer links to Britain, and those who considered it more important to conciliate imperial interests and the English-speaking opposition.

Politicians who sought to gain and to hold a parliamentary majority had to attend to the demands of the three political movements represented in parliament: white landowners, the white working class, and the mainly English-speaking members whose interests were linked to the mining industry. These three movements could be brought into harmony, but only with great effort and on a very fragile basis. And their interests could not be harmonised at all, if the further demands of educated Africans, or Indians, or the African working class or the peasants were attended to. From the inception of Union, therefore, ministers of the cabinet worked in two main directions: seeking ways to satisfy the demands of the major white political interests, and developing means of coercing the rest of the population. The 1911 Mines and Works Act, for example, gave Union-wide effect to the job colour bar which was already in force in the Transvaal mines. However, it did not satisfy the labour aristocracy in the mining industry, always nervous of being diluted in numbers and in wages by the wider employment of black miners. In the middle of 1913 Johannesburg miners went on strike, won concessions from the state, and organised themselves for a further strike. In the interval, the government mobilised the Union Defence Force, and in January 1914 when a strike broke out again, the UDF marched into Johannesburg, aimed cannon at the miners' headquarters, broke up the strike and deported the leaders of the movement. If the mine-owners were satisfied by this demonstration of state support, the labour aristocracy was outraged – and in any case it was black miners whose interests were most seriously affected. Not only were a range of semi-skilled and skilled jobs permanently barred to them, but the mining industry was now better able to control black wage levels through agreement among employers. White miners and their working class allies could now organise themselves politically – and they did so very efficiently, winning the Transvaal provincial elections in 1914 for instance – but no such alternative was available to blacks.

The government moved from the mining industry's needs to those of white farmers, introducing and enacting the Native Land Act in 1913 which, as we have seen, consolidated the control of white landowners over their land, and made it almost impossible for African agricultural tenants to survive, unless they agreed to become wage labourers. Yet even this draconian measure was insufficient to satisfy landowners entirely. During 1912 Hertzog had been squeezed out of the cabinet, for expressing anti-imperial sentiments which upset English-speaking whites; and in January 1914 the Nationalist Party formed itself around him, in opposition to the governing South African Party. The Nationalists had their heartland in Hertzog's Orange Free State, whereas the SAP continued to be popular in the Transvaal, where the alliance between gold and maize had first emerged, and where landowners had gained the most advantage from that alliance. Once established, however, the Nationalist Party won support in the other provinces, wherever the sentiments of republicanism or the needs of Afrikaners were thought to be at risk. In any case, if politics was the art of balancing three major interest groups, inevitably those three groups would tend to crystallise out, the better to press their demands.

The outbreak of the Great War in 1914 provoked a further re-alignment of the party system. Constitutionally, South Africa was at war with Germany as soon as King George V declared war. The government was anxious to demonstrate its imperial loyalty,

General Hertzog's cabinet, 1924. Hertzog is in the front row, third from left. Centre at the front is Governor-General, the Earl of Athlove

and attacked German forces in South West Africa. Not all Afrikaners felt so committed: a detachment of the UDF crossed the border to join the Germans; other Afrikaners rebelled and attempted to declare a republic; Hertzog and his supporters sought neutrality. The government's decision to send an army to occupy South West Africa alienated many of its earlier supporters. And in 1915 when elections were held, the Nationalists won 26 of the 130 seats, forcing the SAP (54) into a tacit alliance with the Unionists (40) in order to be sure of a majority. The powerful Labour Party was, for the moment, so badly divided on the war issue, that it won only four seats. Meanwhile the easy conquest of South West Africa was followed by Smuts' participation in the East African campaign, which persisted to the end of the war, and which was much more difficult to explain in terms of purely South African interests.

By the end of the war, then, the South African Government was an active (and publicly honoured) participant in the British imperial alliance – but losing the sympathy of the Afrikaner constituencies. White landowners were inclined to believe that they could gain even more from Hertzog than from the SAP (especially after Botha died in 1919, leaving the leadership to the more aloof Smuts); white labour was alienated by the manifest influence of mine-owners over the SAP; the government depended increasingly upon the tolerance of the official opposition Unionists; and outside parliament African opinion was not only hostile, but (by the end of the war) increasingly self-confident, vocal and assertive.

During the 1920s the state modified its shape and its purpose in response to opposition groups. Black opposition was suppressed by the police, by the UDF, and by white volunteers, both in rural areas and in the urban areas which were rapidly attracting a permanent black population. African opinion could not be conciliated without antagonising the parliamentary parties, so an elaborate machinery of pass laws and a reinforced police force were called into existence. Black demands for land, for freedom of movement and association, or for a living wage, were met by force. The government was inclined to respond in much the same high-handed fashion when white workers threatened the peace. During the crisis of 1921–2, when mine managers determined to reduce the proportion and the wage levels of the white miners, the state supported management. The white workers took their revenge in 1924, when the Labour party won 18 seats and – as junior partner to Hertzog's Nationalist Party – displaced the SAP (and the Unionists who had now joined it) from government.

Both the Nationalists and Labour had expressed a vague anti-capitalism in the election, and the Nationalists had linked that issue to anti-imperialism. In reality the new government was caught in the same triangular network which had paralysed the SAP. The white working class was becoming Afrikaner in its ethnic

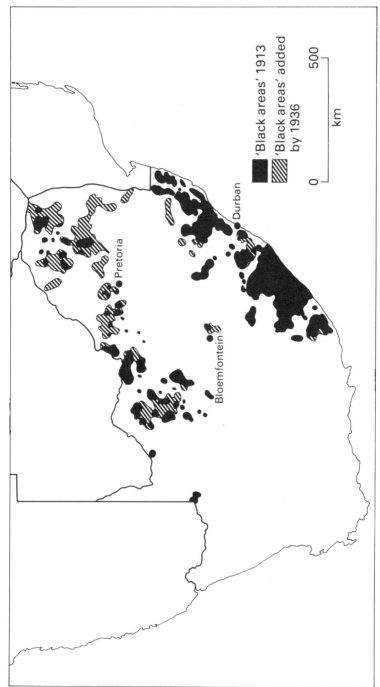

Map 9 South Africa: 'Native Reserves', 1913 and 1936

'Black areas' 1913

'Black areas' added by 1936

0   500
        km

Durban

Pretoria

Bloemfontein

composition, and the coalition partners were anxious to relieve the misery of the unemployed poor whites. However, white unemployment was not to be relieved by attacking capital investment, nor by untying the imperial connection. Instead, the Pact government entrenched the position of those white miners who had kept their jobs despite the retrenchment of 1921; it attempted to create new job opportunities in manufacturing, and through the reservation of jobs in the public service; and the general loosening of commonwealth constitutional links satisfied the demand for greater autonomy. Now these measures irritated mining capitalists, but did not drive them out of business: the real victims were blacks whose lives were hedged around by an ever-increasing network of economic, political and social constraints. Two slogans were used to justify the policies – 'civilised labour' to ensure a living wage for a large range of white workers, and 'segregation' to exclude blacks from jobs, from permanent urban residence, and from many social and economic opportunities. In brief, the Pact government set about controlling the rapid urbanisation and diversification of the economy, ensuring that blacks should take part in these processes only on terms which were acceptable to employers and to white workers.

Since the Pact government refrained from any direct assault on existing capital investment, and its own legislative programme was soon enacted, the parliamentary divisions were increasingly irrelevant. Black – or any other – militancy could be controlled by the Riotous Assemblies Act (1927); the network of pass laws limited the mobility of African men; the government was committed to industrial development, symbolised by its establishment of ISCOR – what else was there to argue about? Feelers were put out from both sides of the parliamentary division, and eventually during 1933 and 1934 the existing parties merged into the United South African National Party, with Hertzog as Prime Minister and Smuts as his deputy, and only a few diehard imperial loyalists (the Dominion Party) and republicans (the Purified Nationalists) remaining outside the grand coalition or Fusion. For a while it seemed as if the absolute unity of the white population was within reach, since the new party included representatives of white labour, mining capital, and landowners. The stage was set for a final, and comprehensive, strategy to deal with the majority of the population.

The package of legislation which passed through parliament in 1936 dealt with two dimensions of African life which seemed as yet unclear. Industrial relations had been clarified by the solidification of the industrial colour bar, and arbitration procedures which ignored African unions; the lives of urban Africans were determined by pass laws and residential segregation, a structure which assumed that Africans were inherently rural and came to town only for limited periods of employment in limited capacities. What remained unclear was how African rural area were to be controlled, and how Africans were to relate to the political system. The Native Trust and Land Act committed the government to acquire further land for African occupation – on a scale which would eventually bring about 13 per cent of the South African land surface under African occupation. The Representation of Natives Act removed Cape Africans from the common voters' roll, and provided for their separate representation in both houses of parliament. The government was unmoved by the massive opposition of Africans to each of these measures. The value of African (and coloured) votes had already been cut in half by the enfranchisement of white (but not black) women in 1930; they possessed far too little electoral power to divert the Fusion government from its purposes. At the same time a Native Representative Council was set up, whose members could advise the government on matters concerning Africans – but whose advice could be ignored. Created in defiance of African opinion, the NRC was most unlikely to influence future government policy.

Demonstrating its disregard for African opinion, and abolishing white poverty, the Fusion government had little to fear from parliamentary opposition. The Purified Nationalists were slow to gather Afrikaners to their republican banner, the Dominion Party could hardly expect to win many seats except in Natal, and white trades unionists saw little point in breaking with a government which guaranteed not only jobs but also incomes.

Once again it was war which prompted a re-alignment of parliamentary parties. When world war broke out again in 1939, Hertzog (again) attempted to keep South Africa neutral, but a majority of the United Party (and a narrow majority of parliament) supported Smuts and the Allies. Hertzog's faction of the United Party was eventually merged into the Purified Nationalists under Dr D. F. Malan's leadership. During the war, the drain of manpower into the armed forces placed a strain on mining and manufacturing, and led to a discreet employment of Africans in a wider range of jobs than had been available in the 1930s – but the government still outlawed any strike action by African unions. Although the government supported the Atlantic Charter with its resoundingly democratic aspirations – and the government was accused by Afrikaner nationalists of jeopardising white security on that account – in reality the state remained firmly committed to preserving the existing pattern of race relations. That policy was good enough to win the general election of 1943, when the Nationalist opposition was itself divided: but in the long run it has never been sufficient for a political party merely to preserve the status quo.

When general elections were called again in 1948, the Nationalists had a programme summed up in the vague term 'apartheid', which served just as well as Hertzog's slogan of 'segregation' in 1924; and by the narrowest of majorities, Malan's Nationalists came to power with the support of the survivors of Hertzog's faction. The Nationalist Party has won every subsequent election, and since 1948 the shifts in government policy have owed nothing to the interaction of political parties in parliament, and everything to strategic and tactical decisions made within the Nationalist Party to meet the increasingly committed opposition of extra-parliamentary forces.

In retrospect, three circumstances may be seen to have favoured the entrenchment of a state explicitly committed to racial separation wherever possible. One of these is the 1910 constitution, which by enfranchising all adult white males, ensured that the interests of landowners, of white workers, and of the capital invested in mines (and then in manufacturing) would persistently demand attention. Conversely, the exclusion of all but a handful of the coloured and African population from participation in politics guaranteed that the burden of white demands would be carried by the disfranchised majority. Second, the over-representation of rural white voters ensured that landowners would hold a disproportionate share of political power. Conversely, the increasing Afrikaner proportion of the white population, and the steady drift of Afrikaners into urban employment, ensured that mainly rural political parties would possess a bridgehead to urban constituencies, which were in any case liable to be divided between working class and lower middle class interests. Third, the constitutional and political link with imperial Britain proved to be a source of stability to the political system, rather than a means of changing it. African appeals to Westminster were always turned away empty-handed; and imperial officials made sure that South Africa's neighbours, under colonial administrations of various kinds, would not embarrass the Union government. As each new anti-imperial government came to office – in 1910, in 1924, and then in 1948 – it turned from hostility to acquiescence in the imperial relationship. Though Afrikaners held office from 1910 onwards, it took half a century for the republic to come into being: the imperial links were allowed to fade away, rather than being snapped.

The cost of such a political process, however, was the persistent and ruthless alienation of the whole disfranchised population; not only Africans, but equally Indians (despite the representations of the Indian Government on their behalf) and coloureds (culminating in the removal of coloured voters from the common roll during the early 1950s). The impossibility of conciliating black interests meant a massive expansion of the forces of internal repression, until there was hardly a branch of government which was not directly involved in maintaining control over the black majority, whether in the rural reserves, or on white farms, or in the shanty towns and mining compounds.

In this sense, many of the Nationalist government's measures of the 1950s merely put the finishing touches to machinery which already existed. Racially mixed marriages were banned – but inter-racial sexuality had already been prohibited by the Immorality Act of 1927. The Population Registration machinery of the 1950s merely made it more difficult for individuals to sneak across the barriers of race which already existed. The provision of different syllabi for African school children (and then the provision of separate universities for different races in the late 1950s) took to a logical conclusion the actual segregation which already prevailed in almost every school in the country. The disenfranchisement of coloureds followed logically from the earlier removal of Africans to separate electoral rolls and representation. All of these measures were implicit in the 1910 constitution, and in the interaction of political forces represented by that document.

By the 1950s, then, all three enfranchised white groups had seized the opportunities presented to them by the constitution, and had entrenched their interests very deeply. The white working class – by now overwhelmingly Afrikaner – shared power in a government committed to protecting their jobs and their wage levels. White landowners had clear title to most of the land, and coercive powers over the rural labour force. International capital was reconciled (mainly by the state's manifest and ruthless control over unskilled labour) to taxes which subsidised and protected manufacturing industry. A fearsome battery of uniformed forces and bureaucrats and repressive laws controlled the lives of the population. Two circumstances, however, made it necessary for the government to seek a fresh approach to political institutions: the deterioration of South Africa's international position, and the massive development of internal opposition. A constitutional arrangement which was not very unusual in 1910 had become – by the middle of the century – offensive abroad, and intolerable at home.

Chapter 14

South Africa's regional hegemony

From its inception in 1910, the Union government enjoyed wide influence in the southern African region, for a number of reasons: its military power, its economic strength, and the capital invested in it and through it. On the other hand, South Africa's neighbours remained formally the dependencies of European imperial powers; and even in the smallest and most isolated of these dependencies, the permanent inhabitants were not merely cyphers in their own affairs. It may be helpful to see each of these territories in the context of a triangular relationship, each involving its inhabitants, the imperial power, and lastly the influence of the Union government.

Namibia (South West Africa)

The German conquest of Namibia (South West Africa) began with annexation in 1884, and was incomplete at the turn of the century. As in other German possessions (New Guinea and Tanganyika especially), a determined drive towards commodity production, by German settlers or by forced production, provoked substantial rebellions in the first years of this century. The Herero in central Namibia, and the Nama in the south, had both been forced to acknowledge German colonial authority, but as settlers and companies acquired land and cattle, both communities rebelled in defence of their remaining herds and pastures. They rebelled separately in 1904, and the cumulative effect of their rebellions interrupted production for at least three years. The military campaigns against them were ruthless, almost genocidal. Hostilities ended formally in 1907, apart from some small-scale guerilla operations. In 1907, then, the colonial authorities were strong enough to impose a brutal labour code, and to turn their attention to the dense agricultural settlements of Ovambo speakers along the northern border of the territory. Herero and Nama were left in

Chained Herero tribesmen taken prisoner by the Kaiser's troops, 1904

possession of their remaining lands and herds, while Ovambo labour was recruited into the large-scale diamond- and copper-mining ventures which flourished during the last years of German rule.

British and South African authorities were scarcely involved in these events. The Cape (and therefore South Africa) retained the harbour of Walvis Bay; but the Germans built their own harbour nearby at Luderitz Bay, to provide independent access to the sea. The territory attracted capital directly from Germany, and labour from within its own boundaries, and developed trading links directly with Hamburg. Although the economies of Namibia and South Africa were very similar, there were very few links between them. Even the diamond-mining companies were rivals rather than allies, at least until 1914.

When the Great War broke out, all German colonies were attacked from the closest British bases. Botha and Smuts mobilised the Union Defence Force, and rapidly overwhelmed the small detachments of Germans in Namibia. Conquest on behalf of Britain was followed by administration on behalf of the new League of Nations, under a system of mandates which camouflaged the expropriation of German colonies. The Union took over Namibia as a 'going concern', leaving most of the German settlers and traders in possession, but bringing in Afrikaners mainly as public servants. This approach to matters of state reassured the remaining settlers. Secondly it made it very difficult for the African communities to mount effective resistance. In 1922 for example, the small Bondelzwarts community rebelled; but the Union Defence Force attacked swiftly by land and by air, inflicting heavy casualties and bringing the rebellion to an abrupt end. Three years later a possible rebellion in the Rehoboth community was forestalled by the rapid mobilisation of the Union armed forces. Before long 'business as usual' resumed in the area, in the forms of settler pastoralism and mining with Ovambo migrant labour.

The generation between the wars was probably the high-water mark of Union control in the affairs of Namibia. The League of Nations supervised the mandate through the Permanent Mandates Commission, composed mainly of representatives of the great European colonial powers, who seldom asked difficult questions. The remaining Germans accepted the new regime, with a few nostalgic regrets; the Nama and Herero were little disturbed in their residual lands; and Ovambo labourers had no effective voice, whether through their chiefs at home, or on contract in mining compounds, or in the Katutura barracks outside Windhoek. Nothing was permanently settled, but there were no immediate challenges to South African authority. Nevertheless the incorporation of Namibia was far from complete. One element of distinctiveness was the survival of a German community which maintained educational and some mercantile links with Germany. More important, the bulk of the territory could only be exploited through pastoralism, and the Herero and Nama groups retained some autonomy on their own lands. The migrant labour system which enmeshed the Ovambo communities did not carry them outside Namibia itself. Although black Namibians and black South Africans shared many similar experiences, they did not share them together. Until the middle of this century, what happened in the mandated territory was not incorporation into South Africa, but rather a separate and parallel exploitation.

A concerted attempt at incorporation occurred only after the Second World War, by which time it was too late to be successful. The United Nations proposed a trusteeship system to replace the old League of Nations mandate system, and Smuts's government resisted such a move. In 1949 an open break occurred. Dr Malan's Nationalist Party government, with a slender parliamentary majority, formally incorporated Namibia. As a condition of incorporation, Namibia's white inhabitants were allowed to elect six members to the Union parliament (all of whom proved to be supporters of the Nationalist Party). Although the United Nations refused to acknowledge the incorporation, economic and social planning proceeded on the assumption that the incorporation would be permanent.

In order to legitimise the incorporation, the Union government began as early as 1946 to hold meetings at which the people were encouraged to request formal annexation. The whites, and especially the new Afrikaner residents, were firmly in favour. It is unlikely that many Africans favoured the loss of separate, mandate status; but there was an interesting pattern in the responses which were recorded. The public meetings which boldly rejected the Union government's advice were pastoralists, mainly Herero. No such embarrassments were recorded in meetings with agricultural peoples. It seems likely that the government's control over the agricultural communities, through the migrant labour system, and through the appointed chiefs, was quite tight, whereas pastoral communities still preserved some degree of economic and political autonomy. During the 1950s, when more explicit opposition was voiced, pastoral spokesmen were prominent among the petitioners to the United Nations: Ovambo opponents of the Union regime found it much harder to reach an international audience. Once the Ovambo spokesmen did make themselves heard, however – from the 1960s onwards – they moved rapidly to militant and uncompromising positions. These events will be treated in a later chapter. Here it is sufficient to note that the Union government proposed full annexation very late – so late in the day in fact that internal and international forces were able to impede these moves.

Mozambique

A long line of British officials and British colonists looked acquisitively at Mozambique from the 1890s onwards. Rhodes and several British Government officials were irritated that Mozambique prevented the complete encirclement of Kruger's Transvaal Republic. After Union in 1910, that argument became irrelevant, but Botha and Smuts inherited the old ambition to replace Portuguese by South African control. As late as 1919, during the settlement following the Great War, they hoped to squeeze the Portuguese out of southern Mozambique and (if necessary) hand over part of Tanganyika as compensation. Since Portugal had remained neutral during the Great War, however, there was no obvious pretext for a wholesale confiscation of territory, and the Portuguese managed to hold on. From the Union's point of view, matters could be a lot worse. Portugal had, after all, succeeded in conquering the Gaza kingdom in 1895, and a series of rebellions was put down in the early years of the twentieth century. The Portuguese authorities could clearly maintain some kind of colonial order. Portugal had neither the capital nor the manpower to transform Mozambique unaided, and Mozambique depended very heavily indeed on the Union economy, if any revenue was to be generated at all.

One of the essential elements of the colonial economy in Mozambique was hiring out African labour to Union employers, and especially to the Witwatersrand gold fields. This flow of labour was organised largely by chartered companies from the 1890s onwards, which enjoyed powers and privileges very similar to those of Rhodes's British South Africa Company. Their revenue came mainly from capitation fees charged for each Mozambican labourer recruited. The colonial state also benefited from this enterprise, since the capitation fees were payable in gold, and provided Portugal with much of its foreign exchange. The other essential element in the colonial economy was revenue from the railway line running from Maputo (Lourenço Marques) to Johannesburg. This was the shortest line to the sea from the mining centres, and it suited both the Portuguese and the mining industry to use it fully. In 1903, immediately after the South African War, the British and the Portuguese negotiated a *modus vivendi* – in effect an economic treaty – regulating both labour recruitment and proportions of railway traffic. With occasional modifications, that agreement survived until Mozambique's eventual independence. It acknowledged Portugal's dependence upon the South African economy, and it fixed the rewards which Portugal could win from its inert co-operation. Until Mozambique's independence, the relationship suited both governments. Some white South Africans distrusted the Portuguese policy of assimilating 'evolved' Africans into white colonial society; but they were comforted by the fact that a mere 5 000 Africans had achieved that status after four centuries of colonial interaction in south-east Africa.

The High Commission territories

At the time of the Great War, the British Government encouraged South African intervention in Namibia, and South African aspirations in Mozambique; but there was less enthusiasm for South African attempts to incorporate British dependencies in the region. Swaziland, Botswana (Bechuanaland) and Lesotho (Basutoland) were all listed in the Schedule to the Act of Union, as territories which might be added one day. English-speaking politicians in the Union were not very enthusiastic about transfer, but Afrikaner politicians tended to see the territories as potential land for white agriculture and pastoralism. As early as 1911, the Union government of Botha and Smuts requested the transfer of Swaziland. Botha's own closest supporters were farmers in the eastern Transvaal, some of whom owned land also in Swaziland, and many of whom saw Swaziland as their natural hinterland for expansion. Swaziland had been administered by the Transvaal in the 1890s, at least half of its land had been alienated to whites, and if Zululand could be added to Natal (in 1897), then why not Swaziland to the Union a generation later? To Botha and his followers, the case for annexation seemed overwhelming.

The Swazi chiefs naturally saw matters in a different light. From the 1890s they had protested against their being placed under the Transvaal, and they continued the tradition of resistance into the twentieth century. By the time of Union, Swazi chiefs were already aware of the Union's desire to incorporate their country, and of the likely disadvantages for them of such a move. Throughout the 1920s and the 1930s, the Swazi leaders opposed the notion of their country being transferred to formal control by South Africa, arguing in their petitions to the British Government that the Swazi objected to the numerous anti-African pieces of legislation operating in the Union. The British, always using the argument that they could not transfer any of the territories to South African control until the Union governments produced an acceptable African policy, could not dismiss the Swazi chiefs' objections lightly. However, although South Africa's political ambitions in Swaziland were frustrated, and although Swaziland therefore remained outside the Union, South Africa's economic expansionism during the first half of the twentieth century enabled it to control the destiny of Swaziland and resulted in the creation of what has been described as a 'dominance-dependence' relationship between South Africa and Swaziland today. To that extent, the Swazi chiefs' success was clearly rather limited.

South Africa had equally strong claims to Lesotho, which had been a part of the Cape in the 1870s, and which was entirely surrounded by the Union. In this case, however, the claims were pressed less resolutely. There was very little arable land in the territory, and the laws provided that the land could not be alienated from Sotho ownership. There were no obvious mineral resources to exploit, and even if any were found, South African mining capital could enter the territory without difficulty. There were, in other words, no obvious prizes to be won by incorporation, and in many ways it was convenient to leave the British Government to control a poor and sometimes turbulent society. The slight uncertainty as to the ultimate destiny of the Sotho people, however, reinforced the British Government's reluctance to attempt any measure of economic or social development. With the passage of time, therefore, the territorial economy sank ever deeper into dependence upon the wages of migrant labourers, to purchase food and other daily essentials. The Basutoland National Congress, representing the major chiefs of the kingdom, voiced opposition to incorporation whenever the issue arose: what they could not do was to mobilise the British authorities into serious planning for the territory's economic development.

The case of Botswana was (and remains) more complex. If Zimbabwe (Rhodesia) remained outside the Union, then Botswana and Zimbabwe might, under imperial guidance, provide a counterweight to Afrikaner and republican enthusiasms in the Union. Little land had been alienated to white settlers, but that land – the Tuli block – was closer to Bulawayo than to Pretoria. The BSA Company retained some vague rights, dating from Rhodes's duel with Kruger in the 1890s. All these circumstances pulled Botswana into a northern alignment, while most of its transport and economic links were to the south. If the uncertain future of the other High Commission territories encouraged inertia in British officials, the double uncertainty of Botswana's future promoted paralysis among officials.

Some Tswana enjoyed a flair for publicising their points of view. Paramount Chief Khama of the Ngwato was highly regarded by some British politicians at the turn of the century. Tshekedi Khama, regent of the Ngwato from 1926 until 1950, was highly literate, scholarly, and determined to preserve the territory's separate status. Transfer would certainly provoke hostile publicity in Britain. However, if the possibility of transfer was postponed, it was not ruled out by the British Government. Accordingly, the British officials would attempt nothing in Botswana which might differentiate the territory from its larger neighbour. Nor were any steps taken which might imply that transfer would never occur. If the Union government relied on British officials to maintain order in Botswana, the British also relied heavily on the Union for support.

This relationship was revealed quite dramatically in 1933, when the imperial government wished to overawe Tshekedi Khama. A naval detachment landed at Cape Town, and caught the train to Mafeking before setting out on a show of force on the fringe of the Kalahari desert. The need for South Africa's good will was also underlined by the fact that the administrative headquarters of the protectorate were in the little town of Mafeking, which was actually inside the Union. It is not very surprising, then, that as late as 1950 the British should depose Seretse Khama from the Ngwato paramount chieftaincy, as a punishment for marrying an English woman. His 'offence' was perfectly legal in British and in colonial law, but would have been illegal within the Union.

To avoid dependency, it was not enough to do nothing. The longer the territories languished in the backwaters of the regional economy, the harder it would be to emerge. One mechanism of Union control was the South African Customs Convention, initiated in 1903, and revised with few amendments until the present day. Union officials collected all customs duties at the coast, on goods destined both for the Union and for the protectorates. Customs revenue would then be distributed among the consenting governments in fixed proportions. This arrangement had the advantage of convenience, and in simple financial terms it may have been an advantage to all the participants. However, it also meant that the protectorate authorities had absolutely no control over the customs policies which regulated tariff levels. South African customs policy, for example, might aim to levy large duties on articles consumed mainly by Africans: it would certainly try to protect South African manufacturers from overseas competition. African consumers, and potential producers in the protectorates, could not be protected from South African economic policies. Similarly, the three small economies were entirely at the mercy of South African monetary policy (since they shared the same currency) and railway policy (since they had no harbours, nor could they build their own railways), and these policies were, of course, shaped by Union interest groups.

The protectorates also depended upon South African educational institutions for the secondary and higher education of young people – apart from a few who found their way to Britain or the United States. At Fort Hare University College these young people mingled with blacks from the Union itself, and from Central and East Africa, acquiring a better education than most universities provided between the wars. Conversely, some of the South African-educated elite attached themselves to the protectorate chiefs, as advisers in dealing with the Union government. The distinct identities of the territories were blurred by these exchanges, in much the same way that the meeting of migrant labourers in the mining compounds created some sense of a regional destiny distinct from the separate destinies of each territory. None wanted to be governed by the Union government: but that did not mean that they thought of the future as separate sovereign states.

Steadily, therefore, the protectorates were subordinated to the needs of South African capital and the South African state. Lesotho came to rely upon the earnings of thousands of young men (and smaller numbers of young women) on white farms and in the mining compounds. Smaller numbers of labourers were recruited from Botswana, and from Swaziland. In these cases, there were other mechanisms of dependency. Botswana's main source of income was the sale of beef, and Johannesburg was the obvious market. That market could be closed, by simply refusing to let Botswana beef enter the Union, through the (real or imagined) risk of animal disease entering the Union. Even if cattle were then smuggled across the border, the risk was great and the profits were reduced. Swaziland's agricultural and pastoral products were equally tied to the Johannesburg market, making the kingdom equally vulnerable to South African pressures. By the 1950s the idea of formal transfer was abandoned by Britain: but two generations of neglect and of subordination to South African economic interests had left the three High Commission territories in a weaker international position than they had experienced in the pre-colonial years.

The Rhodesias

The most important imperial piece of the southern African chessboard was Southern Rhodesia (Zimbabwe). In theory at least, the British authorities had three options in determining the fate of the Zambesian region. First, Southern Rhodesia could be added to the Union, where its white population might strengthen the non-Afrikaner forces at work in the electoral system. This option gradually faded away as the white Rhodesian population grew in size and in self-confidence. Second, Southern Rhodesia could become the centre-piece of an association of British dependencies, from Botswana through Northern Rhodesia (Zambia) to Nyasaland (Malawi). This option was occasionally considered but not implemented until the 1950s. Third, Southern Rhodesia (and to a lesser extent the neighbouring British dependencies) could be left under the control of the British South Africa Company. The only attraction of this unpopular system of administration was that it would save a great deal of money, needed to buy out the Company's chartered rights in the region. When the original charter expired in 1914, it was grudgingly renewed in London to run until 1923.

At the beginning of this century, the Company's financial prospects in Rhodesia were bleak. The 'second Rand' failed to appear, and small-scale mining companies were struggling to show a profit. Railways and the slow growth of urban centres at Salisbury (Harare) and Bulawayo did not immediately promote white agriculture or pastoralism, although some Shona and Ndebele producers benefited from the new market opportunities. Economic development through increased peasant production would be a slow process, yielding small returns on the Company's capital outlay. By about 1908 the Company had begun to implement a quite new policy, selling blocks of land along the railway line to white settlers. That strategy did not lead to a quick increase in production, but it did increase the cash value of land, and permitted the Company to enjoy the profits of land transactions. At the same time the peasant producers were squeezed by taxation and forced recruitment, so that they yielded short-term labour for the struggling gold mines, rather than crops for local markets. That overall strategy was reinforced by bringing in the Liebig beef company as a great ranching company in the dry regions of western Rhodesia. By 1910 therefore the peasant-production strategy was as dead in Rhodesia as it was in the Union. In both countries, economic development was to be accomplished by white enterprise and black labour.

If the development strategies were similar, they were not entirely compatible. For example, the small Rhodesian gold mines needed even cheaper labour than the Witwatersrand gold mines, and this led to serious rivalry for recruiting rights in Zambesia as a whole. Again, the Union government was anxious to settle poor Afrikaner landowners in Rhodesia, whereas the Company (and the white farmers in Rhodesia) were more anxious to recruit farmers from Britain, who would bring some capital and drive up land values. Incorporation into the Union would probably mean disaster for Rhodesian mining interests, and difficulties for white farmers.

In spite of a great deal of sympathy for the white Union, therefore, the settlers in Rhodesia preferred to see themselves as a distinct and 'British' community. They made their wishes known in 1914 when the option was presented to them; and again at the end of 1922, 60 per cent of the settlers voted to stay out of the Union. In 1923 the British government acknowledged the logic of the situation, and conceded responsible government to the settlers. British policy was as limp in Rhodesia as it was in the protectorates, but a determined settler population seized the initiative, so that settler self-government proved the least inconvenient method of ensuring order in Rhodesia. Naturally, they adopted many of the Union's tactics for controlling the black majority – land apportionment, coerced labour, narrow opportunities for African advancement – but the evolution of a distinct settler economy lead the settlers to resist appeals to join the Union. As Afrikaners increased their hold on the Union government, there was a cultural prejudice in white Rhodesia, reinforcing economic arguments for a separate status.

Just as Rhodes had spoken rather vaguely about a linked series of British dependencies from the Cape to Cairo, so Smuts would toy with the vision of a United States of Africa based upon the Union. The continued separation of Rhodesia from the Union made nonsense of such expansionist visions. Zambia (Northern Rhodesia) and Malawi (Nyasaland) could not be linked constitutionally to the Union, so long as Rhodesia separated them. What exactly should happen to the British dependencies of Central Africa remained a matter of unhurried debate.

In the event, no firm decision was reached until the 1950s. This meant that throughout the first half of the twentieth century the political future of Northern Rhodesia, for one, remained uncertain. Compared with its southern counterpart, Northern Rhodesia had a relatively small white immigrant population. It seemed likely, therefore, that the territory would be 'developed' as an African country in the future. Yet the situation was compounded by the ambivalence of British official attitudes. While wishing to include Southern Rhodesia and to exclude Northern Rhodesia from the newly-formed Union of Southern Africa, the British were at the same time building a Northern Rhodesia that was increasingly dependent upon the south not only through the communications network that had been established since 1910 but also in terms of the mining, agricultural as well as educational policies that were pursued in the two Rhodesias.

In Northern Rhodesia, as also in Nyasaland, the European settler population attempted during the 1930s and 1940s to secure some form of closer relationship with Southern Rhodesia. Indeed, as early as 1936 a suggestion had been made by Stewart Gore-Brown, a leading settler politician in Northern Rhodesia, that a Central African Federation be formed. In Nyasaland, on the other hand, the European population advocated what they called amalgamation, which was firmly opposed by the Africans. By 1949, Nyasaland's Europeans had settled for federation, a scheme also gaining popularity among the Northern Rhodesian European settlers.

In both Northern Rhodesia and Nyasaland, African opposition to the prospects of any move towards closer union of any sort was firm from the outset. Whether it was described as amalgamation or as federation the process would have meant the same thing for the African population in practical terms – the achievement of European domination and the subjugation of African interests to those of the Europeans throughout Central Africa. The British Government displayed a somewhat similar attitude in the north to that which it held further south in relation to the High Commission territories. While assuming a posture of protecting African interests – in Northern Rhodesia especially – it did nothing to stop the settlers from pursuing domination. Arguing that they were opposed to a move that would culminate in the transfer of power to a white minority, the British looked more favourably upon federation (rather than amalgamation, which might have ended in the south absorbing the north completely). In the end a Central African Federation of the Rhodesias and Nyasaland was proclaimed in August 1953. In the formal sense, then, Central Africa had been excluded from South Africa's expansionism.

South African expansionism

Ronald Hyam, the historian of British imperialism in Africa, describes these events as 'the failure of South African expansionism', since none of the British dependencies scheduled for incorporation was actually transferred to the Union. Even the mandate over Namibia has not been translated into permanent incorporation. None of the southern African boundaries drawn by the end of the nineteenth century has been amended. On a constitutional interpretation, therefore, Hyam is justified.

In political and economic terms, however, there is much more to be said. As Chanock points out, Rhodesia and the High Commission territories gave the British Government an influence in South African affairs which it would not otherwise have possessed. It was half a century before Afrikaners declared their republic, and Afrikaner suspicion against British capital and British connections was blunted by that influence. Further, the formal failure of South African expansionism conceals a more profound feature of regional relations in the twentieth century. South African capital was free to operate throughout the region, and apart from capital invested in Rhodesia, there was no other rival source of economic growth in the region. South Africa's mines especially drew hundreds of thousands of migrant labourers from throughout the region (Rhodesia again being the exception), and inhibited the development of alternative kinds of production, so that South African interests were clearly dominant throughout the region. By means of customs, monetary, and railway policies, South African interests have prevailed, where a more balanced regional development might have occurred. Any drive towards economic independence had to wait until political independence was achieved – and by that time two generations of subordination had distorted the economies of most of the societies in southern Africa. When the South African Government began to devise a new development strategy for the whole region in the 1950s, it could accurately describe the protectorates as African areas firmly within the South African economic system. The accuracy of that description is the most depressing conclusion to be drawn from observing the inertia of British and Portuguese colonial policy for the first half of the twentieth century, while rapid economic growth gave the Union a dominant role in the region.

Chapter 15

Internal opposition

Strictly speaking, we could trace internal opposition back to the foundation of the Cape Town garrison in the seventeenth century, when Khoi groups resisted the occupation of their land, and when free burghers opposed the privileges of the Company's officials. However, opposition has changed its form and purpose many times since then, and this is especially true in the hundred years following the mineral revolution. In this chapter, we will be concentrating on the internal opposition since the 1880s, seeing how new circumstances led to new conflicts and forms of organisation.

In the 1880s, in the oldest colony, there were a number of well-educated Africans, including Mfengu and Xhosa in the east and coloureds in the west, who thought of themselves as representing the present and future aspirations of Africans generally. Their education admitted them to clerical and professional employment, and their jobs admitted them to the franchise. They usually linked themselves with Cape liberal politicians – professional and merchant men – and shared many of the optimistic views of that group. The Jabavus, Sogas, Walter Rubusana and others assumed that a general liberalisation would eventually enfranchise more Africans – in the Cape and beyond – and it was not necessary to do more than encourage white people in that direction. They did not have a distinct voice in Cape politics, and they did not see themselves as an opposition. During the South African War for example, Jabavu's newspaper *Imvo* opposed the imperial cause (and was suppressed) while *Izwi* supported the empire. It was only in the years leading to Union that this group realised that South African affairs were running against them. Time was not on their side. They protested against the racial provisions of the Act of Union (and against many of the Union government's actions), but even then they shared a platform with the old white Cape liberals, and were slow to form a distinct movement.

Outside the Cape, African opposition was still voiced mainly by chiefs in the 1880s. The Tswana chiefs – Khama, Sechele and Gaseitsiwe – successfully negotiated with Britain, against incorporation into Rhodes's territories; and their successors (especially Tshekedi Khama) continued that diplomatic and defensive campaign through the twentieth century. In Lesotho it was the 'sons of Moshoeshoe' who warned against moves to incorporate them, just as the royal family and leading chiefs of Swaziland were doing. The crucial role of chiefs in the 1880s is suggested by Zululand. By removing Cetshwayo, and subdividing his kingdom, the British authorities unleashed internal civil war which neutralised Zulu power in the 1880s. The removal of Sekhukhune from the Pedi chieftaincy in 1879 also neutralised the most powerful African society within the Transvaal.

The crucial role of chiefs is not very surprising, when we remind ourselves how late the independent chieftaincies survived. The Shona were conquered only in the 1890s (and had to be conquered twice), and Lobengula's Ndebele also went under in the 1890s. Portuguese conquest of the Gaza kingdom occurred in 1895, and was insecure for some years thereafter. Maharero led the Herero, and Hendrik Witbooi the Nama, against Germany as late as 1905. It was only the defeat of the chiefs, and their exile, which forced opponents of the colonial regimes to find alternative leaders.

Colonial and settler authorities continued to see kings and chiefs as the most likely leaders of revolt. In Rhodesia, the authorities resolutely refused to allow Lobengula's sons to be recognised by the Ndebele, preferring to send them away to school. Maharero's exile in Botswana and Witbooi's death removed the most likely leaders of renewed resistance to Germany. In Zululand, Natal officials insisted on putting Dinuzulu on trial, although there was no evidence to suggest that he had led the Zulu during the Bambatha campaign of 1907. In the Cape, resident magistrates kept a close watch on the southern Nguni (and East Griqua) chiefs. And undoubtedly the chiefly titles, and their holders, continued to enjoy the loyalty of many people, even after the chiefs lost their power to act independently.

By the end of the nineteenth century, however, new forces were forming. The western-educated clerks and journalists and teachers of the Cape were more visible than the chiefs, and spoke to a much wider audience. As individuals in the other territories returned from tertiary education, they also became prominent spokesmen: John Dube, for example, returned to Zululand from the USA in 1909, determined to apply some of the measures developed by black Americans. As conditions and prospects for western-educated people declined, so they were pushed towards outspoken opposition.

Social conditions and relationships were changing in other ways too. As numbers of men and some women were drawn into urban wage employment, they began to see themselves in a fresh light, confronting daily problems which the chiefs were quite unable to resolve. Miners, domestic servants and laundry workers lived –

for shorter or longer periods – quite outside the communities of their birth, in barracks or dormitories or shacks, among people from many different backgrounds. Even if the chiefs visited them in town, there was nothing the chiefs could do to improve urban living conditions. The migrants might cling to their family ties – but they also needed support among themselves.

There were also people who left their rural homes but did not find a niche in the labour market, and therefore turned to robbery, or illicit alcohol, or protection rackets. Johannesburg was the Mecca for these activities but they flourished around all the urban areas. Groups like 'the regiment of the hills' which van Onselen has traced through Johannesburg police records, were certainly opposed by the state; but we should not consider their actions to be 'opposition' to the state, since they were willing to rob or defraud everyone, irrespective of race, sex or creed.

In the early years of this century, there was opposition from chiefs, from the educated, from urban and rural workers, and from the unemployed. In isolation from each other, they could accomplish almost nothing. Was there some way they could combine? The South African War prompted the formation of congresses – the African Peoples Organisation in the western Cape in 1902, led by Dr Abdurahman and comprising mainly coloured people, and African congresses in the OFS, Transvaal and Natal. These associations were mainly led by the western-educated, and they responded angrily to the betrayal of African aspirations, notably Britain's acceptance of a racially exclusive franchise in the ex-republics. The particular grievances of members – exclusion from land and from trade – seemed to hinge upon exclusion from the franchise; and it was these measures (rather than industrial grievances) which drew most of their fire.

These articulate men were brought together, with a few of the diehard Cape liberals, in protest against the Act of Union. Their protests were over-ruled, and the new Union government proceeded to tidy up some inconsistencies in industrial and agrarian laws. It was clearly necessary to form a Union-wide and permanent association, to express African dismay and to seek amelioration. They met in January 1912 at Bloemfontein, agreed to create the South African Native National Congress, and proposed an ad hoc constitution. Paramount chiefs were to be life-time members of an upper house, and it was expected that Lewanika of the Lozi, and Letsie II of Basutoland would belong, as well as the paramounts of Tswana and Sotho and Nguni communities. The scope of the SANNC was conceived as Pan-African, rather than merely Union-wide. Indeed the aspiration of many leaders was to achieve common and non-racial equality with whites, rather than an exclusively African identity, even though it might require a mobilised African movement to reach that goal.

First ANC delegation to Britain, whose unsuccessful attempt to persuade the British Government and the King was cut short by war in 1914. Left to right – Mapikela, Rubusana, Dube, Msane and Plaatje.

The inclusion of tribal leaders acknowledged their continuing prestige – and the impossibility of reaching rural Africans by other channels of communication. Inter-ethnic tensions persisted, and the executive committee had to balance them – four members from the Cape, including Rubusana (but not Jabavu, who refused to join), four from the Transvaal, including Makgatho, one from the OFS, and the Rev. John Dube from Natal as President. Though the African National Congress – as it came to be known – was widely spread, it did not have deep roots.

Strategies of opposition

This shallow membership did not seem to matter at first, since most leaders believed that their rulers could be persuaded to amend their policies, by appeals to reason and humanity. When appeals failed to move the South African Government in 1914 and 1919, the ANC sent respectful delegations of well-spoken men to London to address the British Government, or the King. Only slowly did they realise that neither the King, nor the British Government, nor the South African political leaders would act on their behalf. The issues closest to ANC's heart – land, trading rights, job discrimination and the franchise – were subject to ruthless government action in the first years after Union.

Meanwhile other groups were taking actions and devising tactics which were worth thinking about. Indian indentured labourers in Natal from the 1860s sometimes stayed there when their indentures expired, and they were supplemented by others who came as merchants and clerks and professionals. Though they were usually British subjects, they experienced a wide range of discrimination in Natal and in the Transvaal (where a few had managed to settle). In the face of discrimination, and led by M. K. Gandhi, a young lawyer, they organised peaceful non-cooperation tactics, forcing the Transvaal and South African Governments to arrest them in large numbers. Later on in India, these techniques were perfected into satyagraha (passive resistance, or moral resistance) and undermined British imperial control. In South Africa, however, this technique was not effective.

ANC leaders established and maintained close relations with the APO under Abdurahman. However, although coloured people suffered much the same discrimination as other Africans, their situation in the western Cape was rather different and consultations did not lead to close co-operation. Essentially the ANC must either mobilise African mass support, or else find allies within the enfranchised white population. It was the second alternative – seeking white allies – which the ANC mainly preferred.

There were strong and committed enemies of the South African Government within the white population. The industrial working class as a whole was suspicious about the influence of capitalists over the state, and disappointed at Botha's and Smuts's collaboration. Strikes broke out on the Witwatersrand in 1907, 1913 and 1914, in protest against the dilution of the white labour force. However, the white miners preferred to struggle (and even to lose) on their own, rather than enlist African allies. If African workers were to be unionised, they would have to organise themselves.

It was, of course, difficult to mobilise African industrial workers even around Johannesburg. As contract workers from different parts of the region, spending only a few months together, and under the constant observation of employers, they could not easily agree to action. Their discontents were commonly expressed by short outbursts of anger, and ill-prepared action. After the South African War, for example, many simply stayed at home or worked in non-mining jobs. At the end of the First World War there was a more organised strike by black miners, whose living costs had increased during the war, but whose wages did not rise. The strike was suppressed violently in 1920.

Shortly afterwards, in 1921, the white miners struck once again, in protest against dismissals and dilution. On this occasion the strike escalated into a revolt – the famous Rand Revolt – before Smuts sent in the army to restore order. Within a few months, the white miners were seeking to regain by the ballot box what they lost in direct action. Eventually, in 1924, the Labour Party won enough seats to become junior partner in Hertzog's Pact government. However, there was absolutely no prospect of sympathy from the Labour Party, which indeed preferred to keep Africans out of jobs which white workers wanted. So what could be learned from these struggles?

No clear 'lessons' could be deduced. Both white and black workers had used the strike strategy: but it did not yield results, perhaps because black and white did not strike together. White workers gained more through voting in elections – but African votes were so few that the same option was not really available. In any formal political alliance, representatives of African voters would form only a tiny minority.

In any event, it was not the ANC who took initiatives as a rule. Their commitment to the cause of individual westernised men, and their confidence in rational argument, as well as their pride in their own individual accomplishments, made them reluctant to initiate mass protests. The leaders did, however, adopt causes which emerged spontaneously from other oppressed groups. In 1913, women in the OFS marched peacefully against the extension of pass laws against them, and the ANC endorsed these protests. When miners struck work, ANC leaders would represent them. In brief, the leaders tolerated local mass protests, and even used these as evidence that humane change was necessary: but they would not incite such protests.

The leaders of the ANC were particularly weak in industrial matters which were usually outside their personal experience as pastors and teachers and clerks. They were overshadowed in this area by a quite new movement. In 1919, dock workers at Cape Town struck work, in favour of wage increases, and from this episode Clements Kadalie emerged onto the national stage. A young migrant from Nyasaland, with a secondary education and clerical experience in Rhodesia, he founded an organisation known as ICU. Though not at first its secretary, he was always its dominant personality.

The ICU flourished in the Cape, where workers in Cape Town, Port Elizabeth and East London were eager to form large associations, and where the co-operation of a few whites could be expected. From the Cape it spread rapidly to the Witwatersrand and to Durban. At its peak it may have enrolled 100 000 members; but it was known to many more, who might well follow where it led. The question was where it would lead – the same question which ANC leaders had failed to resolve. If it were purely an industrial organisation, then it should negotiate wage settlements for its members. If it were a political association, then it could bargain with Hertzog or prepare for extra-parliamentary agitation. In the event, all three tactics were used, none of them to great effect. Hertzog was surprised to enjoy ICU support in his 1924 election campaign; but he had no doubt that ICU was a threat to his coalition, and once in power he tried to harass and weaken it. When the small Communist Party protested against ICU indecision and financial muddle, Communists were expelled – but Kadalie was also uneasy with his few white liberal advisers. No clear strategy was laid down.

Kadalie hoped for international support, seeing (probably correctly) that ICU was too weak to force general economic or political changes on a stubborn South African Government. Once again he faced a choice, whether to seek support from Communist or non-Communist unions in Europe. And while he was away in Europe, his organisation began to break up. By the time he gained a little support from the British Labour movement – and the aid of a full-time organiser from Scotland – it was too late. The provincial branches were pulling in separate directions. In the absence of a clear strategy, or of significant gains in wages, the rank and file grew impatient. In 1929 ICU broke up, leaving separate organisations in Rhodesia, Natal, the Transvaal, the Orange Free State and the Cape itself.

Among the white population, ANC members made individual friends and allies, usually professional or academic, and sometimes involved in the small Communist Party. Few institutional links grew up, such as the Joint Councils of Europeans and Africans, and these were merely consultative. Not surprisingly, some blacks considered these white sympathisers to be a conservative influence on the ANC. That suspicion may have been unfair, but it is clear that the white allies brought no great strength to the alliance.

Individual ANC members were involved in ICU, though the ANC itself stood aside. The ICU experience suggested that African workers could easily be mobilised, but that the state was too strong and ruthless to be overthrown – or even redirected – without a very long and painful struggle. Oppressed by this realisation, the ANC fell into decline, responding only to grave government initiatives.

The most alarming of these initiatives took the form of four pieces of draft legislation published by the government in 1926, though not enacted for ten years. In these bills, it was clear that Hertzog was anxious to dismantle Cape African voting rights, to extend (but then finally to limit) African land, and to separate African from coloured and white political institutions and movements. The ANC leaders could not accept these proposals, either separately or as a package: but it was not clear what could be done about them. Opposition was expressed by an All-African Convention led by Professor Jabavu (son of Tengo Jabavu) who stood outside the ANC: but this opposition failed to deflect the government from its purpose. By 1936 when the modified bills became law, there was a sharp contrast between the unity of most white political parties, and the inability of the ANC to mobilise an effective defence.

What was the ANC's purpose? During the 1920s and 1930s it was forced into a defensive posture, relying on an eloquent appeal to Christian and humanist principles, defending the old vision of gradual assimilation of a westernised elite, and paternal concern for the majority. As the vision faded from practical politics, the ANC leaders had to take more seriously the option of mobilising mass support for the politics of confrontation. Yet such tactics were distasteful to the leaders, and to their liberal allies in the Joint Councils. These tactics appealed more strongly to the Communist Party, whose vision of the past and the future was stated in terms of class and struggle, rather than race and harmony. Although chiefs and liberals and Christians disliked the language of radicalism and militancy, it was impossible to suppress the debate over strategy and purpose – especially when the ANC President in the late 1920s, Josiah Gumede, voiced the arguments of Marcus Garvey and of the Comintern. Gumede was no more consistent than any other ANC leader, but he encouraged a wider range of strategic opinion. That wide-ranging debate persisted, although radical influences were formally ended in the 1930s – Gumede lost the presidency in 1930, and CP influence diminished with an abrupt reorganisation and purging of members.

The Congress Alliance

These discussions bore no particular fruit until the 1940s, when the war against fascism pointed up the anomalies of a racially-divided and explicitly oppressive South African society. The ANC leaders at last formulated their programme in a document called *African Claims*, and these – non-racial and democratic – aims were very similar to the Atlantic Charter which spelt out American and British purposes against fascism. Nevertheless it was only in 1951 that the ANC – urged on by the ANC Youth League – agreed to a mass campaign of peaceful disobedience. In that campaign, launched in mid-1952, hundreds of volunteers courted arrest. But even when the gaols were full to overflowing, Dr Malan's Nationalist government declined to compromise. What the campaign did achieve was enormous publicity for the disabilities which Africans suffered, and for the ANC as a champion of equality. Membership shot up to 100 000: the ANC could no longer be dismissed as a mere elitist association.

Devising effective campaigns, the next step, was more complex. Boycotts of schools – protesting against inferior curricula and miserable conditions – failed to rally sufficient support. Protests against forcible resettlement schemes, though popular, were beaten by superior government force. An organisation now existed; but where could it go?

Sharpeville, some of the dead and wounded

During 1955 the ANC took part in a Congress of the People, which wrote a charter for a congress movement. Other congresses involved were representing coloured and Indian movements, a few communists, and the few non-racial trade unions. Coloured people were willing to join in, especially as they had lost their common roll franchise. Indians, who were divided sharply by internal economic circumstances as well as religion, were more ambiguous, and the SA Indian Congress was not supported by all possible members. The Congress of Democrats, though enthusiastic, represented a tiny fraction of the population; and the Congress of Trade Unions – excluded from the white Trade Union Council – was itself suffering from harassment. The social democratic Freedom Charter, which gave more detailed expression to congress policies, still did not clarify strategic and tactical choices. The government placed 156 leaders on a long trial for treason (and therefore kept them out of circulation). Meanwhile many ANC members resented the influence of non-Africans in determining congress policies, and argued for more direct action.

During 1958 a split within the ANC gave rise to the Pan-Africanist Congress, a more exclusively African movement, outside the Congress Alliance. In 1960, it organised anti-pass law campaigns, again using the technique of non-violent non-co-operation against passes, which were symbolically as well as substantively important. On 21 March, at Sharpeville, police massacred unarmed demonstrators; and in the aftermath both the ANC and PAC were declared illegal organisations. When several congress leaders were captured at Rivonia (outside Johannesburg) and placed on trial in 1964, an era was brought to a close.

In reviewing the ANC's legal career, it is important to notice that it was never the most militant of the day. Mine and dock workers struck work again and again, without ANC instigation – and the ANC could only endorse the campaigns which others began. Even at the time of its greatest public recognition – the 1950s – it was overshadowed by peasant rebellion in the Transkei. The ANC followed while others led.

The leaders only very slowly escaped from the rationalist, preaching style and tactics of its founders. Even the most famous president – Albert Luthuli – who presided over the transition in the 1950s, was firmly in the Christian, chiefly and cautious tradition. The suspicion of all non-African allies was also a long tradition – for which there were often sound reasons – but this was usually overlaid by a passionate commitment to the gradual achievement of a non-racial, democratic social order.

By the late 1950s, though, the ANC had finally achieved a programme, and an appreciation of the tactics which might bring it to fruition. Most people were willing to follow, in a campaign against the whole edifice of racial discrimination. The popularity of

194

Albert Luthuli, President-General of the African National Congress and winner of the Nobel Peace Prize

the PAC suggested that people would follow a clear lead, whether the strategy was devised by the Congress Alliance or by a more narrowly African leadership. At least, after half a century, the ANC and PAC were able to bring their wishes forcibly to the government's attention, no longer as courteous requests but as demands. It is no wonder that they were banned at that point. Nor is it an accident that the government then initiated the most drastic and destructive policy change since Union: Bantustans.

Chapter 16

Bantustans

Origins of the Bantustan programme

When Dr Malan's Nationalists won the 1948 election, they were ill-prepared to govern. Only once before (in 1924) had government changed hands through an election, and the Nationalist victory came as a surprise even to themselves. The electoral slogan of 'apartheid' suggested that the Nationalists would have even less sympathy for Africans than any previous government. They won the elections with a minority of the votes cast, relying mainly upon rural constituencies; and this emphasised their isolation from the powerful mining, manufacturing and commercial interests of the urban areas. This was the first white government since Union to have no English-speaking members. Their first priority was to establish their authority, not only over the mass of the population, but also in the eyes of the powerful urban interests which supported the opposition United Party. As a rural organisation, they had little experience or understanding of the urban areas where population had recently been growing rapidly, and where social problems were most acute.

The policy of apartheid had not been spelt out, and might mean little more than the 'segregation' programme which won Hertzog the 1924 election. Many of the Nationalists' measures showed little imagination, and an inflexible determination to finish off the repressive programme where Hertzog had left off. They moved grimly to transfer coloured voters to a separate voters' roll, in spite of some opposition from ex-servicemen (the Torch Commando) and from the courts. The programme of population registration made it more difficult for people of mixed race to smuggle themselves across racial boundaries; and a stricter application of the pass laws, and of urban residential segregation, made it more difficult for rural blacks to smuggle themselves into urban areas in search of employment. Massive arrests for breaches of the pass laws, and occasional prosecutions under the Immorality Act (which forbade sexual relations across racial boundaries) effectively separated the races from each other on most occasions. As the Nationalists gained strength in parliament, they also moved towards the old Afrikaner ambition of a republic, which was achieved in 1961, although South Africa was then prevented from rejoining the Commonwealth. All these measures appealed to the old values of rural Afrikaners, and especially to those who had flirted with semi-fascist organisations during the war; but they had little effect beyond tightening the existing mechanisms of social control. They made it clear what people should *not* be doing, but they did not re-direct people's energies into new directions.

A series of long-term social changes in the country posed problems which mere repression could not resolve. One fundamental crisis was the acute and deepening poverty of the rural reserves, from which there were steady flows of blacks into urban areas, whether or not the pass laws permitted them to do so. If urban Africans were the most vocal in expressing their opposition to the regime, the tensions arose from both rural and urban conditions. Some Nationalists recognised the inadequacy of simple apartheid to cope with these tensions, and in 1950 they succeeded in having a new Minister for Native Affairs appointed, with a more complex understanding of the situation and total self-confidence. Dr H. F. Verwoerd was an unusual Afrikaner in Malan's government, being an urban academic, with all the clear vision and dogmatism which academics often bring to politics. He commissioned a comprehensive 'development' plan for all the African areas (the Tomlinson commission), and embarked upon a programme of 'separate development' which claimed to be a progressive and adaptive strategy, as distinct from the old emphasis on preserving white privilege and black subordination. Increasingly his vision dominated the Nationalist Party programme, especially after he became Prime Minister in 1958, and even after his assassination in 1966. His role as the architect and implementer of separate development may perhaps be compared with that of Milner half a century earlier, as architect and implementer of British imperial policy in the region. Both had a background in journalism, so that they were the best propagandists for their own policies.

The Bantustan programme, however, could not move too far away from the interests of the Afrikaners who voted the Nationalists into power. Since 1948, the drift of Afrikaners into mining and other urban employment has continued and even accelerated. A new policy for the control of the black population therefore could not make concessions which would damage the interests of white farmers, or of the white working class; and if capitalist production was to be sustained, the new policy would also have to be acceptable to the managers of capital. There was rather little room for manoeuvre between these political pressures. Much of the legislation associated with the Bantustan policy was therefore essentially negative in its effect. A separate curriculum for black schoolchildren merely isolated them further from free access to the world's stock of knowledge. Separate universities for each racial group isolated students from each other and from contemporary ideas. The Suppression of Communism Act (1950) did not suppress communism, but it made life very difficult for political associations involving more than one race in its membership. Placing barbed wire along the racial fences did not have much influence on the shape of political struggles.

The crucial piece of legislation, attempting a new policy dispensation and throwing a fresh light on other pieces of legislation, was the Promotion of Self Government Act of 1959. This Act provided for the grant of self-government (and eventually independence) to particular groups of Africans, defined in tribal terms, and based upon the surviving rural reserves. As Verwoerd and his supporters explained it, there were really only two alternatives for South Africa's political future. One was a single common citizenship of a unitary political system, in which blacks must eventually have political and social equality: but the whites would not agree to such a strategy. The other was to divide the country into a series of related states, so that each community could be politically independent of all the others. Such a strategy might be clumsy and artificial, but it was said to offer a measure of dignity and autonomy to each community in the country.

The reason for the importance of this legislation is not that it actually changed South African reality: rather, it insisted upon a quite new perspective on unchanging conditions. Africans were mobilising through the ANC and the PAC: the government could now argue that Africans should seek equality and dignity through their own ethnically defined states, instead of demanding equality within a unitary political system. Foreign investors were becoming nervous: the government could now reassure tham that there was a credible plan to channel opposition into safe directions. The United Nations was objecting to racial discrimination: and the government could reply that there would be no further discrimination once everyone in South Africa had his or her own democratic rights within a series of interlocking states.

In other words, the Bantustan programme provided a lot of new cards for South African diplomats, for South African security forces, and for anxious investors. As a debating device, it enabled South African representatives to defend pieces of legislation and administration which were quite indefensible on any other grounds. Was it not reasonable, Verwoerd asked, that the citizens of a foreign country should relinquish their South African citizenship and their hopes for South Africa's future? If blacks had their own homelands, was it not reasonable to exclude them from permanent residence, schools, accommodation, and skilled jobs outside their own homelands? Were they not similar to the *'gastarbeiters'* from

Mediterranean countries who came to work in Germany, France and Switzerland? The Bantustan strategy was therefore a direct challenge to the popular mass movements of the ANC and PAC which threatened sweeping changes. If Africans could be manipulated into tribally-defined political channels and institutions, they would no longer threaten existing conditions. In general, the Bantustan programme was an elaborate device for conserving the status quo by making it look different. In order to make the strategy credible, all that was necessary was to find some support among blacks.

The Transkei

The Transkei presented both the most acute crises and the most promising opportunities for implementing the Bantustan project, and it was the Transkei which was selected as the first subject of the experiment. It was in this region that peasant production had first occurred among African communities, and after almost a century the consequence was an extremely impoverished rural population, severely divided within itself, and relying massively upon the wages of migrant labourers to buy food. In 1960 much of the rural Transkei was still in a state of rebellion, and a state of emergency gave the Union authorities wide powers to restore South African (and chiefly) control. The Transkei had also a long experience of local self-government (in the form of the Bunga, or assembly), and there were acute rivalries between the (government-appointed) chiefs of the tribal groups which made up the Transkei's population. With so many tensions operating, it should not be too difficult for the South African authorities to find some groups who would co-operate in implementing the self-government plan; and the state of emergency allowed the authorities to act without much risk of being reported in the newspapers. In 1963 then, the Transkei became the first self-governing territory to be blasted into orbit. On its fate would hinge the entire plan of a constellation of satellite states, which were to circle round the South African state, seemingly independent, but held firmly in place by the forces of economic gravity.

Some features of Transkei politics were unusual by any measure. In the Legislative Assembly chiefs (appointed by Pretoria) outnumbered elected members by 64 to 45. Whites could not vote, but they administered the government departments, on secondment from South African departments. The urban areas remained South African enclaves, surrounded by a black and Transkeian countryside. The countryside itself was fragmented, and separated by slices of South African territory, while some of the Transkei land was still owned by white farmers. The Transkei was a rural reserve which had to import food, and prospects for other kinds of

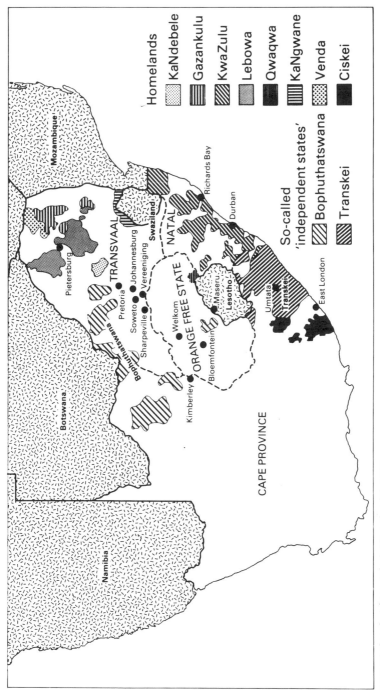

Map 10 South Africa: 'Black Homelands', 1982

Homelands

KaNdebele
Gazankulu
KwaZulu
Lebowa
Qwaqwa
KaNgwane
Venda
Ciskei

So-called
'independent states'

Bophuthatswana
Transkei

Mozambique

Richards Bay

Durban

TRANSVAAL

Swaziland

NATAL

Pietersburg

Johannesburg

Pretoria

Soweto

Vereeniging

Sharpeville

ORANGE FREE STATE

Welkom

Maseru

Lesotho

Umtata

Transkei

East London

Botswana

Bophuthatswana

Kimberley

Bloemfontein

CAPE PROVINCE

Namibia

economic production depended upon the South African policy of promoting industrial production on the borders of the homelands. The prospects for self-sufficiency were bleak indeed, even if all potential Transkei citizens remained outside the homeland: if they were all forced to come 'home', congestion would grow even more acute. Most of the elected members saw these as sufficient reason for rejecting separate independence. They argued that the Transkei could reasonably become a new province of South Africa: full independence would simply isolate them from other forces for change in South Africa, without enabling them to achieve economic viability of any kind.

When the Territorial Assembly convened, Chief Kaiser Matanzima presented the pro-independence line, arguing essentially that the half-loaf of illusory independence was better than no political bread, and that an independent Transkei would be able to continue to make demands upon Pretoria. This view commanded very little support, but a narrow majority was assembled, comprising the majority of the chiefly members and a small minority of the elected members. Once that majority was put together, and independence was endorsed, Matanzima's government had great sources of strength: most of the Transkei's revenue came from Pretoria, the chiefs depended upon the Transkei government for their appointments, and a web of security measures could be used to confound the popular opposition. Since the government owed little to the electors, the obvious way to remain in power was through repression rather than mobilising popular support; and since independence the Transkei government has passed security measures even more repressive than those of South Africa.

Bantustans proliferate

Black politicians in other reserves noted the South African Government's determination to have its way. Most of the small and fragmented reserves had little chance of standing out against the policy, and some have reluctantly accepted the notional status of independence: Bophuthatswana (a string of blocks of land running westward from Pretoria) in 1977, Venda (in the northern Transvaal) in 1979, and Ciskei (west of the Transkei) in 1981. Some leaders, however, have opposed the policy. When the Zulu were lumped together as KwaZulu, Chief Gatsha Buthelezi was elected chief minister at the head of Inkatha, a widely based and popular mass movement. Inkatha's view has been that self-government is a useful means of decentralising decision-making from Pretoria to each homeland, and should be seen as essentially similar to provincial government: but that any step towards independence would be a denial and betrayal of Zulu rights and prospects within South African society as a whole. By means of this delicately balanced

Chief Gatsha Buthelezi

argument, Buthelezi has been able to become the best known and probably the most popular black spokesman operating within conventional politics.

Some of the conditions constraining homeland politicians are suggested in the two tables. The first point to notice in Table 1 is that the total area of the homelands is less than a seventh of the total land area of South Africa. That amount of land might have been viable in the nineteenth century, before the massive increases in population, and before the destructive effect of migrant labour: but in the twentieth century they are far too little to be the basis of self-sufficiency, especially in the absence of massive capital investment. Most of the homeland governments (and most loudly the Transkei) have requested further land, both for historic reasons and for some prospect of self-reliance in food. These requests have always been refused, and only marginal quantities of land have been transferred. The second remarkable feature of the first table is that a high proportion (from 40 per cent to 90 per cent) of the 'citizens' of each homeland live outside its borders. In addition, a substantial proportion of the resident population is outside at any given time, earning money as migrant workers.

Table 2 provides more detail on how people survive. The value of goods and services produced inside each homeland is never much more than a third of the total in each case. The bulk of people's income is earned by commuters who leave the homeland (usually on a daily basis) to work in the cities and factories on the border, or by migrants living much further away. The incomes earned in this humiliating manner are absurdly small. It is certainly true (as South African spokesmen frequently argue) that *cash* incomes of black South Africans are higher than those of many Africans elsewhere in

Table 1: Homeland populations

Name of territory	Area (1976) '000 ha	Population (1976) de jure	de facto	Migrants as % of total
Bophuthatswana	3 800	2 103	1 158	4.6
Transkei	4 100	4 250	2 411	15.0
Ciskei	533	872	479	5.3
Gazankulu	675	814	334	22.4
KwaZulu	3 100	5 029	2 710	10.3
Lebowa	2 200	2 234	1 388	14.2
QwaQwa	48	1 698	91	8.5
KaNgwane	370	590	209	3.9
Venda	650	449	339	17.6

the continent. On the other hand these cash incomes are no longer supplemented by domestic food production as they were earlier this century, and as they still are in many other African countries: so for most black families, the cash income is the sole means of support. Equally, for each of the homeland governments, it is the income deriving directly or indirectly from South Africa which comprises the totality of their revenues. Many of the enterprises sponsored by homeland governments – casinos, hotels, tourism and golf courses – rely on well-to-do consumers from South Africa. To consider their potential for 'development' without including the South African dimension is a meaningless exercise.

The beneficiaries of the Bantustan programme are, in the main, the South African Government. Homeland governments have the power to enact their own security laws, on attaining independence; but the independent homelands have in fact enacted security measures which are at least as strict as those of the republic itself. There is no risk of the homelands providing refuge for underground members of the ANC or the PAC, or indeed any other underground organisation. Homeland leaders have also carried responsibility for arguing their way into international organisations (the United Nations and the Organisation of African Unity), which would tend to legitimise the South African strategy. As it happens, no such recognition has occurred. During 1976 the Government of Ecuador explored 'matters of common interest' with the Transkei, but formal diplomatic recognition did not follow, and it is difficult to imagine what matters the Ecuadorian and Transkeian spokesmen discussed. Finally, the South African authorities benefit enormously from the extent to which the homeland programme does help to divide black opinion within South Africa. These divisions are hard to measure, because we must assume that there would be some ethnic tension even within a unitary South African political system: but it is almost certain that the existence of homeland governments, however dependent they may be, serves as a focus for ethnic sentiment and for inter-ethnic suspicion.

The Bantustan programme relies upon the existence of some residual reserve land. When Verwoerd and his colleagues turned their attention to the politcal destiny of coloured and Indian citizens, there was no territorial focus for them to build on. A Coloured Persons Representative Council was elected in 1969, but the Labour Party – which won that election and the following one in 1974 – declined to co-operate to make the Council work. The government could offer them no land, and only the prospect of employment preference in the western Cape province. The Labour Party took the view that coloured people would be better represented by membership of the South African parliament; and in the 1970s they came more explicitly to the conclusion that coloured people could not be fully autonomous so long as Africans were the

Table 2: Gross national income of the homelands, 1975

Name of territory	Gross Domestic Product (Africans) R'000	Commuter incomes R'000	Migrant incomes R'000	African incomes, per capita R
Ciskei	29 333 (27%)	50 193 (47%)	27 816 (26%)	223
KwaZulu	157 212 (20)	333 960 (42)	303 857 (38)	277
QwaQwa	5 286 (32)	1 600 (10)	9 810 (59)	183
Lebowa	79 873 (23)	55 944 (16)	207 427 (60)	224
Venda	19 032 (22)	3 816 (4)	63 980 (74)	225
Gazankulu	17 695 (16)	13 760 (13)	76 488 (71)	272
KaNgwane	9 703 (28)	16 728 (48)	8 393 (24)	169
Transkei	198 566 (34)	7 700 (1)	372 552 (64)	218
Bophuthatswana	120 945 (35)	172 077 (49)	55 188 (16)	310

victims of discrimination. Economically the 1970s were prosperous for coloured people, many of whom have the educational background to benefit from shortages of semi-skilled and skilled labour: but even rising prosperity has not won the coloured people to the government's vision of their future.

An Indian Council was also established in 1968, by nomination of the government. For Indians too there was no land, and only the chance of employment preference in Natal. South Africans of Indian descent, however, since the days of Gandhi, have been infinitely divided by wealth, by occupation, by religion and even by caste. Such a fragmented community has never been able to reach consensus in its response to government proposals: Indians have been among the most militant opponents, and among the most quiescent supporters, of separate development. Neither Indians nor coloureds can logically contemplate a future without some alliance with Africans, even though a few members of each community have toyed with the idea.

Bantustans and international relations

It has been an article of faith of Bantustan supporters that human beings of different racial backgrounds simply co-operate with each other within unitary political systems. This argument, which evolved out of South African politics, was not restricted to South Africa itself, but in principle applied to the whole of mankind. The only other slice of mankind available for South African officials in the 1960s and 1970s was Namibia. The Odendaal Commission in 1963 explicitly recommended the application of separate development to Namibia's black population, dividing them into half a dozen distinct homelands, even though the total population of Namibia was less than a million souls. By the late 1970s, there were proposals for constituting a series of 'second-tier', ethnically-defined administrations, within a federally-constituted territorial assembly. Although these proposals have been overshadowed by persistent warfare in northern Namibia, the logic of a federation of races was endorsed by the Turnhalle alliance of political spokesmen (considered in Chapter 17). Whatever happens in Namibia in the future, the habit of thinking in ethnic terms has received powerful encouragement there during the 1960s and 1970s, and this habit will not easily be uprooted.

The Tomlinson Commission, which provided the blueprint for separate development, assumed that the High Commission territories of Swaziland, Botswana and Lesotho (which were still under British control at that time) would fit neatly into the regional pattern. When they attained their own independence, the new governments were hostile to such a limited view of their future. Nevertheless the South African authorities held out the prospect of federating each of the newly independent countries to its neighbouring homeland: Bophuthatswana in the case of Botswana, QwaQwa in the case of Lesotho, and KaNgwane in the case of Swaziland. While the independent governments may have been attracted by the prospect of territorial expansion, and perhaps by a substantially increased population, they were asked to pay too high a price: nothing less than the full recognition of separate development as the most humane strategy for multi-racial societies.

Only in one of these cases has there been any serious prospect of success. In 1982, without warning, the South African Government suspended the KaNgwane homeland authority (which had declined to co-operate in its own exclusion from South Africa), and offered to Swaziland not only the whole of KaNgwane, but also a slice of territory which formed part of KwaZulu. The effect of this offer would have been to enlarge Swaziland, and to give it independent access to the Indian Ocean: in exchange, presumably Swaziland would have had to accept a permanent role as buffer between ANC activists in Mozambique, and South Africa. Swaziland would also have been required to endorse, in a spectacular and public fashion, the whole strategy of separate development. To achieve this coup, however, the South Africans had to confront opposition from KaNgwane itself, from KwaZulu, from a lot of whites, and from the courts. Before this opposition could be overcome King Sobhuza died, and negotiations were shelved – at least for a while.

In making a judgement of the Bantustan strategy, it is important to establish exactly the purpose of the programme. If it was to provide substantial independence for defined groups of Africans, then the policy has certainly failed: the homelands are at least as dependent upon the South African economy now, as they ever were; and any real independence would require not only massive investments of capital, but also a great transformation of social relations in order to disengage from the South African economy.

However, the Bantustan strategy had at least two further objectives. One was to divide the black population into smaller, more manageable components, and to confound all attempts at black unity. Since black unity would have been difficult even within a unitary system, it is difficult to guess whether or not Bantustans have complicated an already difficult aspiration. The second objective was to give the South African authorities some room for manoeuvre in international (and especially in regional) affairs. In this respect the strategy has certainly enjoyed some limited success. South African diplomats and apologists have had a number of effective rhetorical cards added to their hands. If we consider the Bantustan strategy as a massive confidence trick, rather than an attempt to transform human relationships and conditions, we must concede that it was a clever operation.

Chapter 17

The Bantustan programme founders

For all the cleverness of the Bantustan concept, it was only a paper solution to substantive problems, lacking the capacity to change reality. Three irreversible developments rendered the programme unworkable, and gave rise to hostile reactions to the government's policies and officials. We will consider each of these developments in turn.

Rural underdevelopment

African populations in southern Africa were able to cope with substantial losses of land in the nineteenth century: the Transkei and Zulu areas were producing a surplus of grain as late as the end of the nineteenth century, and it is only in the twentieth century that the reserves were obliged to import food in order to feed their people. The reasons for this sharp decline are worth noting. First, the population itself began to increase, creating dangerously dense rural settlement patterns. This problem could have been averted, if Africans had been allowed to purchase land outside the reserves, or to remain as tenants on white-owned farms. Neither of these measures was permitted by the Union government, although a long series of government reports pointed to the shortage of land for African production (from the South African Native Affairs Commission in 1905, and the Economic and Wage Commission of 1924, to the Tomlinson Commission in the 1950s). Any increase in agricultural opportunities for Africans would damage the interests of white farmers, and was therefore politically impossible.

There is probably no land which cannot be made to produce wealth; but some land needs massive capital investment and careful husbandry to become productive. Many of the African reserves could have continued to produce a food surplus, if capital had been available, and if advice had been given for the transition from extensive to intensive production. In reality, neither capital nor technical advice has been made available on an adequate scale, since a self-sufficient black population would not yield the harvest of labour migrants which mines and factories and white farms demanded. Further, the selective recruitment of healthy young men – leaving sick men, old men, women and children in the reserves – made agricultural production even more difficult than it might have been.

Although the governments of southern Africa have been committed to the virtues of capitalist production in general – private ownership of the means of production, and reliance upon wage labour – they have been slow to promote capitalist production in the African reserves. Even the Glen Grey policy, whereby some Africans became smallholders and others were dispossessed of land rights, has not been implemented vigorously: a large proportion of land in the present homelands is still owned on communal terms. The effect has been to create a rural society suffering the worst features of both individual and communal tenure systems. People hold on to the last traces of their rights to land, and therefore inhibit the most productive use of it: but chiefs and other holders of power contrive to increase their access to land, in order to run cattle on it. The result of these processes is a very curious rural settlement pattern, with a tiny proportion of the population occupying land which yields a sufficient living, a substantial number living on inadequately small plots, and an ever-increasing number living on blocks which have no arable land whatever. Naturally, the quality of harvests has deteriorated as the land is abused by desperate people. Suffering a shortage of capital and technology, the African areas are now carrying more people than they can feed.

Urbanisation

Throughout the twentieth century, official policy has chosen to see urban Africans as temporary residents whose real homes are in rural areas. That was probably an untrue impression at the beginning of the century, since small numbers of Africans (especially clerical and professional, and runaways) had severed their ties to land; but so long as the numbers were small, it was plausible for whites to think of Africans as inherently and immutably rural. By the time of the 1921 census, however, more than 400 000 Africans were living in (or close to) metropolitan areas, and legislation between the wars enabled municipal authorities to deport unemployed Africans back to rural areas. Such legislation had little effect in the face of rural poverty, and the number of urban Africans had doubled by 1936. That population had nearly doubled again (to a million and a half) by 1951, and the Nationalist government determined to apply 'influx control' more strictly through the pass laws, to minimise the urban African population by ensuring that no African could remain in an urban area without employment. By the 1950s, however, large numbers of African women were employed as domestic servants in all urban areas, and the government was no longer dealing with a population of rootless bachelors. By 1980, in spite of ruthless pass campaigns, more than 7¼ million Africans were settled in towns as against nearly 14 million rural residents. Given the miserable living conditions of most black rural areas, it is unlikely that the tide of urbanisation can be reversed.

Most urban Africans did in fact retain some rural links, either by sending small children to be raised in the reserves, or by maintaining personal connections in order to be able to retire to rural areas. It was wise to maintain those links, since the threat of being 'endorsed out' of urban residence was always present. Especially in the mines, but also in some manufacturing, it was bachelors who came to urban employment, usually for a fixed term of years. For these reasons, most Africans remained in touch with their rural kin, probably more closely than (for example) Afrikaners who came to town in the 1920s onwards. Nevertheless the urban Africans were becoming a permanently urbanised community, with their own worries, their own ways of eking out a living on the fringe of the law, their own folk literature, and their own music, all very different to those of their rural kin. Youngsters grew up 'street smart', familiar with the ways of the police, and able to evade police controls: none of these skills was useful if they visited the countryside.

Urbanisation on this scale made nonsense of the essentially rural concept of Bantustans. KwaZulu and Bophuthatswana were enlarged during the 1970s, so as to include peri-urban areas outside Durban and Pretoria; but in other urban areas the ethnic mixture was too complex to allow any such administrative solution. A more general strategy from the 1950s onwards was to destroy the old squatter settlements in the urban area itself, and to establish urban Africans in separate towns and townships some distance away from the urban centre. Home-ownership (but not land-ownership) was offered as an inducement to people to feel pride in their surroundings; and in any case a separate African township was much easier for the police to control than a scatter of black neighbourhoods within a racially-mixed urban area.

The development of security controls did not, however, solve problems; it merely suppressed the evidence. We have seen that the essence of the migrant labour scheme was that rural societies should subsidise the mining industry by enabling the mines to pay only enough to keep a bachelor alive. With the increasing proportion of women, and of families, it was absolutely essential that a family-wage (as distinct from a bachelor-wage) be paid. Whether or not urban workers felt militant, they simply could not afford to accept less than the family-wage. The obvious way of dealing with such tensions would be to permit trade unions to represent workers

in particular kinds of employment, and the authorities have moved cautiously towards this system – but to permit trade unions to operate freely would deny the Bantustan concept that people can (and should) organise themselves only on the basis of ethnicity, not of social class. There is no easy resolution of this problem which the authoritires have created for themselves. By the late 1970s an uneasy paper solution had been found: to permit some trade unions to operate, but to persecute the elected leaders of these unions. In the long run, this is no kind of solution.

The question of maintaining social order in turbulent townships could be resolved very easily, if it were not for the Bantustan ideology. Municipal councils, representing township residents, might well defuse some of the tensions of rapid urbanisation; but if the authorities allowed municipal authorities to function openly and freely, that would mean an admission that there were permanently urbanised Africans, for whom homeland self-government was fundamentally irrelevant. By the late 1970s an uneasy compromise had been reached, whereby municipal authorities were coming into existence, but either they were not acknowledged or their elected spokesmen were persecuted, or else both occurred. In brief, 'urbanisation' is not in itself a problem: but it has created demands and expectations which cannot be satisfied

Contrasting ways of life: Cape Town with the Houses of Parliament in the foreground, an African shanty town near Johannesburg, and a new African location within the logic of the ideology of tribally separate development, an essentially rural and nineteenth-century view of human relationships.

Manufacturing

We have seen in earlier chapters that manufacturing did not occur on an important scale until the 1920s. In common with many other industrialising societies, South African manufacturing began with a strong emphasis upon textiles, and by drawing large numbers of women into wage labour. Once begun, the manufacturing revolution occurred very swiftly, breaking out from textiles into heavy industry, and offering employment to more than 140 000 people by the beginning of the world depression (in 1929). After some delay during the depression, manufacturing continued to expand rapidly from the 1940s onwards. By the 1970s, black miners were only a small minority of the total black labour force. There were more jobs for black South Africans in manufacturing, in government service, and in domestic service, than in the mines; and substantial numbers of people were also employed in the construction business, and in trade, as well as in white agriculture. Further, since the mines persisted in recruiting a large number of workers (a quarter of a million men a year) from outside South Africa, there was a great difference between working conditions in the mines, and in other sectors of the capitalist economy. If mining was still overwhelmingly important as an earner of foreign exchange, it was no longer dominant in the domestic economy.

It is impossible here to trace all the implications of the rapid evolution of manufacturing, but even a brief discussion may indicate what social pressures it has created. First, manufacturing requires a very large labour force indeed, since South African manufacturing is less capital-intensive than manufacturing in western Europe or Japan or the United States. It is quite impossible for this whole sector to be reserved for white employment. Manufacturing also commonly involves the development of skills in the work force, so that labour migration is not a satisfactory way of mobilising the appropriate quality of workers. Second, there are important economies of scale in most manufacturing processes, so that large-scale production of goods is often a great deal cheaper than small-scale production. Manufacturers, therefore, unlike gold-mining managers, are always anxious to find new consumers for their products. A badly paid black labour force is unable to purchase consumer goods, so there is some logic in demanding that labourers be better paid in manufacturing than in a purely mining or a purely export economy. Third, the effect of the evolution of manufacturing has been to intensify the attraction of living outside the rural reserves (since by the late 1970s wages in urban areas were at least three times as high as rural wages). Manufacturing can therefore be seen to intensify the underdevelopment of the homelands, and to accelerate the urbanisation process. Taken together, rural underdevelopment, urbanisation, and manufacturing, have persistently undermined the credibility of the separate development programme.

Violent reactions

So far, we have argued against the possibility of separate development, simply in general terms. These arguments would carry little weight, if not for widespread outbreaks of violent opposition during the 1970s. It is the open expression of hostility to the government and its programmes which is the most convincing evidence of the developing crisis in South African affairs. After Sharpeville both the ANC and the PAC were banned by the government. Both went underground, and in the early 1960s there were sporadic acts of sabotage which gave evidence of their survival outside the law. However, the arrest of leading ANC members (including Nelson Mandela a year earlier) at Rivonia outside Johannesburg in 1963, and their subsequent trial and imprisonment, seemed to have ended the ANC's capacity to influence events within the country. Throughout the 1960s the security forces gave the impression of having suppressed organised resistance within South Africa, although both the ANC and PAC preserved their organisations outside the country. From today's perspective, it is the sullen quiescence of the 1960s which seems extraordinary, rather than the outbursts of anger in the 1970s.

A series of strikes broke out in and near Durban during 1973, and were suppressed by managements and by police; but so massive was the support for strike action that official attention was wrenched on to the misereable salaries and working conditions of which the strikers complained. Since trade unions were prevented from playing any effective legal role, the strikes also focused the government's attention on the need for some means of representing the interests and demands of workers, before a crisis was reached. Buthelezi and his party, Inkatha, were drawn into the area of wage negotiations, in the absence of industrially based bodies. Since 1973, strikes among black workers have become more common, so that the government finds it difficult to ignore the need for a workable system of industrial relations. However, to concede the need for trade unions is to undermine the Bantustan theory and the Bantustan authorities. In effect, trade unions have been permitted to all employees, but any elected trade union leader who is vigorous in representing workers is likely to be gaoled or detained.

The international as well as the national publicity which attended the Durban strikes also helped to put pressure on

Nelson Mandela in captivity following his arrest at Rivonia, 1962

employers to raise wages for black workers. Once again this tendency provoked political difficulties. During the mid-1970s, black wages seem often to have risen faster than white wages (although the wage differential was not significantly narrowed); and it was precisely in these years that the right-wing spokesmen for Afrikaners in politics began to win large-scale support among white Afrikaner workers. The black workers' strikes therefore decidedly sharpened the contradictions inherent in the government's policies: how to retain popularity among white electors without provoking violent reactions among blacks and without shaming the Bantustan representatives.

These contradictions were further revealed from 1976 onwards, in a nation-wide wave of school boycotts and strikes and demonstrations. These began in schools in Soweto, the black city outside Johannesburg, and moved rapidly from protests against the use of Afrikaans in schools to demonstrations against the education structure, against the police, and against the whole strategy of white supremacy and ethnic disunity. Although it was schoolchildren who initiated the boycott, the protest gained massive support from Africans, coloureds, and Indians throughout the republic and from all age groups, although it remained primarily a youth movement. In this crisis, the Bantustan structures proved quite useless. Almost all Bantustan authorities stayed away from the urban areas, and even Buthelezi, who could command large audiences in Durban and Johannesburg, began to lose popularity among the young. In the absence of any subtler method of maintaining social control, the state had to rely on the police, whose background and training make them insensitive to popular sentiments and as likely to provoke violence as to suppress it.

The large scale of these outbursts, and their frequency, could not be dismissed as mere errors in a workable system. Through first-hand experience, urban blacks were being reminded that the system of economic discrimination and of Bantustan political structures was inherently incapable of responding to their needs. This had been pointed out by the several thousand blacks in the black consciousness movement (and through the Black Peoples' Convention which was founded in 1972). Neither BPC nor Inkatha had recommended violent opposition to the state, but the massive and spontaneous expressions of hostility proved their analysis to be correct. The question then arose: how were black interests to be stated and defended?

It was at this point that the weaknesses of Inkatha's position became clear. Unlike the political parties governing other homelands, Inkatha did enjoy large-scale support: but that support was restricted to a tribally-defined constituency, and because it insisted upon the common interests shared by all Zulu, it was caught in another dilemma. The most militant black actors on the

Black demonstrators voice their protest against the Government in Soweto, 1976

public stage were wage workers, whereas the most influential members of Inkatha were small traders and businessmen and professionals. Inkatha could not take up the explicitly working-class interests of most Zulu, without antagonising the royalist, traditionalist, and petty bourgeois elements within Inkatha itself. On critical issues such as the proposed transfer of territory to Swaziland, Inkatha could give a clear lead: but in industrial and urban issues, such clarity was impossible.

Although the churches had been somewhat overshadowed by the violent events of the 1970s, a distinctively Christian opposition survived. A Christian humanism infused the rhetoric of the ANC, from its inception until it was outlawed: conversely a humanist strain of Christianity inspired many of the individual churchmen who defied apartheid from the 1950s onwards. By their individual examples, these churchmen demonstrated the universal and revolutionary values of Christianity; but they chose the role of individual witnesses and critics rather than leading popular mass movements. Only in Zimbabwe did Ndabaningi Sithole and Abel Muzorewa try to move from Christian criticism to political leadership, and both failed in the attempt.

The events of the 1970s demonstrated that the ANC and PAC, though banned and harassed for more than a decade, and deprived of legal organisation within South Africa, had not been forgotten. Early in 1978 there was an attendance of thousands at the funeral of Robert Sobukwe, the imprisoned leader of the PAC. While Bishop Desmond Tutu was a welcome member of the funeral crowd, Buthelezi was forced to leave. The ANC emerged even more powerfully from the shadows, also disavowing any connection with Buthelezi (a former member before the ANC was banned), and claiming responsibility for many of the acts of sabotage against government property and government buildings which occurred from the late 1970s onwards.

It is worth pondering the fact that, since the ANC has been banned from formal political life, and has adopted a more explicitly class-based interpretation of social and political change, it has lost nothing of its earlier appeal among working-class blacks. If the Bantustan governments have won small numbers of chiefs, and of professional and clerical workers and traders to a reluctant alliance with the South African authorities, this makes little difference to the broad appeal of the ANC and perhaps PAC. On the contrary, the more profound trends in the life of South Africans – rural underdevelopment, urbanisation, and the diversification of the economy – continue to create impoverished rural, permanently urban, and permanently proletarian blacks; and the Bantustan programme cannot possibly meet their needs, because the programme does not even acknowledge their existence

During 1982 the South African government put forward a

complicated constitutional plan, which was alleged to represent a solution of internal tension. In November 1983 the proposal was put to a referendum of white voters. The essence of the package was to create three houses of parliament, one each for whites, Coloureds and Indians. Power was to be concentrated in the hands of an executive president, almost certainly responsible to the white parliament. This proposal divided Afrikaners very seriously. The 'verligte' supporters of the Government, anxious to show the world that some reform was taking place, considered that the proposal was a necessary demonstration of flexibility. Many 'verkrampte' conservatives, however, objected to even the small tokens of power-sharing which were suggested. Although the white voters became very emotional about the issue, the constitutional proposal does nothing to relieve Africans of their heavy social, political and economic burdens. The fundamental problems of urbanisation, rural underdevelopment, and manufacturing are untouched; and Africans remain subject to the arbirtrary and often oppressive rule of the Bantustan authorities. Just as the Bantustan programme was a window-dressing means of answering the problems of the 1950s, so the power-sharing proposal of 1983 is an unrealistic attempt to cope with the rebellious mood of the 1970s. For opponents of discrimination, the reality remains the same: avoidable poverty, unequal power and arbitrary administration. And because nothing is done for Africans, the constitutional proposal actually offers only the illusion of benefit to Indian and Coloured voters, and the illusion of support for continued control by a white minority.

Chapter 18

The African dimension

During 1960 a great number of African colonies achieved sovereign independence: most of the French territories in West Africa, Nigeria the largest population, and the Belgian Congo the most turbulent. The year 1960 was thought to be a remarkable and auspicious one, since the independence of British East African dependencies could not be much longer delayed, .and the United Nations officially declared the 1960s to be 'Development Decade', acknowledging the urgent need for rapid economic growth in most of Africa and many other underdeveloped regions of the world. Such optimistic views, and the fact that even a British Conservative Prime Minister could acknowledge 'winds of change' in the continent, were bound to cause alarm in the white-minority regimes of southern Africa. Neither majority rule, nor the independence of tropical Africa, nor rapid economic development in tropical Africa, were very welcome. We now know that the pace of political change proved to be slower and the extent of economic change smaller than most people expected in 1960. Nevertheless changes in the African dimension profoundly unsettled the status quo in southern Africa, and in many former colonies there has at last been a drastic transformation of political and economic relationships. In this final chapter, we seek to trace these general changes in southern Africa, and to observe their implications for the last of the minority-ruled societies.

Before we look at each of the independent countries in turn, some general features of their polities and economies should be considered. First, the political institutions inherited at independence were mainly those which had evolved during nearly a century of colonial administration. Rural administration was mainly concerned with preserving order, with the ultimate sanction of locally-recruited police and armies which were also geared to protecting the interests of the colonising power. Such administrations were better equipped to preserve the status quo than to achieve the social transformation which some leaders dreamed of. The addition of an elected parliament, and the rapid Africanisation of the bureaucracy, would not automatically transform the nature of the state. Second, the colonial economy usually left subsistence food production alone, and concentrated on increasing the production of export crops or minerals, in an unprocessed condition, for sale on the international market.

The idea of 'development' in 1960 meant little more than intensifying the existing economic strategy, and the need for pay for an expanded bureaucracy made it even more urgent to increase export production. This had a most unfortunate consequence for the balance of each ex-colonial economy. As a rule, the subsistence economy was complex, highly evolved, and quite efficient: export production was often simple, crude, and unprofitable: yet the transport and technical and extension resources would be devoted to the crude export sectors of the economy, leaving the subsistence producers to fend for themselves. Rapidly increasing populations were putting great pressure on food production, which badly needed research and improvement; but no attention could be given to such problems, in view of the urgency of earning foreign exchange through export production. In brief, the political and economic changes of the 1960s would not by themselves change the political and economic relationships in which most African societies were already entangled.

Central Africa

Since 1953 the British territories of Nyasaland, Northern and Southern Rhodesia had been bound together in the Central African Federation, a device whereby settlers (mainly in Southern Rhodesia) controlled the region on behalf of the British Government. Nyasaland labour, Northern Rhodesian copper, and Southern Rhodesian settler agriculture were linked together, but in such a way as to benefit the settlers who controlled the legislature and the executive. Federal institutions were built in or around Salisbury; the railway network and freight rates favoured settler farmers; the power station of the Kariba Dam complex (the largest project of the era) was positioned on the southern bank of the Zambesi; and the federal authorities perceived African protest movements (quite properly) as the main obstacles to continued settler prosperity and dominance. These protests were suppressed mainly by police action, but the underdevelopment which provoked them was not given serious attention.

Belgian control over the Congo was also challenged by a series of protest movements which were not nation-wide in scope, but which did pose a serious problem of continued control. In the middle of 1960 the Belgians abruptly handed over power in an independent Congo to a national movement led by Patrice Lumumba, which was not yet firmly consolidated. While Lumumba had vision and charisma, he had no massive nationalist movement to support him, nor a reliable bureaucracy to implement central

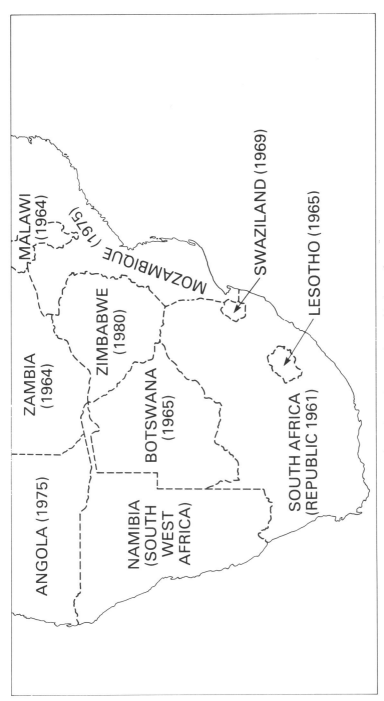

Map 11 Political boundaries of present-day southern Africa, showing dates of independence

government authority. The country's most obvious wealth – copper and other minerals – was concentrated in the southern-most province of Katanga, where Union Minière, the mining colossus, encouraged Moise Tshombe to secede and declare an independent republic. Tshombe enjoyed some local support, but relied more directly upon South African mercenaries and Belgian mining capital. Conor Cruise O'Brien described his government as an extension of the white minority states, with a thin but expensive veneer of African leaders.

The Organisation of African Unity was in no position to assist, so Lumumba appealed to the United Nations for support against the secession. The UN force in the Congo, however, was paralysed by the veiled approval which Britain and France extended to Belgium and to the secessionists. In a long series of crises, Lumumba was assassinated, and although the secession was brought to an end, it was Tshombe who emerged, briefly, as President of the re-united country. Eventually the Commander-in-Chief, General Mobutu, seized power in 1965, and from the capital of Kinshasa began to extend his personal authority over the outlying provinces. These disasters of the first years of independence, and the long agony of getting rid of the mercenary forces, extinguished Lumumba's vision of an entirely independent continent, and encouraged the Zaire Government to concentrate on a mainly passive international policy, relying on United States aid, and ignoring developments further south (except in Angola, as we shall see).

This long crisis made it clear that the Central African Federation was too flimsy to contain all the tensions of the region. In 1961 the British proposed constitutions for both Nyasaland and Northern Rhodesia and after a long political argument, in 1962 these new constitutions were put into effect, so that African majorities entered the two colonial legislatures. In the following year the federation was dissolved, leaving the way clear for the independence of Malawi and Zambia in 1964. Both new governments were anxious, in the long term, to reduce the importance of their links to the south, but neither could make any immediate progress in that direction. Dr Hastings Kamuzu Banda, who assumed the leadership of Malawi, swiftly got rid of the younger, more radical members of the government, and allowed the system of labour migration to continue. For a decade, he conducted diplomatic relations with South Africa in a fashion which embarrassed other African governments and delighted Pretoria; but in the mid-1970s labour migration was stopped. Dr Kenneth Kaunda of Zambia made more explicit his repugnance for apartheid (for example, Zambia's national anthem is the old anthem of the African National Congress) and declined to open normal diplomatic relations; but the disruption of the Zambian economy through declining agriculture, unstable copper prices, and the Zimbabwean civil war in the 1970s made it impossible to sever economic relationships. The opening of the Chinese-built TanZam railway was more a symbolic than a substantive link to the north: South Africa remained the cheapest and most convenient source of manufactured goods and grain, and offered the most reliable railway system to the coast.

The High Commission Territories

As late as 1963 Dr Verwoerd could publicly request the transfer of Basutoland, Bechuanaland and Swaziland from British dependency to incorporation as Bantustans within the South African constellation of states; but the prospect for such a development had probably been dead since 1948, and certainly since South Africa's expulsion from the Commonwealth in 1961. But these territories could no longer remain isolated fragments of the British empire, especially after the collapse of the Central African Federation and the move towards complete decolonisation by Britain. In 1966 Basutoland became independent as Lesotho and Bechuanaland as Botswana; Swaziland followed in 1968. Independence in itself might mean rather little: all three countries relied heavily upon the Customs Union for their revenue, upon the gold mines for employment for young men, and upon South African-controlled communications and transport systems. The responses of the new governments to these constraints suggest the range of policies available to them.

At independence, power passed calmly in Botswana to an elected government, with Seretse Khama as President. Khama was unpopular in South Africa because of his marriage to an Englishwoman, and the new government preserved a dignified distance between itself and its larger neighbour. Within the new administration, however, authority rested with a coalition of well-to-do pastoralists who were socially conservative in outlook and aristocratic in personal style. Government revenue relied very heavily upon the earnings of labour migrants, and in the 1970s the government moved to raise the level of the recruiting fee, and to tax mining incomes directly. These moves emphasised Botswana's economic dependence, and did nothing to reduce it. Within the country, credit and extension services became more directly geared to the needs of pastoral producers, with the effect of widening the gap between them and the majority of smallholders, who had to supplement their direct incomes through wage labour. During the 1970s the internal economy was greatly changed by the opening up of extensive mineral deposits, so that the rural poor could now choose between migration to Johannesburg, or to the mining complex at Selibe-Pikwe: but the essential divisions within the society were not much modified.

Lesotho, the only country entirely surrounded by South Africa, was also the least viable economically at the time of Independence. The extreme shortage of arable land, and of capital to develop it, threw the population into the migrant labour market, with little prospect of any alternative employment. The monarchy – the young king Moshoeshoe II – was curtailed and abolished by Chief Leabua Jonathan, who won the first election and subsequently remained in power.

In Swaziland, in the general elections held on the eve of independence in October 1968, King Sobhuza II's party, the Imbokodvo National Movement, won all the 24 seats in parliament, completely out-manoeuvring the modern political parties led by the educated Swazi. A government led by Prince Makhosini Dlamini as Prime Minister was installed, and King Sobhuza was recognised as the head of state of independent Swaziland. Sobhuza pursued an extremely conservative policy which was reflected by his determination to blend 'tradition' with 'modernity' in his espousal of cultural nationalism within Swaziland. Further, Swaziland's politics were dominated by the royal house and by members of chiefly families, while the economy tended to be controlled by the white settlers, principally from the Republic of South Africa. In his *hamba kahle* (go slowly) approach to relations with South Africa, Sobhuza tolerated the operations of South African companies within Swaziland, and even toyed with the idea of a Swazi 'homeland' being created at some stage in the future. Typical of Sobhuza's gradualist approach was his intervention in 1971 in opposition to any rash action by the Makhosini administration in recovering land from white farmers through the Land Speculation Bill of that year. Swaziland's neo-colonial position *vis-à-vis* South Africa was well known to the king, but clearly he was unable to do anything about it.

Politically, Swaziland attempted to avoid getting involved as a base for anti-South African actions by the liberation movements. Internally, the political and constitutional crisis of 1973 in which the king abolished the constitution, suspended parliament and declared a return to a more traditional government, meant the end of political activities by the main opposition parties. One of the last important declarations Sobhuza made before his death in August 1982 was the 1977 announcement of the replacement of parliament with *tinkundla* (regional committees). These were to incorporate the educated and the uneducated as well as the rural and urban population: their main function was to 'maintain cultural identity and promote peaceful development'. The success of these committees, like the survival of the very institution of kingship itself, still remains to be determined.

The effect of independence in Botswana, Lesotho and Swaziland has therefore had little direct bearing upon the struggles taking place within South Africa itself. The dependence of the economies has dictated that the independent governments treat the South African state with reluctant respect, confining their opposition to statements of dismay. Many black (and a few white) refugees have crossed the borders to escape through Botswana, and smaller numbers through Lesotho and Swaziland; but the independent countries have not offered a platform for organising an armed intervention: they constitute one-way escape routes.

Portuguese collapse

During the late 1950s, independence movements began to emerge in all three Portuguese African colonies, led by individual Africans who had received a formal higher education abroad, and seeking links with the mass of the rural population. Elsewhere in the continent, such fragile movements were often successful in the 1960s, becoming the inheritors of political power through decolonisation. Portugal, however, was to prove the last (as well as the first) European colonial power on the continent. Metropolitan Portugal itself remained a poor and underdeveloped country, which could ill afford to lose the protected markets and revenues of its overseas territories. Throughout the 1960s therefore conflict escalated into bitter civil war. In Mozambique, FRELIMO (led by the American-educated Eduardo Mondlane) began a classic guerilla campaign, leading to the establishment of alternative governments and alternative policies in the liberated areas, mainly in the far north and west. In Angola a similar war developed, but was complicated by the division of the indigenous liberation movement into three, each based on a regional base: Agostinho Neto's MPLA in the east, Jonas Savimbi's UNITA in the south, and Holden Roberto's FNLA on the Zaire border. Since guerilla warfare was also being waged in the West African territory of Guinea Bissau, Portugal found itself committing most of its army to unwinnable campaigns against a series of unpinnable enemies. A small measure of decentralisation introduced by Caetano in 1970 (who had succeeded Salazar as dictator-president) indicated the strains on the Portuguese economy, but did nothing to meet the proliferating crisis. At last, in 1974, the Portuguese armed forces took matters into their own hands, overthrowing the government in Portugal, and moving very swiftly to abandon all overseas territories in 1975.

In Mozambique there was little doubt that FRELIMO should and could form the new administration. Mozambique became fully independent on 25 June 1975 under a FRELIMO regime headed by President Samora Machel. Settlers in Lourenço Marques (soon re-named Maputo) attempted a coup of their own, but were not supported by the South African Government, and the rising quickly collapsed, leading to a large emigration of Portuguese settlers back

Samora Machel, first President of fully independent Mozambique

to Portugal, and across the border to South Africa. The South African Government must have calculated that FRELIMO was either inevitable, or the best prospect for social control; and that some kind of co-existence was possible. FRELIMO was a revolutionary movement, and (because of Portugal's commitment to Nato) it had some links with the USSR. It had also sustained a long campaign to destroy the hydro-electric complex at Cabora Bassa, which was linked to the South African power grid. In government, however,

FRELIMO was obliged to find ways of managing the Mozambique economy, without enjoying the recruiting fees which the Portuguese had levied on labour migrants. The internal restructuring of Mozambique's society and economy – to cope with the departure of Portuguese colonists and technicians as well as to create a more equitable society – took higher priority than the immediate disengagement from South African entanglements. It was still the case that both governments benefited from the smooth operation of the railway and harbour complex, and from the Cabora Bassa irrigation and power-generating system.

The South African reaction was quite different to the more confused situation which prevailed in Angola as the Portuguese forces withdrew without a clear succession. A judgement must have been made in Pretoria that an MPLA administration was both undesirable and avoidable, because a flying column of South African troops was launched directly at the capital Luanda, to pre-empt MPLA assuming office. It was not far outside Luanda that the column was halted, by MPLA and Cuban forces who flew in swiftly to protect the new government. Since then, South African forces have operated freely in southern Angola, allegedly in support of Savimbi's UNITA movement, but clearly on their own initiative. The intervention in Angola has had a dramatic effect on international relations. South African officials assume that the United States either endorses or acquiesces in the Angolan adventure; and the Western powers as a whole have observed matters without protest. African governments however – including many who have no sympathy with MPLA – can only be appalled at such intervention. As the Organisation of African Unity crumbled and almost collapsed in the late 1970s, a more pacific South African government might perhaps have established 'normal' relations with some African governments; but a South African government committed to indefinite adventurism has paralysed its diplomatic offensive on the continent.

Zimbabwe

The independence of Mozambique was an important incident in the decline and fall of Rhodesia as a white-minority regime, and almost certainly accelerated that process. When Ian Smith's Rhodesian Front regime declared itself independent in 1965, it counted upon a half-hearted protest from Britain and the unpreparedness of Africans generally. The first assumption proved accurate: British governments declined to intervene militarily (although the Falklands War in 1982 suggested that the military difficulties were less of an impediment than was claimed at the time), and applied economic sanctions in such a way as to be irritating rather than effective. The swift arrest and imprisonment of African leaders within the country also paralysed black resistance for a while. Armed resistance was very slow to emerge, until the early 1970s when coherent military forces took shape. The independence of Mozambique, then, made it much easier for one wing of the Patriotic Front to organise itself for operations in the eastern regions, while the other wing of the PF continued to operate under great difficulties from bases in Zambia. Diplomatic sanctions on their own did not, and probably could not, undermine the minority regime: rather they provoked the regime to take firm control over the economy, in order to create a viable basis for long-term survival in isolation. So long as the South African Government and business firms supported the Rhodesian Government and producers, diplomatic isolation was merely an inconvenience.

During the 1970s Patriotic Front forces did establish themselves, and did begin to command popular support in rural areas. The Rhodesian forces were well armed, and enjoyed some support from mercenaries and from South Africa; but the 'bush war' could not be won by superior arms. As the regime realised that it was being worn down, it moved – too late – towards an 'internal settlement' which would divide African opposition, while leaving Nkomo and Mugabe and their followers out of power. That strategy might have had some success a decade earlier; but by the mid-1970s any African politician who entered relationships with Smith, and accepted implicit South African support, would be discredited at once in the eyes of the people. Abel Muzorewa, who led the internal government with Ian Smith breathing down his neck, became an increasingly sad figure; and when supervised elections were held in 1980, his candidates were routed. To the surprise and dismay of the settlers, of the South African Government, and of the British Government as well, Robert Mugabe's wing of the Popular Front won an absolute majority of seats. Muzorewa's failure to capture seats from Mugabe, combined with the failure of Joshua Nkomo's wing to capture seats outside the Ndebele area, avoided the need for a coalition, which many observers had expected.

With massive popular support, the new government was able to initiate not only popular and overdue policies such as land redistribution but also less popular policies designed to retain the confidence of some skilled whites, and to gain the confidence of international financial institutions. The task of the government was enormously complicated by an open breach with Nkomo, which broke up the governing coalition. At the same time, the presence in the country of hundreds of demobilised guerillas, many of whom had been trained to fight and to do little else, made the problems of rural security acute. A government committed to maintaining agricultural production and yet redistributing land, and to maintaining industrial production despite the loss of skilled manpower, and to equalisation without loss of social control, had a

Robert Mugabe, Prime Minister of Zimbabwe

great deal on its agenda. Apart from allowing formal relations with South Africa to wither away, and developing good relations with Mozambique and Zambia, the new Zimbabwean Government had little immediate effect in regional affairs.

Namibia

While the pastoral people of central Namibia, with fairly easy access to schools and to literacy, were the quickest to express their opposition to the South African occupation, the agricultural population of the northern borderlands moved rapidly from formal opposition to armed resistance. Since Namibia was a mandated territory, with a special relationship to the United Nations, it was natural for protestors to appeal to the United Nations, and to the International Court of Justice, for the removal of the South African occupation. This strategy was shown to be counter-productive when, in 1966, the Court closed the door to political change through judicial decision. Ethiopia and Liberia, appearing before the Court as former members of the League of Nations, were advised by the judges that they had no standing in the dispute. A different strategy was now required, as the United Nations, while expressing disapproval of apartheid in general and the South African occupation of Namibia in particular, was not about to take action to support those opinions. SWANU, representing the young, the educated, and the pastoral communities, stated a dignified protest: SWAPO, representing the dense northern population, moved to armed resistance. It was SWAPO, which was willing and able to train a military arm, which received the recognition and support of the Organisation of African Unity, and of the United Nations, in the 1970s.

The South African Government settled down to fight for Namibia during the 1970s on two distinct fronts. SWAPO forces were fought in the northern regions, and across the border in Angola, in a prolonged war of attrition. The Angolan Government, although anxious to establish normal diplomatic relations with the United States, has had to rely on Cuban and other allies, to protect the country from raids across the border – while the South African Government has pointed to the Cubans as a justification for keeping up a long campaign against 'communism'. Throughout the rest of Namibia acts of violence have been rare, and the war has mainly been contained in the north. Behind the barrier of the South African Defence Force, the administration during the 1970s pieced together a fragile coalition of ethnic constituencies, later formalised as the Democratic Turnhalle Alliance, and representing most of the conservative interests in the country which look nervously at SWAPO. A few small political groups (including the original SWANU, now reduced to a young Herero party) have stayed clear

of the Turnhalle Alliance, without committing themselves to SWAPO: but these middle-of-the-road groups find themselves crushed as the country is polarised into SWAPO and non-SWAPO camps. The South Africans are clearly not willing to risk elections for independence unless they can be sure that their protégés will win (and the disastrous fate of Muzorewa in Zimbabwe makes the South Africans very nervous indeed): SWAPO sees itself as the legitimate anti-colonial movement, which should not need to jump over electoral hurdles as well as conducting the liberation war.

The African dimension

In the early and middle 1960s, it seemed as if the Organisation of African Unity might become the powerful and effective voice of Africa, able to lay down the continental interest in localised issues. As matters turned out, most of the newly independent countries were more closely linked to metropolitan powers and markets than to their neighbours, and a series of localised wars increasingly paralysed the organisation, until the early 1980s when it became difficult for the OAU even to hold meetings. The liberation of Mozambique and Angola, therefore, owed little to OAU support, and the liberation of Zimbabwe owed even less. In each case the society had essentially to liberate itself, and to seek allies outside Africa as well as sympathisers within. The South African Government has therefore been able to disregard the OAU, and to concentrate on individual African governments.

Increasingly, too, the South African authorities have dabbled in clandestine and armed intervention (in Angola, in support of a small rebel movement in Mozambique, and in the early 1980s in the Seychelles and Lesotho). There may be some advantage to the South African Government in some of these adventures, but the overall effect is to convince all African governments that they should steer clear of alliances with Pretoria. At the same time, South African employers (especially in the gold-mining industry) have been encouraged to cut down on migrant labour from outside the immediate region, and to rely instead upon South African (and Basotho) workers, even if this means slightly higher wage rates. While trade has been encouraged, dependence upon foreign labour has not. This also marks something of a retreat from regional economic dominance to a smaller sphere of operations. The 'African dimension' which is crucial to the future of the South African regime, is not so much the attitudes and actions of Africans as a whole, but rather of Africans within South Africa's own boundaries. The fewer migrant labourers come from outside, the more important is labour recruited from inside the South African economy: the less labour is employed, the more machinery is needed, and a skilled labour force to operate it. The fewer goods are exported to the rest of the continent, the more they must be purchased in the domestic market. In all these respects, black South Africans assume a more obvious role than ever before. To put the same point in another fashion: the old pre-capitalist modes of production have now been almost entirely ground down, and black South Africans are committed almost totally to the new capitalist economy, which does have a logic of its own. If all blacks are poor, who is to buy manufactured goods? If all blacks are unskilled technically, who is to operate the capital-intensive machinery?

The general strategy of the South African state during the past twenty years has been to promote divisions within black South African society: the Bantustans imply a black population divided by language and ethnicity, but they also imply a thin stratum of black politicians, bureaucrats, and traders (though probably not producers of commodities), whose self-interest ties them to the white minority, and who may help to maintain social control in the townships and in the countryside. The trends of the last twenty years, however, suggest that this is not a winning strategy. In the Transkei, for example, the benefits for blacks are too few, and too concentrated in a very few hands, to make the Transkei state a source of strength to Pretoria. In KwaZulu, on the other hand, a larger black petty bourgeoisie is unwilling to play the docile role expected of it. In the persistently growing urban areas, in spite of the divisions implied by language and ethnic origin, people organise themselves on the basis of social class which tends to cut across ethnic lines. And in the rural areas the bankruptcy of South African policy is plainly written in the desperate efforts of blacks to escape to the towns, and to avoid being repatriated to their impoverished and miserable so-called 'homes'.

Scholars and journalists are often tempted to regard a particular event or a particular date as a decisive 'turning point'. In reality, every moment is a decisive one. Southern Africa has passed through many genuinely decisive turning-points, but always faces another one. So far, since 1800, all South African governments have chosen to see themselves as physically located in Africa, but somehow separate from it; as outposts of non-African societies, operating non-African economies. African resistance in the nineteenth century was often based on the view that these were external forces, to be held at bay. During the twentieth century African societies have been so eroded and re-shaped, and so entangled in the social relations of capitalist production, that the separation of races has become increasingly arbitrary, artificial, and coercive. The next decisive turning-point must be reached within a very few years. The successful management of a mature capitalist economy requires quite different techniques of social control than the devices which work in an undeveloped capitalist economy. On the one hand, systems of crude coercion may succeed in controlling the people for a very long time, but jeopardise capitalism itself by making it intensely unpopular. On the other hand, the good will of the direct producers may require concessions which the controllers of the state are unwilling to concede.

Most of the arguments among historians of South Africa hinge on this question: does capitalism necessarily produce economic and social and political inequality? Or does it tend in the long run to generate a prosperous and harmonious society? It is this question, which has never been finally settled, that now faces resolution. As the question is resolved, it will be (once again) the creative or destructive forces within the African dimensions of South African society, which determine the issue.

Sources

This text provides one way of synthesising the books which have already been published on South Africa and her neighbours since 1800. To make the best use of this text, it should be read in conjunction with as many other books as possible. South Africa has, however, produced a very uneven historiography, and writers have interpreted events in a variety of ways. Also, until the late 1960s the progress of historical scholarship in the rest of Africa had made little impact inside South Africa itself. The first edition of this text, for example, could rely upon very little information about the lives of the African majority and the actions they initiated. During the past fifteen years, a great deal of good history has been published, giving many new perspectives on southern African affairs. In the list of sources below, we include a fairly wide range of books, including recent texts as well as the older sources.

BALLINGER, M., *From Union to Apartheid*, Cape Town, 1969.
BEACH, D. N., *The Shona and Zimbabwe, 900–1850*, Gwelo and London, 1980.
BENDER, C. J., *Angola under the Portuguese*, London, 1978.
BENSON, M., *The African Patriots*, London, 1963.
BLEY, H., *South-West Africa Under German Rule*, London, 1971.
BUNDY, C., *The Rise and Fall of the South African Peasantry*, London, 1979.
BUNTING, B., *The Rise of the South African Reich*, London, 1964.
CARTER, G. M., *The Politics of Inequality: South Africa since 1948*, London, 1958.
CHANOCK, M., *Unconsummated Union: Britain, Rhodesia and South Africa, 1900–45*, Manchester, 1977.
DAVENPORT, T. R. H., *South Africa: a Modern History*, London, 1977.
DE KIEWIET, C. W., *A History of South Africa, Social and Economic*, London, 1941.
ELPHICK, R., *Kraal and Castle: Khoikhoi and the Founding of White South Africa*, New Haven and London, 1977.
ELPHICK, R., and GILIOMEE, H, *The Shaping of South African Society, 1652–1820*, Cape Town and London, 1979.

FAGAN, B. M., *A Short History of Zambia*, Oxford, 1967.

FIRST, R., *South West Africa*, London, 1963.

GRAY, R., *The Two Nations*, London, 1960.

GUY, J., *The Destruction of the Zulu Kingdom: the Civil War in Zululand, 1879–1884*, London, 1979.

HYAM, R., *The Failure of South African Expansion*, London, 1972.

ISAACMAN, I., *Mozambique: the Africanisation of a European Institution, the Zambesi Prazos, 1750–1902*, Madison, 1972.

— *The tradition of Resistance in Mozambique*, London, 1976.

KADALIE, C., *My Life and the I.C.U.*, London, 1970.

KUPER, H., *Sobhuza II: Ngwenyama and King of Swaziland*, London, 1978.

LUTHULI, A., *Let My People Go*, London, 1962.

MACMILLAN, W. M., *Bantu, Boer and Briton*, London, 1929.

MANDELA, N., *No Easy Walk to Freedom*, London, 1965.

MARKS, S., *Reluctant Rebellion*, London, 1969.

MARKS, S., AND ATMORE, A., *Economy and Society in Pre-Industrial South Africa*, London, 1980.

MARKS, S., AND RATHBONE, R., *Industrialisation and Social Change in South Africa*, London, 1982.

MBEKI, G., *South Africa: the Peasants' Revolt*, London, 1964.

MONDLANE, E., *The Struggle for Mozambique*, London, 1969.

MULLER, C. F. J., *500 Years: South African History*, Pretoria, 1969.

NGUBANE, J., *An African Explains Apartheid*, London, 1963.

NOLUTSHUNGU, S. C., *South Africa in Africa*, Manchester, 1975.

OMER-COOPER, J. D., *The Zulu Aftermath*, London, 1966.

PALMER, R., *Land and Racial Domination in Rhodesia*, London, 1977.

PALMER, R., AND PARSONS, N., *The Roots of Rural Poverty in Central and Southern Africa*, London, 1977.

PEIRES, J. B., *The House of Phalo: a History of the Xhosa People in the Days of their Independence*, Johannesburg, 1981.

RANGER, T. O., *Revolt in Southern Rhodesia*, London, 1967.

ROBERTS, A. D., *A History of Zambia*, London, 1976.

ROSS, R., *Adam Kok's Griquas*, Cambridge, 1976.

ROUX, E., *Time Longer than Rope*, London, 1966.

ROTBERG, R., *The Rise of Nationalism in Central Africa*, London, 1966.

SANDERS, P., *Moshoeshoe, Chief of the Sotho*, London, 1975.

SIMONS, H. J. AND R. E., *Class and Colour in South Africa 1850–1950*, London, 1969.

SITHOLE, N, *African Nationalism*, Oxford, 1959.

SUNDKLER, B. G. M., *Bantu Prophets in South Africa*, London, 1961.

THOMPSON, L. M., *The Unification of South Africa*, Oxford, 1960.

—, *Survival in Two Worlds: Moshoeshoe of Lesotho 1786–1870*, Oxford, 1975.

VAIL, L., AND WHITE, L., *Capitalism and Colonialism in Mozambique*, London, 1980.

VAN JAARSVELD, F. A., *The Awakening of Afrikaner Nationalism, 1868–1881*, Cape Town, 1961.

VAN ONSELEN, C., *Chibaro: African Mine Labour in Southern Rhodesia 1900–1933*, London, 1976.

—, *Studies in the Social and Economic History of the Witwatersrand 1887–1914*, 2 Vols., London, 1982.

VILAKAZI, A., *Zulu Transformation*, Pietermaritzburg, 1962.

WARWICK, P. (ed.), *The South African War*, London, 1981.

WILSON, M., AND THOMPSON, L.,(eds.), *The Oxford History of South Africa,* 2 Vols., Oxford, 1969 and 1971.

Index

African influence in, 179, 181; *see also* Lesotho

Bechuanaland: administration, 116–17, 118–20, 122, 135, 137; agriculture and economy, 126, 137, 145; independence, 225, 226–7; South African influence in, 179–80, 181; *see also* Botswana

bijwoners, 129, 144

Black Peoples' Convention, 217

Bloem, Jan, 51

Bloemfontein, 187

Blood River, Battle of, 76, 77

Bophuthatswana, 202, 204, 206, 208, 211

Botha, Louis, 133, *134*, 135, 161, 163, 164, 175, 190

Botswana: Bantustans and, 207, 208; independence, 225, 226–7; South African influence in, 179–80, 181, 225

Brand, John Hendrick, 80, *81*, 110

Britain: ANC delegations to, *188*, 189; annexations, 78–9, 81–2, 85, 87, 90, 110–12, 116–17, 122, 142–3; Army, strike-breaking by, 162; attempts at confederation, 109–16, 130; attitude to Rhodesias and Nyasaland, 183–4, 229; Cape administered by, 17, 56–7, 68–73, 76–84; creation of post-imperial successor state, 130–8; economic dependency on, 153; High Commission territories, 136–8, 178–81, 207–8, 225–7; imperial interests upheld in post-colonial state, 135–8, 161–2; imperialism, attitudes towards, 109–10, 116, 118–20, 122–3; Indian trade, 15, 17; post-colonial links with, 161–2, 164, 167, 171, 184; as world power, 108

British South Africa Company, 117, 120, 122, 135, 137–8, 179, 181–2

Burgers, T. F., 110

Bushmen, 10; *see also* San

Buthelezi, Chief Gatsha, 202–4, 215, 217, 219

Cape: British administration, 17, 56–7, 68–73, 76–84; early European attitudes to, 14–15; economic impact of diamonds on, 92–5; European settlement, 15–24; government and administration, 56–7, 68–73, 76–84, 92, 94–5, 109, 116, 133, 163, 185; military capacity, 93; population growth, 93–4; rural inequalities, 57–8, 140–1; self-government, 83–4; territorial expansion, 90, 93; trekkers' dependency on, 80–1

Cape Town: dependence on trade, 21–2, 24; Dutch supply station, 15–17; early function and character, 17, 56–8; regional impact of establishment, 17–19

capital: agricultural, shortage of, 85, 143, 209–10; mining, 89, 99–100, 135–6, 150–1, 156

Carnarvon, Lord, 110, 112

caste society, Ndebele as, 49, 51

cattle: diseases, 5, 78, 106, 126, 141; quality, 125; ownership, Basotho system of, 39–40, 44; *see also* pastoralism

cattle frontier, expansion of, 59–67

Central African Federation, 184, 222, 224–5

Cetshwayo, 110, 112, *113*, 114, 123, 186

Chamber of Mines, 99, 128, 155

Chamberlain, Joseph, 122, 123

Chartered Company, *see* British South Africa Company

Chelmsford, Lord, 114

chiefs, African, 185–6; in ANC, 187, 189; in Bantustans, 200, 202; *see also names of individual chiefs*

Christianity, 43, 57, 61, 71, 219

Ciskei, 202

Coloured Persons' Representative Council, 205–7

coloured population: alienation, 171, 172, 189; on frontier, 60

Communist Party and communism, 191, 192, 199

confederacy, Sotho state as, 40, 44

confederation, attempts at, 109–16, 130

Congo, independence of, 222–4

Congress Alliance, 193–6

Congress of Democrats, 194

Congress of the People, 194

Congress of Trade Unions, 194

copper mining, 156

Consolidated Gold Fields, 100, 120

Cubans, 229, 232

customs revenue, 180

Customs Union, 225

De Beers Consolidated Mines, 89, 90–1, 100, 120, 127, 149–50, 155, 156

Delagoa Bay, 14

dependency, 153; ex-colonies, 224, 225–7, 229

diamond mining, 85–95, 99, 127–8, 149–50, 155–6; *see also* gold

Difaqane, see Mfecane

Dingane, 35–6, 41, 76, 78

Dingiswayo, 26, 27, 30, 31, 34

Dinuzulu, 131, 186
disease, 18, 52, 54, 78; cattle, 5, 78, 106, 126, 141
Dlamini, 45, 56
Dlamini, Prince Makhosini, 226
Dube, John, 186, *188*, 189
Durban, strikes in, 215
Dutch East India Company, 15–17, 19–24 *passim*, 56, 68

East India Company, 17, 56–7, 68
Eckstein and Co., H., 100
economy, Bantustans': dependence on S. Africa, 200–2, 204–5, 208
economy, capitalist: African role in, 234–5; establishment and expansion, 19, 20–2, 73; labour regulation for, 71–3; *see also* labour
economy, centralised: Ndebele, 49; Zulu, 28
economy, colonial: dependence on Britain, 153; diversification, 152, 155, 157; emphasis on exports, 221–2; impact of mining on, 92–5, 101, 104, 128, 133, 136, 150, 151–60
economy, ex-colonies', 221–2, 224, 225–7, 229
economy, pre-capitalist, 1–12; impact of market economy on, 75–6; population pressure and, 31–3
education, 93, 101, 141, 172, 180, 185, 186, 198–9, 217
'1820 settlers', 70
elections, 163, 167, 170–1, 197; Rhodesian, 230; *see also* franchise
environment: population density and, 31–3; pre-colonial states and, 25, 31–3; pre-capitalist production and, 1–12
Europeans: exploration, 13; settlement and expansion, 15–24; southern Africa's early unattractiveness to, 13–15; *see also* Britain; Portuguese; white settlers evolution, 10
explosive manufacture, 104, 152
exports: De Beers' contribution to, 149–50; emphasis on, 221–2; gold, 101, 104, 132; increase in, 73–4

FNLA, 227
franchise, 83, 101–3, 120, 123, 163, 185; exclusion of Africans and coloureds from, 136, 170, 171, 172, 187, 192
free trade, 68, 108
freeburghers, 20
Freedom Charter, 194
FRELIMO, 227, 228–9
Frere, Sir Bartle, 112, 114

frontier, colonial: conflicts and warfare on, 23, 24, 76, 77, 79, 81, 82; expansion, 58–67, 69, 73; fragmentation along, 67; government and administration, 60–1, 62, 64–7; interaction and trade along, 71, 75; peasantisation on, 74–6; stabilisation, 69–71
frontier societies, 66–7
Fusion government, 169–70
Fynn, Henry Francis, 30

Gaza empire, 34, 52–4, 120, 186
German South West Africa, 115–16, 126, 131, 138, 145, 167, 173–6, 186; S. African influence in and occupation of, 167, 175–6
Germany: non-intervention in S. African War, 124; rivalry with Britain, 108, 122–3; Transvaal and, 105
Ghandi, M. K., 189
Glen Grey legislation, 91–2, 140
gold mining, 96–107, 128, 129–30, 132, 136, 151–5, 156–7
government and administration: African townships, 212; agriculture and industry encouraged by, 142, 143, 144, 155, 157, 160; Bantustans, 200–2; Cape, by British, 56–7, 68–73, 76–84; Central African Federation, 184, 222, 224–5; colonial frontier, 60–1, 62, 64–7; ex-colonies, 221–2, 224, 225, 226–7, 230, 232–3; German South West Africa, 138, 175; Griqualand West, 85, 90, 109, 112; influence of mining capitalists on, 90, 91–2, 103–4, 105, 128, 133, 135–6, 151–2, 164, 165; Transvaal, 97, 101–4, 105–6, 109, 115, 118, 120–2, 132–5; trekboers and trekker republics, 64–6, 76, 78–81, 110
government and administration, colonial: annexations, 76, 78–9, 81–2; expanding responsibilities, 76–83; institutions of inherited by Afrikaners, 161; labour supply regulation, 71–3; by military officers, 69; self-government, 83–4; trekboers and, 64, 67; *see also* trekker republics
government and administration, post-colonial: African opposition to, 187, 189–96, 215–19; astonishment at activities of, 161; institutions of, 162–3; major interest groups represented in, 164–7, 172; regional influence, 173–84; repression of Africans, 167–72, 192, 197–215, 234; Transkei, 200–2

Malawi, 159, 183–4, 224; *see also* Nyasaland
manatees, 35
Mandela, Nelson, 215, *216*
MaNthatisi, 34, 41, 42
Maqoma, 74, 75
Matanzima, Chief Kaiser, 202
Matiwane, 34, 41
Mawewe, 47, 53
Mbandzemi, 118
Merriman, John X., 133, *134*, 163
Mfecane, 25, 30–6, 37–55
Mfengu, 34, 70, 75–6, 141
Mhlangana, 35
migrant labour system, 91–2, 106–7, 127, 129–30, 131–2, 136–7, 142, 143, 145, 146, 147, 151, 157–60, 176, 179, 181, 204, 225, 233–4
military organisation and power: Gaza, 52–3; Mthethwa, 26; Ndebele, 49, 51–2; Sotho, 39, 43; Swazi, 46–7; Zulu, 27, 28, 29, 35–6, 49, 51
Milner, Lord Alfred, 123, 131, 136
miners, white, 89, 99, 100, 128, 129, 155, 165, 190
Mines and Works Act (1911), 165
mining: economic impact, 92–5, 101, 104, 128, 133, 136, 150, 151–60; expansion, 149–51, 157; industrial structure, 87, 89, 97–9, 100, 149–50, 151, 155–6; labour *see under* labour force; manufacturing industry and, 149, 150, 153, 155, 159–60; Namibia, 175; wages, 89, 100, 106, 128, 129, 159, 160; *see also* diamonds; gold
mining capitalists: consolidation, 156; landowners and, 91–2, 103, 143, 146; relationship with government, 90, 91–2, 103–4, 105, 128, 133, 135–6, 151–2, 164, 165
missionaries, 43, 61, 71, 72–3
Mobutu, General Joseph, 224
Mohlomi, 39
Mondlane, Eduardo, 227
Moshoeshoe, 37, *38*, 39–41; diplomacy, 41, 42; political power, 40, 48; relationship with Africans, 41–2; relationship with whites, 43–5, 78, 79, 81, 82
Moshoeshoe II, 226
mountains, flat-topped, strategic importance of, 39, 41, 42
Mozambique: control over Gaza, 120; dependence on S. Africa, 177–8; independence, 227–9; migrant labour from, 130, 132, 138, 145, 159, 177; Transvaal and, 118

Mpande, 112
Mpangazita, 41
MPLA, 227, 229
Mswati, 46–7, 48, 114
Mthethwa, 26, 27
Mugabe, Robert, 230, *231*
Muzorewa, Abel, 230
Mzila, 47, 53
Mzilikazi, 34, 48–52, 78

Nama, 60, 131, 138, 145, 173, 175–6, 186
Namibia, 156, 175–6, 207, 232–3
Natal: as Crown Colony, 78, 109
Natalia, Republic of, 76
Nationalist Party, 165, 167
Nationalists, Purified, 170, 171, 197–8
Native Affairs, Minister for, 198
Native Land Act (1913), 144, 147, 165
Native Representative Council, 170
Native Trust and Land Act, 170
Ndebele, 34, 41, 48–52, 117, 120, 122, 131, 145, 182, 186
Ndungunya, 45, 48
Ngqika, 74
Nguni, 7, 9, 11, 25–6, 30, 31, 33, 76; *see also* Zulu
Ngwane, 34, 41
Ngwato, 106, 179, 180
Nkomo, Joshua, 230
nomads: hunter-gatherers, 6, 9–11; pastoralists, 10, 11, 18–19
Nyasaland, 130, 138, 183–4, 222, 224

Oppenheimer, Ernest, 156
Orange Free State: African rural impoverishment, 142; claim to diamond fields, 85, 87, 90; government and administration, 81, 109, 133; Sotho and, 82
Organisation of African Unity, 224, 229, 232, 233
Ovambo, 9, 173, 175, 176

Pact government, 169, 190
Pan-Africanist Congress, 194, 196, 199, 200, 215, 219
Pass Laws, 103, 167, 197, 210–11; protests against, 190, 194
pastoralism: African switch from cultivation to, 147–8; impact of mining on, 104, 106; *see also* cattle; sheep
pastoralism, commercial, 19, 20–1, 58; expansion, 22–3, 24, 58–67, 73–4; impact on Africans, 18–19, 125–6, 140; state support, 143
pastoralism, nomadic, 10, 11
pastoralism, pre-capitalist, 3, 5, 7–9, 10, 25

243

white settlers: imperial government and, 110; smallholder settlement policy for, 70; relationship with Africans, 33, 36, 43–5, 110, 112–15, 118–20, 131

wine production, 73, 94, 127

Witbooi, Hendrik, 186

Witwatersrand, gold mining on the, 96–107, 128–30; *see also* gold mining

Witwatersrand Native Labour Association, 129, 130, 132

wool, export of, 73–4, 85

working class: rural, 144; white, political representation of, 164, 167–9, 172, 190

World War I: German South West Africa and, 175; gold prices and, 153, 155; political parties and, 165–7

World War II, 170

Xhosa: commercial pastoralists and, 23; disunity, 62, 63, 75; impact of market economy on, 74–5; imperial conquest, 112; interactions with other Africans, 11, 62–3; land annexed, 81; trekboers and, 62, 63, 64, 66

Zaire, independence of, 222–4

Zambesia, Rhodes' expansion in, 117–18

Zambia, 156, 224–5; *see also* Rhodesia, N.

Zimbabwe, 229–32; *see also* Rhodesia

Zulu: Bantustan policy and, 202–4, 208; defeat at Blood River, 76; environment and, 25; Inkatha and, 217–19; kingdom, establishment and impact of, 26–55; military organisation, 27, 28, 29, 35–6, 49, 52; neighbouring peoples and, 29, 33–55, 114; political significance, 114–15, 186; rulers, *see* Cetshwayo, Dingane, Shaka; white colonists and, 33, 36, 112–15, 120, 131

Zwide, 26, 27, 34, 46